UNDERSTAND BUSINESS FINANCE
A GUIDE FOR MANAGERS

UNDERSTAND BUSINESS FINANCE

A GUIDE FOR MANAGERS

Ernest Jones, FCA, FCCA, FCMA

Pitman

PITMAN PUBLISHING
128 Long Acre, London WC2E 9AN

A Division of Longman Group UK Limited

© Ernest Jones 1991

First published in Great Britain 1991

British Library Cataloguing in Publication Data
Jones, Ernest
    Understand business finance: A guide for managers.
    I. Title
    658.15
ISBN 0 273 03467 7

Printed in Great Britain by The Bath Press, Avon

CONTENTS

PREFACE

Most managers are not so much introduced to business finance as surrounded and, all too often, overwhelmed by it.

At the same time, most accountants were introduced to, and instructed in, business finance in total isolation from either the recipients of what they are employed to communicate or the reality of what they account.

It is to overcome these two differences – to bridge this gap – that I have tried, in the following chapters, to create a framework of understanding, one that management, both non-financial and financial, can recognise as meeting each other's needs and purposes – to provide better questions from which better decisions may be made. Beginning as it does with an assumption of no knowledge, I have placed the manager on the entrepreneurial bar stool of every business and developed each stage of understanding from the following primary propositions:

If it were my money, where would I get it from?

In which areas would I invest it?

How would I measure, progress and control success in financial terms?

The subject is developed through the three primary questions of business investment – the return, the risk and the ready – and these in turn are traced through each aspect of management accounting.

At no time is understanding assumed, but then neither are explanations couched in either a patronising or didactic manner. At the same time it is hoped that the explanations will also serve as a means by which accountants can perhaps measure up to the service for which they are employed. That is, providing better questions for those concerned with decision making and recognising throughout their activities two primary objectives – to make sure that what they present is understood, and to ensure that the presentation or organisation of such information assists in its use.

1 | AN INTRODUCTION TO BUSINESS FINANCE

The purpose of business is to bring money and people together in such a way as to create wealth. Wealth which can be used to provide today's rewards to employees, investors and the government – and therefore the whole community – through the wages, salaries, dividends, interest and taxes paid to them – while at the same time creating the necessary funds for reinvestment in order to enable the business to provide such rewards in the future. It is therefore essential for everyone concerned with business, whether they are investors, managers or employees, to understand business finance – to become commercially aware.

The business model

To do this we need first of all to see how money behaves – what it does in a business – and then to see the purpose of the financial information which is produced about it. To help us do this look at Illustration 1.1. This sets out a model of business investment. What we will do is put a name into each numbered circle – and to discover these names I shall ask you some questions. Mind you, if you prefer not to mark the illustration, why not take a copy?

The sources of money

First, in the case of circle 1, what must we have financially if we start a business? Oh yes. I know we must have policies, plans, ideas and so on, but what else? Yes, we need money. We have a very special word for the area from which we get money and we call it capital. So we can put the word capital into circle 1.

Capital is obtained when anyone starts a business from two sources – themselves and lenders, that is their own savings and borrowings from people or businesses such as banks who do not want their money back immediately. In limited companies these two sources of capital are termed

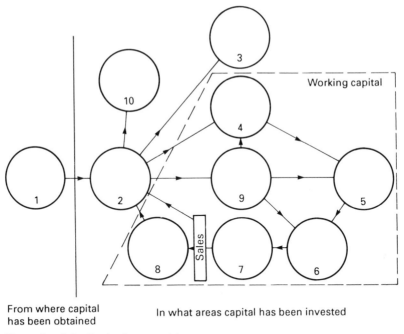

From where capital has been obtained

In what areas capital has been invested

Illustration 1.1 The business model.

the Share Capital (provided by the shareholders, the owners of the business), and loan capital (provided by lenders).

Gearing

It is this division of capital between these two sources which is called the gearing of a business. High Gearing is when the majority (more than 50 per cent) of the capital has been obtained by means of borrowing, whilst the reverse situation is known as Low Gearing. The significance of gearing lies in the relationship between the providers of the capital and its recipient, the particular business. For example, in the case of loan capital, interest must be paid on the amount borrowed over the life of the loan and the amount itself must be repaid to the lenders on the due date.

However, there are no such requirements as regards share capital. We do not have to repay owners – the shareholders – the money they have invested as share capital: it is, as we say, permanent. And their rewards – dividends as they are called – do not have to be paid to them. Owners' capital is, as we say, 'at risk'. It may do well or badly but this will depend upon how the business does.

It therefore follows that a high geared business may well find the need to pay interest on – and moreover to repay – its borrowed capital financially embarrassing and even disastrous during difficult times. It might be said therefore that the need to pay interest on and to repay loans creates pressure on a business.

Gearing questions

Gearing therefore is concerned with pressure. High gearing means more pressure whilst low gearing means less, which brings us to the first principle of understanding business finance – that its understanding rarely supplies answers, just better questions.

For instance, in the case of a high geared business, the question is, can the business take the pressure? There is nothing wrong with pressure – in fact many businesses, like people, work better under pressure – but you must always question their ability to work in this way.

In the same way with low gearing – there is nothing right or wrong about such a situation, just questions which need to be raised. For instance, is the business living under too little pressure, and if so, does this mean that it is not working as hard as it could?

Under-gearing

Finally there can be the situation of 'under-gearing'. This is when a business has good things on which it could borrow, i.e. use as security or collateral, such as land and buildings and it has not done so. And again we are left with further questions. For instance, 'under-gearing' may be a sign that the business is not using its resources as well as it could, or it could be that it is waiting for some event in the future for which funds will need to be raised by means of borrowing and therefore it wishes to preserve its ability to do so.

The use of money

We have now considered the sources of finance so we can turn to circle 2. This relates to the way money comes into the business, in other words, what are we looking for financially to start a business? The answer is of course cash, so we can put the word 'cash' in circle 2.

Of course it is possible to start a business with something other than cash such as office equipment, or machinery, but this presupposes the conversion of cash into such things which are then used in the business. So we shall assume that capital introduced into a business starts as cash. Now we come to the next question: what do we do with the cash we put into a business? Yes, we buy things – but what things? If we sat down and listed the things which we would have to buy in any business we might produce a selection – a 'shopping list' – such as this: land and buildings, people things (like wages and salaries), plant and machinery, materials, merchandise, office equipment, shop fittings, motor vehicles ... And then there are those things like rent and advertising, insurance, and heat and light, things which are often called collectively – and in the case of light appropriately – the overheads!

In fact we could go on and on. However, at this point let us stop and think about the items just mentioned from a cash spending point of view, because if we do we shall find that they fall quite naturally into two main categories. To understand this I want you to think about the items we have mentioned and ask yourself, if it was your money and your business, would you consider these all in the same way?

I believe that if you thought of them in this way you would find that the items mentioned very broadly divide themselves into two. These would be that some are things we buy with no intention of selling, for example the land and buildings, plant and machinery, office equipment and the motor vehicles – what in business we call the 'fixed assets'. On the other hand the other items, such as wages and salaries, materials, advertising, rent, insurance and so on are going into what we do sell.

Fixed assets

We can now fill in some more circles. Circle 3 relates to those items which we have no intention of selling, and we can therefore place in it the words 'Fixed assets'. Next we come to the circles marked 4, 5, 6, 7 and 8 flowing out of and back into cash, with circle 9 in the middle.

Working capital

The circles around which I have drawn a dotted line in Illustration 1.1 are termed collectively 'the working capital'. They show, as circles 4, 5 and 6 respectively, materials, labour and all those other items termed overheads, and these can now be filled in. These in turn are converted into finished goods or services which are shown as circle 7. Such finished goods or services may then be sold for cash which is shown by the line leading from circle 7 back to the cash circle 2.

Credit taken
However, both goods and services are often sold to customers – people and businesses – who do not pay immediately. They hesitate before they pay.

In this country such customers are collectively called the 'debtors' whilst Americans, who shorten everything, refer to them as 'accounts receivable'! These are shown in Illustration 1.1 as circle 8 which interrupts the line between circles 7 and 2.

Credit received

Finally, circle 9 in the middle which connects to circles 4, 5, 6 and 2, stands for the fact that, just as a business's customers do not pay immediately for the goods and services sold to them, neither does a business pay for all its expenses immediately.

It receives materials and merchandise from its suppliers before it pays for them. It also incurs overheads in the form of rent, advertising and other expenses before having to pay for them, and in most cases it does not pay for its labour before the end of the week or month. In all these cases businesses and people, supplying such goods and services, are waiting for their money, and we refer to them collectively as the 'creditors' of the business, or as the Americans would say 'accounts payable'. Circle 9 therefore stands for these creditors and indicates the delay between the receipt of materials, merchandise, labour and other expenses and the subsequent payment for them.

Working capital investment

The investment in working capital is therefore a net investment. It is the total of circles 4, 5, 6, 7 and 8 less circle 9. If we were considering a manufacturing business, working capital would be calculated in the following terms. First, there would be the stocks of raw materials we would have to carry at any particular time. Second, there would be stocks of work in progress – the goods in part production – made up of the cost of the materials, labour and overheads which have gone into them up to their stage of production. Third, there would be the stocks of finished goods – again containing the materials, labour and overheads in the completed items. And finally there would be the debtors or accounts receivable made up also of the materials, labour and overheads and, in this case we hope, the profit contained in the goods sold but unpaid for.

It is from the total of these items that must be deducted the credit the business has taken before paying for its materials, labour and overheads which have gone into its stocks of raw materials, work in progress, finished goods and debtors. This way of looking at working capital is set out in Illustration 1.2.

The working capital of a business, then, can be likened to the financial 'luggage' that it carries on its journey to a sale. In this respect for a manufacturing business there are four pieces of financial luggage, namely the raw

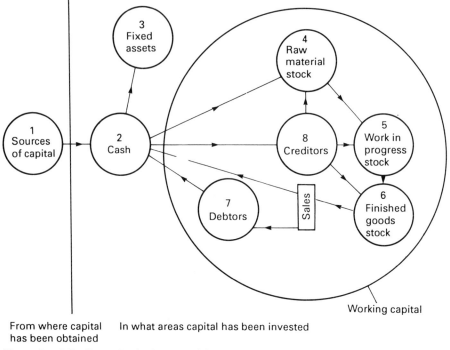

From where capital   In what areas capital has been invested
has been obtained

Illustration 1.2   Alternative business model.

material, work in progress, finished goods stocks and the debtors, and
from the total of these we deduct what it owes the people or businesses who
help it carry its luggage – the financial 'sherpas' as they might be called –
known as the creditors.

Recapitulation

So now we have discovered that when we invest money in a business we
have two investment areas: first, in things we are not intending to sell – the
fixed assets – and second, in things specifically intended to go into what
is sold – the working capital.

Fixed asset questions

The right assets?

Now, to return to the questions. When viewing the fixed assets of a business, there are two very specific questions that need to be posed. First,
because fixed assets are purchased with no intention of their resale, there

is a prime requirement that what assets a business owns in this area are the 'right ones'. After all, once fixed assets are purchased the business is left with them! For this reason it is important that people looking at the fixed assets have the necessary technical knowledge to decide whether they are the right ones. So, for example, the knowledge of an engineer is vital when looking at the plant and machinery of an engineering enterprise, as is the knowledge of a property person when looking at the land and buildings owned by a hotel group.

Their replacement

However, at the same time as posing the first question, there is also the second that needs to be asked when looking at some of the fixed assets of a business, those which over their lives wear out and/or become obsolete. In such cases there is the question as to whether or not the business is preparing for their replacement. In other words, has it got sufficient money set aside for this purpose, either in the form of cash or investments which can easily be converted back into cash? Or is the business building itself in such a way that it will be able to obtain the necessary funds from outside itself when this is necessary, for instance by borrowing on the security of the land and buildings it owns?

These then are the two questions that must be asked when we look at the fixed assets of a business. First, are they the right ones, and second, when it becomes necessary will the business be able to replace those which wear out and become obsolete?

Working capital questions

The cash flow

But what about the working capital? What are the questions that need to be raised here? Once again there are two questions which need to be asked, the first relating to a very important commodity indeed – cash itself.

If you look at Illustration 1.1 you will see just how central cash is to working capital. The line joining each of the circles in working capital is continuously moving out of and back into cash. It is because of this that when a manager or investor considers this area they need to pose the classic cash question which haunts everyone, both in their business and personal lives: 'Will I have the money available to pay the bills (in business "the creditors") as and when they become due?' You will see if you examine the business model that this is very much a timing problem, making sure that money is available as money as and when it is needed. After all, if this is not so and creditors demand their money the business will either have to sell its fixed assets in a hurry – not the best or easiest thing to do in most cases – or get a loan in a hurry, again not the best way to borrow money!

A business that finds itself in such a situation is said to have a liquidity or cash flow problem. This is precisely the same problem that, when it is faced by individuals, is described as 'being skint'.

The question of liquidity has great significance as it might be said that cash is the lubrication a manager needs to make a decision. If cash is not available managers do not make decisions – decisions are forced upon them. It is for this reason that the question of liquidity is so important to ask about a business.

After all, if you do not have the money you may not buy the best materials from the best suppliers but have to deal with those who give the longest credit, however poor the quality of their goods. Or again, you may be forced to sell goods to people who pay the quickest, even if the price you charge them is much less than to people who take longer.

However, as well as the question of liquidity there is the second working capital question – the amount of the investment itself.

Minimising?

To understand this second question let us pretend that we are the manager or investor in a business and ask ourselves how much of our capital would we wish to invest in the working capital area? This is not a trick question – the answer does not differ between large or small businesses or between different types of trade. Every manager and every investor has an identical wish as far as the amount of the investment in working capital is concerned. It is to minimise it as far as possible – to reduce it to nil, or even in some cases to a minus if possible.

The ambition of every manager or investor is to sell their goods or services as soon as possible and to convert the sale back into cash, whilst at the same time maximising the time taken before paying for the materials, labour and other expenses which go into such sales. It is indeed by doing this which enables a business to minimise the working capital investment. And why should this be the ambition of managers and investors alike? Well, ask yourself what is everyone's ambition regarding investment anywhere, whatever the proposition, whether it is on a horse or in a business. The answer is quite clearly to maximise the odds, the return or the profit, on the capital invested.

The words 'odds', 'return' or 'profit' refer to precisely the same thing – the growth the investment creates. After all, if the odds are 10 to 1 this

Illustration 1.3 Comparisons of return on capital employed.

	A Ltd £	B Ltd £
Fixed assets	400,000	400,000
Working capital	200,000	100,000
Total capital employed	£600,000	£500,000
Profits	= £60,000	= £60,000
Return on capital employed	10%	12%

means that if we put £1 on the horse to win and it does, the £1 becomes £11. We still have the original £1 invested and it has grown by £10. So, in the case of a business, profit is the measurement of the growth created on the capital invested – or employed, as we say – over a given period of time.

The purpose of minimising the working capital investment is therefore to maximise the return or profit on the capital employed, because if a business can make the same profit with less capital invested, it must be right.

You can see an example of this in Illustration 1.3 where for A Ltd the profit of £60,000 represents a return of 10 per cent on the total capital employed – fixed assets £400,000 and working capital £200,000, a total of £600,000. However, the same profit made by B Ltd on capital employed of £500,000 – fixed assets £400,000 and working capital £100,000 – represents a return of 12 per cent on the total capital employed.

On the other hand, the desire to minimise the working capital investment must be reconciled with the need to meet the amounts due to creditors as and when they become due. This of course is essential because if it cannot be done the only thing the business then has available to raise cash speedily are things it has no intention of selling – its fixed assets. In working capital there is always a need to strike a balance between minimising the amount invested whilst at the same time avoiding the risk of being unable to meet bills as and when they become due.

Outside investment

Having understood the two major investment areas we still have one more to consider. This is the investment of cash not in fixed assets nor in working capital but in outside investments in the form of shares in or loans to other businesses or individuals.

Reasons

We can therefore fill in circle 10 in Illustration 1.1 as outside investments. Such investments do not normally take place when a business is first started, but when the business has been in operation for some time there may well arise situations where an outside investment might be felt desirable. One reason which might attract a business to invest outside itself is to spread its investment risk, that is to divert some capital away from the main business into one that is totally dissimilar or to gain an interest in a business which is complementary to its own. An investment in the supplier of a key raw material is an example of this type of investment because in this way it may be possible to guarantee supplies if these become difficult to obtain.

It might also be felt desirable to invest in another enterprise in order eventually to take over its control and thus obtain a second, ready-made business. Such control is normally obtained by purchasing more than 50 per cent of the voting shares of the company. In such a case the business in which the investment is made is referred to as a subsidiary company and the investing business as its parent company.

These then are examples of outside investments.

Models for a service industry or retail business

We have now examined business investment in terms of a manufacturing enterprise and a complete example is set out in Illustration 1.4. In the case of a service industry the finished goods circle 7 will be replaced by the term 'Finished services' and in such cases it may also be found that materials are so small as not to warrant a separate circle. However, the model that we have been discussing will be found, with very few exceptions, to be adaptable to every conceivable type of business. Illustrations 1.5 and 1.6 should be examined together to see how the model for a manufacturing business set out in Illustration 1.4 compares with the model of a service business set out in Illustration 1.5. Again, in the case of a retail enterprise material is referred to as merchandise, and as there are no manufacturing processes there will be no finished goods, just saleable merchandise.

It will also be found that, as most sales by retailers are for cash, the interruption caused by credit being taken by customers – set out as circle 8, the debtors – will be the exception and not the rule as in the case of most manufacturing and many service industries. A business model for a retail enterprise is included as Illustration 1.6.

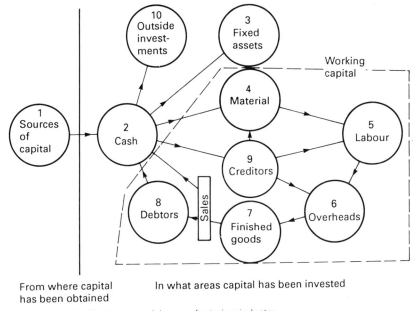

From where capital
has been obtained

In what areas capital has been invested

Illustration 1.4 Business model: manufacturing industry.

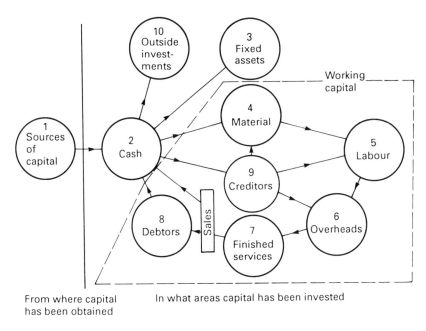

From where capital
has been obtained

In what areas capital has been invested

Illustration 1.5 Business model: service industry.

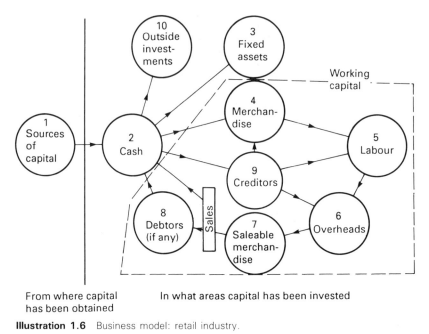

From where capital
has been obtained

In what areas capital has been invested

Illustration 1.6 Business model: retail industry.

Summary of the business model

What must be stressed is that the pattern of investment described above has not been invented by experts but follows the natural investment of cash in any business. After all, even Adam and Eve had fixed assets – they called them trees; they also had working capital which they called apples!

Now to summarise – money in any business can only be invested in three areas, namely fixed assets (things we have no intention of selling), outside investments and working capital. It has always been invested in these three areas and it always will be invested in these three areas. It must also be noted that there is no natural barrier between them. Amounts invested in one can be taken out of that area and transferred to another and vice versa. In other words, when we are looking at business investment we are looking at a very moving situation.

It must also be noted that all the rules regarding how much money we should invest in particular areas are always subject to alteration. Even the rule that we mentioned in this chapter as regards minimising the money in working capital can and may need to be broken. For instance, if someone running a business can see that a material is likely to rise in cost over the year ahead such a person might well believe it right to buy more material than is needed immediately. This will mean holding more stock than is required for immediate use and therefore not minimising the working capital during this period of buying in anticipation of price increases. However, by taking such action, the person running the business would be doing the correct thing, although it would be breaking the rule of minimising working capital.

The money questions

It is the movement of money which is central to an understanding of business finance. It is this movement which calls for the need to control and examine money in business by the techniques which we shall introduce and examine in this and future chapters. It must always be remembered that financial information is produced to meet the natural desire to know what is happening to the business investment. So let us begin by asking, what do we need to know? To answer this question we shall consider ourselves, once again, as if we are starting our own business and seek to answer this primary question: 'What do we want to know about the financial progress of the business?'

The return

Now if you think about this question you will see that it is really asking, what does anyone want to know about investment, and in a business situation your need is no different from that of any investor, whether it is an investment on a horse, in land, in jewellery or in a car. You will find that every time investment proposals are made there are two primary and obvious questions investors ask: What is the return – in other words what are you going to get in return for your investment, the odds on the horse for example. As we said previously in this chapter, if the odds on a horse are quoted as 10 to 1 this means that if you invest £1 on the horse to win and it does, your £1 will grow to £11. You will still have the £1 you invested but it will have grown by £10 – the odds. It is to examine this question of return that in business a statement known as the Profit and Loss Account is produced.

The risk

Whilst the first question is therefore what is the return, the second – which is equally important – is what is the risk of the investment giving you a return, i.e. the chances of the horse winning?

This is, however, a peculiar question because, although we raise it, we are not really seeking an answer. We want to work that out for ourselves.

Consider for a moment a situation in which I recommend a horse and tell you it is bound to win a particular race. Would you take my word? I doubt it. I think you would suspect me. In fact, although you would clearly want to know the chances of the particular horse winning, you would want to do your own homework. And what you would need would be a starting point – which in the case of the horse would be its name. After all, once you know that, you could enquire into whether or not a horse with that name has ever won a race before, who was riding it and who was it riding against when it did.

It is just the same in the case of the chances or risk of a business making profits. What is supplied is a starting point from which to do one's 'homework', which is called a Balance Sheet. This in reality is an agenda setting out the business model we have just been looking at so you can see what the business owns as fixed assets, outside investments and working capital, and how such investments were financed, the share capital and borrowed sources. It is from reading this agenda that the chances of a business making future profits can be considered by asking such questions as:

(a) Has the business the right fixed assets to make future profits?
(b) Are the investments appropriate for the particular business?
(c) Does the working capital investment reveal liquidity and does it seem to be minimised?
(d) And also have all the investments been financed from the right sources – the question of pressure?

The two primary questions, then, of all investors, whether the investment is on a horse or in a business, are the return and the risk. And it is in response to these two questions that in business we produce in the case of the return the Profit and Loss Account, and in the case of the risk the Balance Sheet.

The ready

However, at this stage we have a difference between business and other investment propositions: when we put money into a business something happens to the money itself which does not happen in other investment situations – the money moves.

Business as we have seen is all about the movement of money and this is what makes it different from putting money into other investments. For instance, when you put money on a horse the one thing you do not want to move is the money – you want the horse to move and the money to stand absolutely still!

It is for this reason that we have this third information requirement regarding business: to know exactly how much money we will have as money at any particular point in time. After all, because money is moving all the time within a business we will find that the amount of money in circle 2 in Illustrations 1.1, 1.2, 1.4, 1.5 and 1.6 will not necessarily stay the same. Sometimes the business may be spending money on fixed assets and material and so on, and sometimes money may be coming in from sales or dividends from its outside investments. It is this situation which makes it essential for anyone running a business to try to forecast its cash position over the period ahead so that they can be aware of whether or not the business will have the money to pay its bills as and when they are due. We refer to the statement that sets out this prediction as the Cash Flow Forecast and it could be described as the forecast of the availability of cash within a business over the period ahead.

The Profit and Loss Account, Balance Sheet and Cash Flow Forecast

You can say therefore that a Profit and Loss Account measures the *Return* on and the Balance Sheet sets out the *Risk* in the capital invested within the business, whilst the Cash Flow Forecast lets us know if we will have the money when it is needed – the *Ready*. These three statements form the basis of all financial information in business and might be termed the three Rs of financial literacy! They form a trilogy of information from which all else flows.

We must also recognise that what the interested investor needs to know, the manager needs to know also. After all the manager is simply acting on behalf of the investor and their needs as regards financial information are therefore identical. In later chapters we shall examine each of these three financial statements individually, namely the Profit and Loss Account, the Balance Sheet and the Cash Flow Forecast, and create a real understanding of their content and use to those running a business.

Consolidation and conclusion

However, before we look into these financial statements, we must first consolidate our understanding of the way business money moves. We must recognise the two aspects of money in business which are set out in Illustrations 1.1, 1.2, 1.4, 1.5 and 1.6. These are the sources of money – where we get our capital from – and the application of such money – where it is invested. We must also become familiar with each source – the owners' funds and money borrowed – and each area of application – fixed assets, outside investments and working capital.

In this understanding we must be aware that whether we are looking at a one-man business or a multi-million-pound enterprise our main sources and our main applications of money remain identical. To illustrate this point turn to Illustration 1.7 in which you will find a list of items on which money might be spent in a business and an empty 'balls model'. You should then insert the appropriate number into the appropriate circle in the model. For instance, if you think raw material is a fixed asset item 1 will be placed in the fixed assets circle. Mind you, I may have made a mistake, so I will not help you any more! Again, if you prefer not to mark the illustration, why not take a copy?

When you have completed this test turn to Illustration 1.8 and check your answers. When you have done this proceed to Chapter 2 which deals with the first of the three primary financial statements – the Profit and Loss Account.

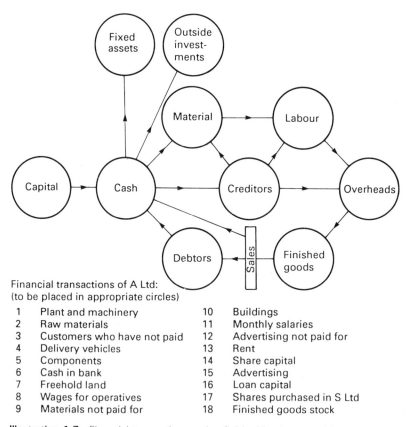

Financial transactions of A Ltd:
(to be placed in appropriate circles)

1	Plant and machinery	10	Buildings
2	Raw materials	11	Monthly salaries
3	Customers who have not paid	12	Advertising not paid for
4	Delivery vehicles	13	Rent
5	Components	14	Share capital
6	Cash in bank	15	Advertising
7	Freehold land	16	Loan capital
8	Wages for operatives	17	Shares purchased in S Ltd
9	Materials not paid for	18	Finished goods stock

Illustration 1.7 Financial transactions and unfinished business model.

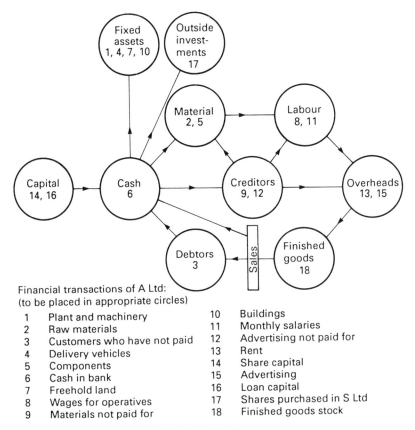

Financial transactions of A Ltd:
(to be placed in appropriate circles)

1	Plant and machinery	10	Buildings
2	Raw materials	11	Monthly salaries
3	Customers who have not paid	12	Advertising not paid for
4	Delivery vehicles	13	Rent
5	Components	14	Share capital
6	Cash in bank	15	Advertising
7	Freehold land	16	Loan capital
8	Wages for operatives	17	Shares purchased in S Ltd
9	Materials not paid for	18	Finished goods stock

Note: Salaries might be considered overheads.

Illustration 1.8   Financial transactions and finished business model.

2 | THE PROFIT AND LOSS ACCOUNT

Introduction

The definition of profit or loss

This chapter is concerned with the return on the business investment which is the measurement set out in the Profit and Loss Account. To begin with we must understand the meaning of return, and to do this let us go back to the simple situation of the return on a horse – the odds. What does it mean when we say the 'odds are quoted at 10 to 1'?

It means, of course, that if you put £1 on the horse to win and it does the £1 will grow by £10, and if it loses the £1 will shrink. In fact it will disappear altogether!

Return is therefore the measurement of the growth or shrinkage of the amount invested, and this is precisely what is being measured in the Profit and Loss Account. The definition of profit and loss is the measurement of the growth or shrinkage that has occurred to the business investment, wherever it may be, over a period of time.

The bias of the Profit and Loss Account

In practice we seldom find a Profit and Loss Account follows this definition – it is biased as it concentrates on one area of growth or shrinkage more than others. This is because people who wish to examine the growth or shrinkage to the business investment are mainly concerned about how much of this is being created by its trading or operating activities.

It is because of this that the Profit and Loss Account concentrates upon the trading or working capital area. It spends most of its time recording whether the products, merchandise or services the business produces, presents or markets have been sold for more than they cost. Look back at the business model set out in Illustrations 1.4, 1.5 and 1.6 to see the area we are talking about. Mind you it does not ignore the other areas – the fixed assets and outside investments – but it only deals with these if something obvious has happened, for instance if dividends or interest have been received on outside investments or losses or profits made on the sale of fixed assets or outside investments.

Capital and revenue expenditure

It is because of this bias that occasionally difficulties of definition may arise. These occur in comparing trading or operating expenses with sales income because of what might be termed the 'mixed' nature of some expenses. Expenses which might be going either into fixed assets, often termed capital expenditure, or into things which go into what is to be sold, often termed revenue expenditure.

The problem which arises is that at times expenditure may be partly capital and partly revenue. However, unless this is correctly defined the wrong costs will be set off against the sales for the particular period and so the wrong trading or operating profit or loss presented.

An example of this is when repairs take place to buildings or machinery and during the process of the repair the particular item is improved. In such a case only the repair should be treated as a revenue expense and deducted from sales in the Profit and Loss Account before striking the trading or operating profit or loss. The improvement part should be treated as capital expenditure and therefore included as a fixed asset.

The period of the Profit and Loss Account

It is also necessary to recognise that because of the bias towards the trading area, the period of these statements is crucial. We normally associate the period of Profit and Loss Account with a year and this is not coincidental or because of a legal or even a taxation rule. It is because, if you are examining the growth of a business within the context of its trading or operating activities, the period measured must extend over its full trading cycle which will normally be the year. Businesses are in most cases seasonal and it is only by looking at the full year that a balanced view of the trading or operating profits or losses can be provided.

It might be said that a month's Profit and Loss Account is just a step along the way! For this reason any statement of profit or loss which does not embrace the full trading cycle – which will usually be the year – must be treated with caution or wrong conclusions may be drawn from it.

The structure of the Profit and Loss Account

Let us now examine Illustrations 2.1 and 2.2. They set out two simple

Illustration 2.1   A Ltd: Profit and Loss Account for the year ended 31 March.

	£000	£000
Sales or turnover		10,000
Less:	£000	
Material costs	4,000	
Labour costs	2,000	
Overhead costs	3,000	9,000
Trading or operating profit		£1,000

Illustration 2.2   B Ltd: Profit and Loss Account for the year ended 31 March.

	£000	£000
Sales or turnover		8,000
Less:	£000	
Material costs	3,000	
Labour costs	4,000	
Overhead costs	3,000	10,000
Trading or operating loss		£2,000

Profit and Loss Accounts showing sales for the period, away from which are subtracted the materials, labour and overhead costs. If sales exceed these costs we have a trading or operating profit as shown in Illustration 2.1; if not we have a trading or operating loss as in Illustration 2.2.

In Illustration 2.1 we show sales of £10,000,000, material costs of £4,000,000, labour costs of £2,000,000 and overheads of £3,000,000, and we have a trading or operating profit of £1,000,000. In Illustration 2.2, on the other hand, we have sales of £8,000,000, material costs of £3,000,000, labour costs of £4,000,000 and overheads of £3,000,000, so in this case we have a trading or operating loss of £2,000,000.

At this stage we are not trying to examine details but principles. It is useful therefore to look back at the business model set out in Illustrations 1.4, 1.5 and 1.6 to see that a trading or operating profit means more comes out of the working capital cycle than goes in, whilst a loss means the opposite. To illustrate this point in more detail, a profit will occur if the total of circles 4, 5 and 6 is less than sales, and a loss will happen if the addition of circles 4, 5 and 6 is more than sales.

Cash and profit and loss

It will be seen therefore that a profit means more and a loss means less cash generated into a business. Mind you we have rather simplified this situation as cash and profit are not necessarily the same. There can be quite a time gap between profit and loss being made and more or less cash being generated.

Matching expenses with sales

For instance, it must be noted that sales in the Profit and Loss Account refer to sales invoiced whether the money has come in or not. In the same way the materials, labour and overhead costs in the Profit and Loss Account are those which relate to – or as we say 'match' – the sales invoiced for the period under review, again whether the money has been spent or not.

This means that you can in fact be making a profit but you can at the same time be short of money, i.e. be skint, and you can be making a loss and you can at the same time have money, i.e. be flush! Profit or loss will eventually effect cash but there may well be a considerable time gap before this happens.

Accruals and prepayments

It is in order to match expenses with sales that there is a need when assessing the profit and loss over a period of time to make sure we relate income and expense to that period. This will very often call for the adjustment of expenses and income so as to ensure that the full amount of each is set out under each head. To illustrate these adjustments let us consider the case of electricity used but not yet billed. In this case it will be necessary to bring in the amount of this expense if the full charge for electricity is to be correctly set off against the sales. This adjustment is referred to as an accrual.

Equally in the case of rent paid in advance it will be necessary to restrict this expense to the rent relating to the period covered by the Profit and Loss Account. It is this adjustment which is referred to as a prepayment. If either of these adjustments is ignored the profit or loss of the business would be misstated.

Accrual adjustment
For instance, if in Illustration 2.3 materials received but not invoiced amounted to £20,000 the material figure of £450,000 would be

Illustration 2.3 A Ltd: Profit and Loss
Account for the year ended 31 March.

		£
Sales		1,000,000
Less:	£	
Material	450,000	
Labour	200,000	
Overheads	250,000	900,000
Net profit		£100,000

understated by £20,000. It should therefore read £470,000, and if this item
was not adjusted, the profits would be overstated by £20,000. In this case
it would therefore be correct for the profit to read £80,000 and not
£100,000 because an accrual adjustment of £20,000 would need to be
made.

Prepayment adjustment

Again, if the overhead expenses of £250,000 included insurance of £3,000
relating to the period 31 March to 30 June a further adjustment would be
required. Overheads would have to be reduced by this £3,000, and if this
were not done profits would be reduced incorrectly for the period ended
31 March by £3,000. To correct this happening a prepayment adjustment
of £3,000 would need to be made to reduce overheads from £250,000 to
£247,000.

Stock and matching

A Profit and Loss Account is concerned fundamentally with the difference
between sales made and the cost of such sales, and it is for this reason that
all expenses deducted from the sales must match such sales. It is because
of this need to match expenses against sales that a certain difficulty can
arise.

For example, at the close of a period it may be found that a business may
have incurred the cost of materials, labour or overheads which have not yet
gone into what has been sold. It is to adjust for such expenses that it is
necessary to take 'stock'. This is the term used for material, labour and
overhead costs incurred during a period but which have not yet gone into
what has been sold.

Types of stock

In a manufacturing business there may well be three types of stock: raw
material stock which is made up of the value of unsold raw material, work

Illustration 2.4 Calculation of materials figure in Illustration 2.3.

Amount deducted from sales calculation:

	£
Opening stock of materials	30,000
Add: Purchases for period (including £20,000 accruals)	470,000
	500,000
Less: Closing stock of materials	50,000
Deducted from sales	£450,000

in progress stock and finished goods stock. Both of these latter stocks will include the value of the labour and overheads as well as the materials which have gone into the finished and partly completed items which have not yet been sold.

At this stage we must understand the logical need for these adjustments. In the case of raw materials, if we take Illustration 2.3 and we suppose the closing material stock at 31 March to be £50,000, this would have reduced the amount deducted from sales to £450,000.

In fact the materials expense set out in a Profit and Loss Account is a calculated figure, and in Illustration 2.3 would have been made up as shown in Illustration 2.4.

Work in progress and finished goods stock

In the case of both work in progress and finished goods stock the valuation of these require a calculation not only of the materials but also the labour and other expenses or overheads which have gone into such partly finished and finished goods. The adjustments required for these closing stocks will therefore reflect all these expense items. At this stage you should note that we shall examine these adjustments and the basis of their valuation in more detail later in our studies.

Cash and profit – the timing difference

It can be seen therefore that because of the need to adjust for accruals and prepayments and to provide the matching adjustments known as stock, the profit or loss determined in the Profit and Loss Account will not necessarily be identified with cash in the bank. There is a timing difference. A business can be making a profit and at the same time be short of cash and vice versa.

To understand this point fully go back to Illustrations 1.4, 1.5 or 1.6 and trace the making of profit or loss and the effect this has upon circle 2, cash. Remember debtors – a sale is a sale in the Profit and Loss Account when a customer is invoiced, not when the sales are paid for. Remember also creditors – a cost is a cost against sales if it relates to the period of the Profit and Loss Account and matches the sales made, whether the expense has been paid or not.

Management judgements

Finally we come to the need to recognise that in determining profit or loss adjustments have to be made based on management judgements.

Stock

In fact we have just been considering an item whose value depends very much upon the judgement of management – stock. After all, in the assessment of stock someone has to consider its quality and quantity before any valuation can take place at all, and both these considerations require judgement. Judgements can never be claimed to be precisely accurate, and yet they have an immediate effect upon the profit or loss shown. Change the stock figure by one penny and you change the profit or loss figure by precisely the same amount. If you doubt this go back to your previous studies and examples on the stock adjustment and its effect on profit and loss set out in Illustrations 2.3 and 2.4.

Depreciation

Again consider the need to take account of the fact that fixed assets lose value. To illustrate this point let us return to the model in Illustration 1.2 where we set out the fact that money in a business is either invested in the things we have no intention of selling – the fixed assets – or into the working capital – the moving area as it might be called.

However, it must be noted that there are many fixed assets which over their lives, although we may have no intention of selling them, lose their value because of wear and tear and obsolescence. They get out of date.

We might say that there is a 'secret shrinkage' which goes on in many fixed assets all their lives. It is to deal with this secret shrinkage – the erosion of value of such investments which goes on all the time – which makes it necessary to bring in another adjustment before arriving at the profit or loss of a business. This adjustment is termed depreciation. To illustrate how this adjustment effects the profit or loss of a business imagine that we have bought a piece of plant machinery for £40,000 and expect it to have a five-year life. We shall also say that we anticipate that the scrap value at the end of five years will be, say, £5,000. So we are expecting a loss of £35,000 over the life of this particular piece of machinery. To account for this we might decide to charge £7,000 each year as an expense called depreciation. The effect of this will be to reduce the profit shown by £7,000 each year over this five-year period.

Depreciation and cash

However, we must note at this point the very real difference between this expense and all the others – the difference of cash. After all, in the case of materials, labour and all the other expenses, cash is or will be directly affected. However, in the case of depreciation, although it reduces profit or increases loss, it has no effect upon the cash – or as we say the cash flow. In fact the cash circle, circle 2 in the model set out in Illustrations 1.4, 1.5 or 1.6 will be increased by the profit made for a period plus any depreciation charged before calculating such profit.

Depreciation has the effect therefore of reducing the profit or increasing the loss shown whilst at the same time conserving the cash within the business. What is happening is that the total business investment is not being increased, it is being conserved, or as accountants sometimes say equalised. The amount being held back as depreciation is equalising what is being lost – what is shrinking away – through the wearing out and/or the obsolescence taking place in the fixed assets.

Purpose of depreciation

The purpose of depreciation is to reduce the amount of profit shown and so reduce the amount available for distribution – the amount available to take out of the business as dividends. For limited liability corporations, this is legally restricted to the profits after depreciation and after taxation.

If this adjustment was not made the profits shown would be that much larger and if these were distributed the total investment in the business would be reduced without it becoming evident until it was too late, when the depreciating fixed assets were totally worn out or obsolete and nothing had been done to make up for the value of the investment lost.

Depreciation and distribution

To help you understand this point turn to Illustration 2.5. Here we see the business model of a newly formed company called J. Bloggs Ltd, the street trader (or barrow boy if you prefer). It is a simple business that buys and sells everything for cash, carries no stock and has no accruals or prepayments.

We will also say that during its first year it buys a fixed asset – its barrow – for £40,000 and involves itself in the following transactions. It buys merchandise – cabbages, lettuce and asparagus in season etc. – for £40,000. It pays wages of £20,000 and it incurs overheads – rent for the lock-up garage and candles for the barrow's headlamps – of £25,000 – which also includes depreciation on the barrow of £5,000. At the same time its sales for the year, again all for cash, amount to £100,000.

In Illustration 2.5 you can see that these figures show that J. Bloggs Ltd has made a profit of £15,000. However, if you consider the cash situation you will see that cash has increased not by £15,000 but by £20,000 – the £15,000 profit plus the depreciation of £5,000. This is because although depreciation is deducted before arriving at the profit it does not reduce the cash in the business.

At the same time, when J. Bloggs comes to decide how much he can distribute – take out as dividends – this is limited to £15,000, the profit made for the period. This means that the company will have £5,000 more cash which it can do anything it wants with except take out of the business as dividends.

You might of course argue that it really represents the fact that the barrow is worth £5,000 less than it did at the beginning of the year. But it is still the same barrow and does the same work. It is just a bit older and

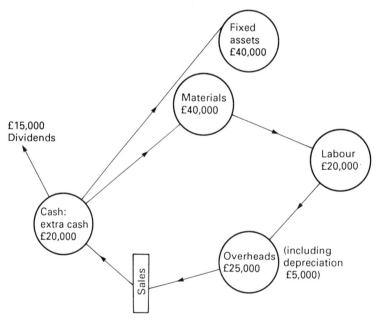

Profit = £15,000 (sales £100,000 less material £40,000 plus labour £20,000 plus overheads £25,000).

Cash increase = £20,000 (profit £15,000 plus depreciation £5,000).

Note: It is assumed there are no debtors, no creditors, no accruals, no prepayments and no stocks.

Illustration 2.5 J. Bloggs Ltd, the street trader.

perhaps looks it! However, the business has £5,000 it has to decide what to do with.

Depreciation and investment

For instance, it could be used to add to the fixed assets or to invest in another business as an outside investment or in carrying stocks of say tinned carrots or in allowing some customers credit – time – before paying for their purchases. The money held back as depreciation can therefore be used to do any of these things. However, whether the money will be available when it is needed to replace the barrow when it wears out will depend upon how well these investments turn out. For example, will people want to buy tinned carrots from a barrow, or will customers, given time, eventually pay?

Depreciation is therefore a forcible retention of profit and enables a business to reinvest the amount by which profits have been reduced by the expense known as depreciation. It must, however, be noted that deducting depreciation does not guarantee that the money will be there when it is needed for replacement. This will depend upon how and where the money held back as depreciation is invested.

Depreciation as a management judgement

This then is what depreciation is, but it must also be noted that the amount deducted in the Profit and Loss Account will depend upon management judgement. The law says a limited company must bring in the expense known as depreciation but the amount is left to the judgement of management. For instance, in the case of a fixed asset costing £40,000 three judgements will be required: first the fixed asset's life, second its scrap value, and third how the difference between the cost and the scrap value should be deducted in the Profit and Loss Account each year.

Methods of depreciation

Illustration 2.6 sets out the two best-known methods of depreciation, referred to as the straight-line and the reducing-balance methods, and these should be studied carefully. You will see that in the case of the straight-line method the depreciation is spread evenly over the life of the fixed asset, whereas by using the reducing-balance method more will be deducted in early than in later years over its life. This latter method is sometimes preferred as it means that as a fixed asset gets older and needs more repairs the total deducted from the profit for depreciation plus repairs will be more evenly spread than under the straight-line method.

It must also be noted again that depreciation is only one of the judgements that may be necessary before measuring profit or loss.

Illustration 2.6 Depreciation methods.

Basic data:

Cost of fixed assets	£40,000
Life expectancy	5 years
Scrap value at end of life	£5,000

Depreciation methods:

1. *Straight line:* $(£40,000 - £5,000) \div 5$
   Annual depreciation charge $\qquad = \quad$ £7,000

2. *Reducing balance* (assuming depreciation to be written off at the rate of 20% per annum):

	Depreciation charge
Year $1 = £40,000 \times 20\%$	$= £8,000$
Year $2 = (£40,000 - £8,000) \times 20\%$	$= £6,400$
Year $3 = (£40,000 - [£8,000 + £6,400]) \times 20\%$	$= £5,120$
etc.	

Doubtful debt provision

For instance, it may be believed that certain sales included in the sales figure may not be paid for, where there are debtors who are suspected as being doubtful. In such cases a deduction from profit will need to be made to account for such doubtful debts and again the figure will be based upon the judgement of management.

For example, suppose that at the end of year a company's debtors – amounts due from its customers – amounted to £30,000 and that of these debtors, £3,000 worth of them were considered doubtful. In such a situation a deduction termed 'provision for doubtful debts' of £3,000 would need to be made before the profit or loss for the particular year was presented.

You will see from this that the doubtful debt provision is unlike the provision for depreciation as it is not cumulative. We have seen how the charge for depreciation adds up year by year to a cumulative total, but this is not so in the case of the provision for doubtful debts. This will only affect the Profit and Loss Account if the amount required needs to be changed.

For example, suppose that, after providing £3,000 as the provision for doubtful debts in year 1, it was found that at the end of year 2 a provision of £4,000 was now required. The adjustment needed in year 2 would be to include a further provision for doubtful debts of £1,000. You can see in Illustration 2.7 how this adjustment is made over a series of years and how it affects the Profit and Loss Account.

Bad debts and doubtful debts

It must also be appreciated that some doubtful debts may well become bad.

Illustration 2.7 Provision for bad and doubtful debts.

The following facts relate to the debtors of A Ltd over its first three years:

Year	Debtors at year end £	Provision for doubtful debts £	Bad debts £
1	60,000	3,000	1,500
2	75,000	4,000	1,700
3	90,000	3,500	2,400

Profit and Loss Account (extracts):

		£
Year 1 *Deduct:*	Provision for doubtful debts	3,000
	Bad debts	1,500
Year 2 *Deduct:*	Provision for doubtful debts (£4,000 − £3,000)	1,000
	Bad debts	1,700
Year 3 *Add back:*	Provision for doubtful debts (£3,500 − £4,000)	500
Deduct:	Bad debts	2,400

In other words no judgement is needed – there is proof that the customer cannot ever pay. In such a case the amount due will be 'written off', that is it is included as an expense called a bad debt, and the provision for doubtful debts can then be reduced by the same amount. This is also illustrated in Illustration 2.7.

Other judgements

Many more judgements might be necessary and these will be referred to as appropriate in our studies. However, the point to recognise is that the profit or loss presented in a Profit and Loss Account is influenced by judgements and can therefore never be claimed to be a precisely accurate measurement.

Understanding the Profit and Loss Account

We have seen therefore that to use a Profit and Loss Account five points need to be understood:

(a) *Definition.* First, the definition of profit and loss – the growth or shrinkage to the investment in a business over a period of time.

(b) *Bias.* Second, that the measurement of profit or loss is biased towards the working capital area of investment because of the need to concentrate upon the trading or operating profit.

(c) *Period.* Third, the period of the Profit and Loss Account – the year – which has not been chosen accidentally but because most businesses operate seasonally.

(d) *Profit and cash.* Fourth, the difference between profit and loss and cash. You can be making a profit and yet be short of money; conversely, you can be making a loss and yet have money in the bank.

(e) *Judgements.* Fifth, the judgements which go into the calculation of profit or loss so preventing it from being precisely measured – the judgement of stock, depreciation and doubtful debts for instance.

Organisation of data

Now let us consider the second stage in using financial information. Whilst the first stage is to understand what is presented the second is to organise the data so that it can be used effectively. To help us approach this problem let us examine the relationship of expense to income. By this I am referring to the fact that broadly speaking business expenses relate to sales in two ways:

(a) *Variable expenses.* First we have those expenses that move in direct sympathy with sales income. We refer to these as variable expenses, for instance the material and the labour costs in the goods we sell or the salesman's commission based on the sales made during the period.

(b) *Fixed expenses.* Second we have expenses which have no such relationship. In fact this second group of expenses relates simply to time, for example the insurance for the year, the administrative salaries for the month, the rent for the quarter. It is these expenses which are often termed the fixed expenses for the period.

The breakeven chart

We can illustrate this relationship by looking at the chart set out in Illustration 2.8. Here we show a vertical axis AB measuring money values, and a horizontal axis AC measuring units produced and sold for the year. Line AD describes the variable expenses which move in sympathy with what is produced and sold, whilst fixed expenses for the year are shown as the distance AE. So EF is the line describing the total cost for the year depending upon the units sold.

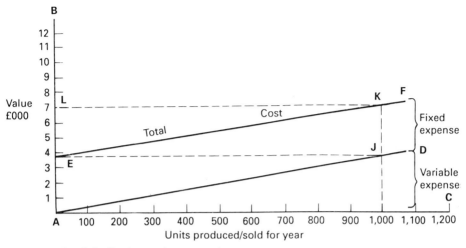

Illustration 2.8 Breakeven chart: stage I.

We can see from this chart that if we produce and sell nothing the cost will be AE, the fixed cost for the period. It also shows that if we produce and sell 1,000 units the cost would be 1,000 units worth of the variable expense, point J, plus AE, which is shown as point K. This we can trace to the vertical axis at point L showing a cost of £7,000.

The breakeven point

We can also expand this picture by drawing in the cumulative sales value line as shown in Illustration 2.9 as line AG. This shows that as we sell we reach the point H when line AG intersects with the total cost line EF. This is known as the breakeven point, the point where the difference between the sales income and the variable expenses equals the fixed expenses for the period – in this case the year – under review. It is this difference between the total variable expenses and the sales income which is referred to as the contribution.

Illustration 2.10 sets out the arithmetical calculation of the breakeven point for your interest. However, this calculation and its use will be dealt with in more detail when dealing with marginal costing in Chapter 7.

Variable and fixed expenses

An understanding of the relationship of expense to income is vital if you are ever going to be able to read and understand a Profit and Loss Account. To appreciate the need for this division of expenses in relationship to sales

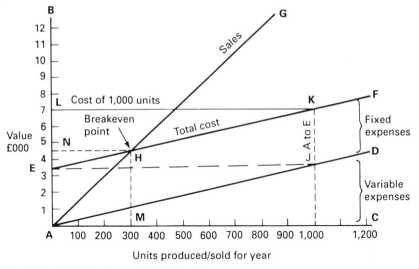

Illustration 2.9   Breakeven chart: stage II.

let us examine Illustration 2.11. This sets out the results of A Ltd over the last three years. In (a) no division is made between the fixed and variable expenses, whilst in (b) such a division is made.

In (a) where no division is made, the percentage of each expense to sales is of little significance as both fixed and variable expenses are mixed together under each heading, with the exception of materials and labour costs.

However, once the division is made significant facts are revealed such as:

(a) Material costs – which should be variable – do not vary in proportion to sales as they should and we need to know why.
(b) Administration fixed costs do not remain fixed – again we need to know why.
(c) Sales variable expenses do not vary with sales – again why?

Illustration 2.10   Breakeven calculations.

Assume following facts for B Ltd which produces one particular service:

	£
Sales price per unit	10
Variable cost per unit	6
Difference or contribution	£4

If fixed expenses for year are £720,000 the breakeven point calculation is:

$$\frac{£720,000}{£4} = 180,000 \text{ units}$$

or a sales value of £1,800,000 (180,000 units × £10 per unit).

Illustration 2.11 A Ltd: profit summaries.

(a) Profit summary:

	Years					
	1		2		3	
	£	%	£	%	£	%
Sales	10,000	100	12,000	100	15,000	100
Material costs	4,000	40	5,600	47	7,000	46
Labour costs	2,000	20	2,400	20	3,000	20
Administration costs	500	5	700	6	800	5
Selling costs	1,500	15	1,800	15	3,000	20
Subtotal	8,000	80	10,500	88	13,800	91
Trading profit	2,000	20	1,500	12	1,200	9
	£10,000	100	£12,000	100	£15,000	100

(b) Re-analysis of profit summary:

		Years					
		1		2		3	
		£	%	£	%	£	%
Sales		10,000	100	12,000	100	15,000	100
Material costs	– Variable	4,000	40	5,600	47	7,000	46
Labour costs	– Variable	2,000	20	2,400	20	3,000	20
Administration costs	– Fixed	500	5	700	6	800	5
Selling costs	– Fixed	500	5	500	4	500	3
	– Variable	1,000	10	1,300	11	2,500	17
Subtotal		8,000	80	10,500	88	13,800	91
Trading profit		2,000	20	1,500	12	1,200	9
		£10,000	100	£12,000	100	£15,000	100

Control of expenses

From this it can be seen that by reorganising the information so as to divide expenses between those which vary with sales as opposed to those which are fixed for the period we discover the two golden rules of expense control:

(a) *Golden Rule Number One*: Variable expenses should be controlled with activity. In other words if sales double, variable expenses should also double and vice versa.

(b) *Golden Rule Number Two*: Fixed expenses should be controlled as an amount – they should not move in sympathy with activity. Just because sales rise or fall this should not necessarily affect the fixed expenses. They should remain the same.

The profit and loss division – the gross profit

The need to strike relationships between expense and sales income is responsible for the development over the years of Profit and Loss Accounts which divide profits before and after administrative, selling and distribution expenses.

Profit before such expenses is often termed the 'gross profit' which is a very similar measurement to the contribution referred to earlier. It is calculated by deducting from sales, in the main, those expenses like materials or merchandise and manufacturing labour which will be of a variable nature. However, the gross profit of a manufacturing business will also include the deduction of manufacturing overheads some of which will be of a fixed nature. Nevertheless gross profit as a percentage of sales should remain reasonably constant from one period to another and if not there will be the need to ask why. It should also be comparable between businesses in the same industry.

Trading and profit and loss account

Where it is felt useful to set out the gross profit businesses will sometimes produce internally for management information what is termed a Trading and Profit and Loss Account. An example of this is set out in Illustration 2.12.

It must be noted, however, that we are at the beginning of our studies of this subject and we shall be developing each area in greater depth at later stages. However, even at this initial stage it can be seen that in the control of expenses – and therefore profits – there are 'two bites necessary at the cherry'. First, variable expenses and therefore the contribution or gross profit, when this is presented, should be controlled as a percentage of sales. If this percentage changes we should want to know why. Second, fixed

Illustration 2.12 A Ltd: Trading and Profit and Loss Account for the year ended 31 March.

	£	£
Sales		10,000,000
Less: Material costs	4,000,000	
Manufacturing labour costs	2,000,000	
		6,000,000
Gross profit		4,000,000
Less: Administration expenses	1,500,000	
Selling expenses	1,000,000	
Other expenses	500,000	
		3,000,000
Net* profit		£1,000,000

*The term 'net' is used to describe that profit is not an average but a net amount for the period involved, having been calculated after both variable costs and fixed expenses have been deducted.

expenses should be controlled as an amount and any changes should be justified. Remember that there is no justification simply in the level of activity. For instance, just because sales increase, administrative overheads do not necessarily need to increase in proportion.

The full Profit and Loss Account

'Below the line' items

It must also be noted that as well as trading or operating items a full Profit and Loss Account will also include income and expenses unconnected with the sale of goods, merchandise or services. Examples of these items are investment income such as interest or dividends received, the profit or the loss on the sale of fixed assets or outside investments, or the payment of interest on loans. These are often termed 'below the line' items and are shown in the more detailed Profit and Loss Account set out in Illustration 2.13. Here you will see a Profit and Loss Account set out for presentation to the shareholders of a limited liability company.

Terminology and layout

You will note how the term 'Turnover' is used in place of the word 'Sales', a case of duplicate jargon as they mean precisely the same thing – sales invoiced during the year.

You will also note that investment income is added in below the line. This would include dividends and interest on outside investments. There are also two items referring to a profit and a loss on the sale of machinery and equipment. These would be the difference between the cost of the particular item less the accumulated depreciation and the amount received on their sale. For example, a machine costing £40,000 with depreciation to date amounting to £35,000 giving a book or written-down value of £5,000 is sold for £6,000. A profit of £1,000 on the sale of the machine would be shown in the Profit and Loss Account.

Taxation

It will also be seen that this illustration includes the corporation tax calculated on the profit for the year as a deduction headed 'Taxation'. This taxation expense will not have been paid at the year end and in fact the precise amount payable will be subject to agreement with the Inland Revenue.

Illustration 2.13 C Ltd: Profit and Loss Account for the year ended 30 September (layout in accordance with Companies Act 1985, Format 1).

	£000	£000
Turnover		170,000
Less: Cost of sales*		100,000
Gross profit		70,000
Less: Distribution costs (these include sales expenses)	12,000	
Administration costs	18,000	30,000
Trading or operating profit:		40,000
Add: Non-trading income		
Investment income	5,000	
Profit on sale of machinery	500	5,500
		45,500
Less: Non-trading expenses:		
Interest on loans	7,000	
Loss on sale of equipment	1,000	8,000
Profit before taxation		37,500
Less: Taxation		12,500
Profit after taxation		25,000
Less: Proposed dividend		5,000
Retained profit		£20,000

*Includes the cost of: materials, manufacturing labour, manufacturing expenses i.e. factory rent, rates, depreciation of plant and machinery, etc.

If a retail operation, the cost of sales figure would include merchandise cost only. In the case of most service industries there is no direct cost of sales and so no gross profit is shown.

(If shares issued numbered 100,000,000, earnings per share = 25p, i.e. profit after taxation £25m divided by shares issued 100m.)

Dividends

Profits after this deduction are referred to as profit after taxation. From this are deducted the dividends for the year, leaving the profits retained. Such dividends will include both interim dividends paid during the year and any final dividends declared but unpaid at the year end.

In many cases limited companies will declare and pay an interim dividend before the year end based on the expectation of sufficient profits for the year to cover such a distribution.

Earnings per share

It is the profit after taxation which is often referred to as 'the bottom line figure'. In Illustration 2.13 this amounts to £25,000,000. It is this figure divided by the number of shares issued to the shareholders from which the earnings per share is calculated. Again this calculation is shown in Illustration 2.13 and shows an earnings per share of 25p.

Consolidation

The items above will be explained in more detail in your future studies but at the present time they are introduced to complete your view of the Profit and Loss Account. To consolidate your understandings of the measurement of profit and loss turn to Illustration 2.14. Here you will see a list of items of expense and income and your task is to list these in the form of a Trading and Profit and Loss Account. When you have completed this compare your answer with that shown in Illustration 2.15.

Illustration 2.14 A Ltd: transactions for year ended 30 June 19...

	£
Materials — opening stock	10,000
Labour for year — manufacturing	60,000
Administration overheads recorded for year	40,000
Cash paid to suppliers of material	110,000
Purchases recorded for year	130,000
Closing material stock	15,000
Depreciation for the year	5,000
Materials delivered but no invoice received	1,000
Cash received from debtors	210,000
Insurance paid for period after year end	500
Interest on loans to business for year	150
Dividends received for year	100
Sales for year	260,000

Illustration 2.15 A Ltd: Trading and Profit and Loss Account for the year ended 30 June 19...

	£	£	£
Sales			260,000
Less: Materials			
Opening stock	10,000		
Add: Purchases	131,000		
	141,000		
Less: Closing stock	15,000		
		126,000	
Manufacturing labour		60,000	
			186,000
Gross profit			74,000
Less: Overheads		39,500	
Depreciation		5,000	
			44,500
Trading profit			29,500
Add: Dividends received			100
			29,600
Less: Interest paid on loans			150
Net profit			£29,450

Conclusion

We have now completed our studies of the Profit and Loss Account – the measurement of the return on the business investment. But what about the risk or the chances of the profit or the loss being made? To answer this question we need to go on to Chapter 3 which deals with the Balance Sheet.

3 | THE BALANCE SHEET

The last chapter looked at the question of the return on the business investment measured in the Profit and Loss Account. So now is the time to look at the second primary question, the 'Risk' – the chances a business has of making a profit. And here we have a very different situation because, unlike the question of return which is set out in the Profit and Loss Account, risk is something you have to work out for yourself. No one can measure the risk for you. Well, they can, but would you believe them? And the answer to that question is in all cases 'No'! This is especially true if it is your own money you are risking. This then is the problem of posing the question of risk. You want to know the answer but you need to work it out for yourself.

Risk – the starting point

However, you have to start somewhere. As I pointed out previously in the case of a horse, you start with its name because from that you can start 'doing your own homework', working out the risk for yourself. For instance, you can find out whether a horse with that name has ever won a race, who was riding it and what the state of the course was when it did win. And that is precisely what everyone concerned with investment needs to do as far as risk is concerned – work it out for themselves. However, as in horse racing, you need a starting point. In the case of a horse it is its name whilst in the case of a business it is the Balance Sheet.

The model and the Balance Sheet

To illustrate the Balance Sheet turn to Illustration 3.1 which sets out the business model of a company called 'A Ltd'. The model of this company shows the investment within each circle as at the date selected – in this case 31 December. However, it does more than that because it also tells us from where this money came. It defines the capital circle.

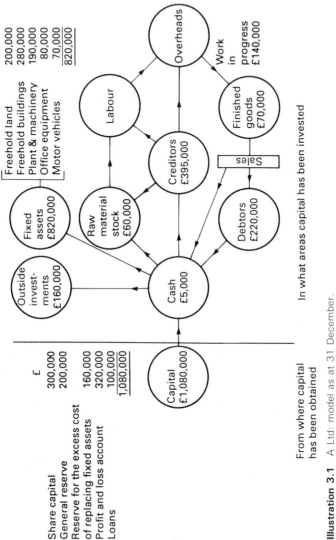

	£
Share capital	300,000
General reserve	200,000
Reserve for the excess cost of replacing fixed assets	160,000
Profit and loss account	320,000
Loans	100,000
	1,080,000

Freehold land	200,000
Freehold buildings	280,000
Plant & machinery	190,000
Office equipment	80,000
Motor vehicles	70,000
	820,000

Capital £1,080,000

Outside invest-ments £160,000

Fixed assets £820,000

Cash £5,000

Raw material stock £60,000

Creditors £395,000

Labour

Overheads

Work in progress £140,000

Finished goods £70,000

Debtors £220,000

Sales

From where capital has been obtained

In what areas capital has been invested

Illustration 3.1 A Ltd: model as at 31 December.

It is indeed this model which is presented in the statement referred to as the Balance Sheet. And just like the model the statement is divided into two, describing where the money is invested in the business in one half and from where that same money has been obtained in the other, at a particular point in time. It is this statement which provides the starting point for anyone wishing to question the chances – the risk – of a business making a profit.

The Balance Sheet as an agenda

After all, if profit is to be made the business must invest its capital in the right places, but equally important it must obtain its funds – its money – from the right sources. This therefore is the purpose of a Balance Sheet – to serve as an agenda from which questions can be raised regarding the uses and sources of money invested in a business.

However, before we examine these questions let us first see how a Balance Sheet is read.

Reading the Balance Sheet

As already stated a Balance Sheet summarises the financial model that we studied in Chapter 1. In this we saw how a business invests its cash into two main areas – in those things it has no intention of selling called 'fixed assets' and in those things it has every intention of selling – its 'working capital'. We also have a third area which might apply to a business once it has been established. Money can be put into outside investments which if they are not intended for sale are included by accountants as one of the fixed assets. However, they do require separate consideration from the other items included under this head.

So now turn to Illustration 3.1 again and look at the model in more detail. Here we see amounts placed in each circle and if we then turn to Illustration 3.2 we see these same amounts set out in a Balance Sheet form.

Components of a Balance Sheet

Fixed assets

In the first place we find that A Ltd on 31 December owns the following fixed assets: Freehold land £200,000, Freehold buildings £280,000, Plant and machinery £190,000, Office equipment £80,000, and Motor vehicles £70,000, giving a total of £820,000.

Illustration 3.2   A Ltd: Balance Sheet as at 31 December.

	£		£
Fixed assets			
Freehold land	200,000		
Freehold buildings	280,000		
Plant and machinery	190,000		
Office equipment	80,000		
Motor vehicles	70,000		820,000
Outside investment in C Ltd			160,000
Working capital			980,000
Current assets	£	£	
Stocks: Raw material	60,000		
Work in progress	140,000		
Finished goods	70,000		
Debtors	220,000		
Cash balances	5,000		
		495,000	
Less: Current liabilities			
Creditors		395,000	
			100,000
			£1,080,000
Financed by:		£	£
Share capital			300,000
Reserves: General reserve		200,000	
Reserve for the excess cost of replacing fixed assets		160,000	
Profit and Loss Account		320,000	
			680,000
Long-term loans			100,000
			£1,080,000

Valuation of fixed assets

At this stage we must also be aware of the conventions of valuation which we use in Balance Sheets. Such conventions are important to understand because, unless they are, the wrong impression may be gained as to the value of the items that we are looking at.

The convention in the case of the fixed assets is cost or revaluation value less depreciation to date. So in the case of a machine bought for £40,000 and depreciated at £7,000 per annum, the value on the Balance Sheet at the end of the third year of owning it would be: Cost £40,000 less depreciation to date £7,000 times 3 years equalling £21,000 – giving a net figure of £19,000.

From this it must be recognised that this will not necessarily be the value of such items if they were to be sold underneath an auctioneer's hammer. It is this 'convention' value which is often referred to as the 'written-down' or 'the going concern value'. It is the value based on the assumption that the item will not be sold but will be kept during its working life by the business. We will talk about revaluation value later in this chapter.

Outside investments

So we have arrived at the total of the fixed assets of £820,000. We can see from Illustration 3.2 that A Ltd also has an outside investment in 'C Ltd' valued at £160,000. This value is again based on the convention of cost or revaluation value. Nowadays it is listed under the title Fixed assets, as you will see when we consider an alternative presentation format.

Current assets

At the same time A Ltd also owns current assets, such things as stocks, debtors (that is people and businesses that owe money for sales made to them) and of course the cash and bank balances the company owns at the Balance Sheet date.

The word 'asset' is a financial term which refers to things of value. A fixed asset is something of value which the business has no intention of selling whereas current assets are things of value which either are cash or which the business has every intention of converting into cash.

If we look at the model again in Illustration 3.1, these items, included under the heading of current assets, are found in the outside circles of the working capital cycle. They are, in the case of A Ltd, stocks of raw materials £60,000, stocks of work in progress £140,000 (this is the stock partly completed and will include the material, labour and the overhead costs incurred up to the point of production reached), finished goods stock at the value of £70,000 (again made up of the appropriate materials, labour and overhead costs which have gone into these items) and the debtors (people or businesses who owe money at the Balance Sheet date for goods or services sold to them which they have not paid for yet) which amount to £220,000. Finally, we include cash and bank balances of £5,000 making a total of £495,000.

This means that the current assets include items which are not strictly part of the working capital as we have previously defined it. Cash and bank balances are in fact neither one thing nor the other as they might become fixed assets or working capital. However, for Balance Sheet purposes they are included with the current assets. The reason for this will become clearer when we consider the question of liquidity later.

Here again in the case of current assets we have to consider the financial conventions of value for these items, especially those which apply to the valuation of stocks. The stocks are valued in the following way.

Valuation of raw material stock
First, in the case of the raw material stock, the value is based on what the

materials cost when they were bought, or their net realizable value now if that is lower. An example of this is set out in Illustration 3.3(a).

Valuation of work in progress and finished goods stocks

In the case of work in progress and finished goods the convention is that, before we value these items at all, we must be satisfied with the answer to two questions:

(a) First, are the items which are in the process of production or which are at present produced and are included as work in progress or finished goods stocks saleable or will they become saleable? Have they passed the necessary technical inspections?
(b) If the answer to that question is 'yes' then the second question is raised: When these items are sold will they be sold at their 'normal sale price'?

If it is considered that both these questions can be answered in the affirmative, then the value of such items will be based upon the material and labour costs that have gone into their manufacture, plus the manufacturing and administrative overheads which are felt applicable up to the point of production reached.

However, if we are unable to give affirmative answers to these two questions then the value must be based on what we believe is a reasonable valuation in the light of the condition of the stocks concerned. Again, an example of how finished goods and work in progress stocks are valued is set out in Illustration 3.3(b).

Valuation of debtors and cash

Having considered the conventions of valuing stock, we come to those which we use for debtors and cash. In the case of cash this will be the amount owned either as cash in hand and/or in the company's bank account(s) at the Balance Sheet date. However, in the case of debtors the value would be based on what is due to be paid by those people and businesses who owe the company for goods, services or merchandise it has sold to them less any adjustment for doubtful debts.

This would mean that if debtors outstanding amounted to £240,000 but £20,000 were considered doubtful we would value them at £220,000 on the Balance Sheet. The £20,000 would have been charged through the Profit and Loss Account, as you will remember from the last chapter, as a 'provision for doubtful debts' and deducted before arriving at the debtors or 'receivables' figure shown on the Balance Sheet.

Valuation of temporary investments

It is also right to mention that if a business holds investments it does not

Illustration 3.3 Stock valuation.

(a) Raw material stock valuation:

Cost when purchased	50p per kilo
Cost at Balance Sheet date	40p per kilo

For Balance Sheet purposes raw material stock value is taken as 40p per kilo – the lower of cost or net realisable value (assumed to be value at Balance Sheet date).

(b) Work in progress and finished goods value:

Example	Material	Labour	Manufacturing and admin. overheads	Total stock value
	£	£	£	£
Finished goods stock value calculated per unit as	40	10	8	58
Work in progress stock (assume half completed)	40*	5*	4*	49*

*These figures assume that all material costs incurred at the beginning of manufacturing process and that labour and overheads are incurred in direct proportion with manufacturing progress.

intend to keep – amounts invested for periods of less than a year – they would be summarised under the current asset heading. In this case their value would be based on their cost or value at the Balance Sheet date.

Current liabilities

So we have now considered the current assets which total £495,000. However, to complete the presentation of the working capital items including cash we need to discover what is owing to creditors – or the amounts due within twelve months from the Balance Sheet date. This comprises the inside circle of the working capital cycle, set out in Illustration 3.1, which will be made up of items listed under the collective name of 'current liabilities'. A liability is a financial term for sums of money which are owed by a business. A loan with more than one year before it is due for repayment is a liability and so is a creditor for materials payable next month. However, such a loan is a long-term liability and it is not repayable for at least twelve months whereas the material creditor is termed a current liability as it is payable within the next twelve months.

In the case of A Ltd the current liabilities include creditors for materials, labour and overheads. They might also include amounts owing for corporation tax or dividends declared but not yet paid, and indeed any other items repayable within twelve months from the date of the Balance Sheet. In this particular case they amount to a total of £395,000.

So we have a picture of the investment in A Ltd as follows: Fixed assets £820,000, outside investments £160,000 and net current assets of

£100,000, that is current assets £495,000 less current liabilities or, as they might be described, 'amounts falling due within a year' £395,000. All this brings the total for the 'top half' of the Balance Sheet to £1,080,000.

The risk questions

This half of the Balance Sheet then sets out where the money is invested, and from this we can pose several risk questions relating to the possibility of the business making profit.

Fixed asset questions

For example, in the case of the fixed assets, are they the right ones, because if they are not, the possibility of profit will be that much less? And second, does the business seem able to replace its fixed assets as and when this becomes necessary? Of course these questions cannot be answered simply by reading the Balance Sheet. The question of whether or not a business has the right assets will require technical more than financial knowledge, and a physical inspection of the land, buildings and plant and machinery would be necessary before conclusions could be drawn. However, a Balance Sheet provides a starting point for such questions.

Again, in the case of the ability of a business to replace its fixed assets, further information will be required, and certainly an examination of the pattern of replacement over past years will be useful in answering this question. In fact an examination of a series of past Balance Sheets will often provide much evidence of value when examining whether or not the business has a record of fixed asset replacement. It will reveal the pattern of such replacement.

Net asset questions

In the same way with current assets and current liabilities questions need to be raised. For instance, in this area perhaps the first concern will be liquidity – the ability of the business to pay its creditors as and when they are due.

The liquidity ratio

Indeed liquidity is such a central question that when Balance Sheets are studied the relationship of current assets to current liabilities is often expressed as a ratio. It is also the reason why cash and bank balances are included with the working capital items under the heading current assets so as to provide a complete view of liquidity. The word 'ratio' in finance refers to an index used to establish comparisons. So in our example in Illustration 3.2 the ratio would be set out as £495,000, the current assets, divided by £395,000, the current liabilities, giving an index of 1.25.

You will see if you turn to Illustration 3.4 this ratio compared with the same ratio relating to the last four years. The trend can then be examined. This shows that current assets are not covering the current liabilities as much as they did, so the question is why? Was it planned or does it indicate a liquidity problem? Notice the questions that are then posed: Is the overdraft increasing or bank balance in hand reducing, and/or is there a delay in the time being taken to pay creditors?

We shall be looking at these and other interpretation questions later in our studies but at the present time all you need to understand is the questions that stem from financial information.

Minimising investment in working capital

Of course liquidity is only one question that concerns us in this area. You will remember from your previous studies that there is also the need to minimise the investment in working capital which forms the major part of the net current assets.

So the second question is the one regarding minimising the investment discussed in Chapter 1. Can the business reduce its stocks, shorten the credit time taken by its customers or lengthen the credit obtained from its suppliers? After all, if the investment in working capital can be reduced the money saved can perhaps be invested in better fixed assets and so improve profitability. It could even be taken out of the business altogether, which, if profits can be maintained, will improve the overall measurement of profits to the total capital employed. Again this was discussed in Chapter 1 and an example provided in Illustration 1.3.

Illustration 3.4 Current ratio.

	Years				
	1	2	3	4	5
Current assets / Current liabilities	2.11	1.86	1.64	1.42	1.25*

$$*\text{Calculation} = \frac{£495,000}{£395,000}$$

Questions arising:
1. Was the change planned?
2. Does it indicate a growing inability to meet the current liabilities out of the current assets? Are there signs of an increasing overdraft or falling cash/bank balances and/or a delay in the payment of creditors?

The sources of funds

This then is how one half of the Balance Sheet should be read but how about the other, the one which sets out from where the business obtained the money which it has invested?

In our first look at the sources of capital when we examined the business model, we considered only two: the owners' funds which, in the case of a limited company, are termed the share capital, and borrowed or loan capital.

Profits retained

Of course at that time we were looking at an initial investment in a business. However, as a business continues we find that these two original sources of capital – share capital and loan capital – will be increased in the years ahead by a third source, one which arises from the retention of profits which is sometimes called, in the case of limited companies, the 'reserves'.

Profit and cash

To understand this third source let us go back to the business model in Illustrations 1.4, 1.5 or 1.6. The trading or operating profit of a business can be traced on this model as the difference between what goes into the working capital cycle and what comes out from selling the products, services or merchandise of the particular business. If more comes out than goes in we have a profit; if more goes in than comes out we have a loss. This means that, if we look at the model shown in Illustration 3.5, the profit will be represented by the cash circle getting larger. Note the dotted lines in the illustration: whilst a profit will be represented by the cash circle getting larger, note the smaller dotted circle representing a loss.

We are of course over-simplifying the situation because, as we have discussed, investment in a business is always moving, and if you remember your Profit and Loss Account studies, there is often a time gap between profit and cash. However, if we could leave our working capital and fixed asset investments in all areas except cash at precisely the same level – profit eventually would be reflected by more cash and loss by less cash in the business.

The destination of profits and losses

Having examined the nature of profit and loss let us look at what happens to such profits or inflated cash or such losses or deflated cash.

First, in the case of profits, some will have to be paid out as taxation calculated on such profits and some will also have to be paid out as dividends

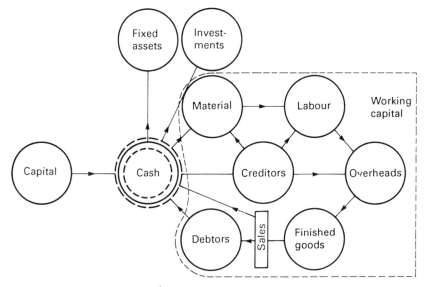

Illustration 3.5 Effect of profit/loss on cash.

to the shareholders. However, any that is left over, the profits retained, will go to increase the fixed assets and/or outside investments and/or working capital. In other words retained profits will be represented by more cash and this will be used in precisely the same ways as additional cash obtained from share or loan capital.

In the case of losses, no one wants them, so they have to be retained! This means that a loss will lead to less cash being invested in fixed assets and/or outside investments and/or working capital.

Profit as a source of capital

Retained profits are perhaps the most important source of capital within any enterprise once it has been established, and is for most businesses the major source of capital used for expansion. If you think of yourself starting a business, once you have invested all your own capital and what you can borrow from other people, from where else would you obtain permanent capital? And the answer is from retained profits.

It must, however, be noted that this source of money does not happen at the close of the year – it is happening all through the year. For this reason it is not just necessary to plan the making of profits, it is just as necessary to plan the continual investment of such additional funds which such profits are creating within the business.

It is also equally necessary to plan carefully the investments we reduce when losses are being made, so that we do the least possible harm to the future potential of the business.

'Reserves'

It is unfortunate that in this area of capital source we find confusion caused by the term used. The word 'reserves' seems to provide a particular mystery to many people and it is necessary to rid ourselves of this if we are to appreciate this vital source of money. It must be understood that the word 'reserve' in finance is simply a term used to describe retained profits, the third source of capital, not how it is applied.

The word 'reserve' therefore does not have its military meaning referring to unused resources. In fact retained profits – the reserves – are fully used within the enterprise, in fixed assets, outside investments and/or net current assets which include the working capital in the same way as any other source of capital such as share or loan capital.

Profit/reserves and cash

In other words, it does not mean when reserves are shown in a Balance Sheet that this amount of money is lying idle within the business available for investment in any new project that may come to mind. The location of the funds represented by the retained profits – the reserves – will be in the three main areas, that is in fixed assets, outside investments and/or working capital. To determine whether or not there are some sources available to finance any particular project or to meet any future contingency, the investments in fixed assets, outside investments and working capital must be individually studied. This will enable someone to see whether there is any cash available or any assets on which the business could borrow money.

Named reserves

In the past it was the practice to name the reserves, although recently this has become less 'fashionable'. However, you may still come across examples such as the 'general reserve' or the 'reserve for the excess cost of replacing fixed assets'. In such cases it must be particularly noted that such names refer to the rationale behind the retention of the profit and not to where the money is invested. For example, the general reserve refers to the general need to retain profit so as to increase the overall capital invested in the business, and the reserve for the excess cost of replacing fixed assets refers to the need to retain profits and increase the capital in the business simply to keep pace with the forecasted additional cost of replacing fixed assets. If you remember Chapter 2 you will recall that depreciation only takes care of the original cost of fixed assets. However, when fixed assets require replacing some may cost more to replace than they originally did to purchase because of new technology or inflation.

Illustration 3.6 A Ltd: summary of Profit and Loss Statements.

Years	1	2	3
	£	£	£
Before taxation			
Profits	120,000	130,000	
Losses			40,000
Less: Taxation	40,000	60,000	
After taxation			
Profit	80,000	70,000	
Loss			40,000
Less: Dividends	20,000	20,000	
Profits retained	£60,000	£50,000	
Losses retained			£40,000
Balance sheet:			
Profit and Loss Account	£60,000	£110,000	£70,000

The building up of reserves

Reserves are cumulative and they grow or are reduced depending upon the profit or loss retained at the close of each period. To illustrate this situation turn to Illustration 3.6 where we see a series of profits and losses for A Ltd over its first three years. We see that in Year 1 the profit retained is £60,000 and the Balance Sheet for that year would show Profit and Loss Account £60,000. In the second year the retained profit figure is £50,000 and in the corresponding Balance Sheet the Profit and Loss Account figure will stand at £110,000, which is £60,000 plus £50,000 from Year 2.

In the third year A Ltd suffers a loss of £40,000 so the Profit and Loss Account figure on the Balance Sheet now reads £70,000, that is £110,000 less the £40,000 loss for Year 3.

The sources of capital defined

The need to separate the sources of capital from their specific location is fundamental in understanding a Balance Sheet. The sources of capital for A Ltd are those shown in Illustration 3.2. These are Share capital £300,000, the Reserves and Profit and Loss Account £680,000 and loans of £100,000, a total of £1,080,000.

In Illustration 3.2 you will note that two reserves named General and Excess cost of replacing fixed assets are shown together with the Profit and Loss Account. It is becoming more and more common to find retained profits are left without any set names such as these and simply to refer to them as Profit and Loss Account. There is, however, one other profit which we have not mentioned which may appear on a Balance Sheet: the one referred to as the revaluation reserve.

Revaluation of fixed assets

The revaluation reserve refers to the adjustment required when a revaluation of fixed assets takes place. In the case of land and buildings it is recommended that limited companies should revalue these frequently and when this happens a further profit may well appear on the Balance Sheet. An example of this is shown in Illustration 3.7 in which the figures before and after revaluation are set out and the profit on revaluation of £150,000 is shown among the sources of capital.

The purpose of such revaluation is to provide investors and managers with a more up-to-date value of the capital employed against which profits can be compared and the value of the business may be more correctly assessed. This once again is a matter to which we shall return in later studies.

Shareholders' funds and gearing

Finally, it must be noted that retained profits including profits on revaluation increases the value of the shareholders' investment in the business. After all, profits retained in a business represent the sacrifice of the shareholders. These are profits which could have been taken out by, or as we say distributed, as dividends to the shareholders.

In the same way, profits on revaluation represent a growth to the assets owned by the shareholders, although unlike other profits they may not be distributed as dividends. This therefore means that when gearing is calculated the proportion of the total capital provided by shareholders will be made up of the retained profits and all the other reserves, including the profits calculated on revaluation, plus the share capital. An example of gearing in such circumstances is set out in Illustration 3.8.

Illustration 3.7 A Ltd: Balance Sheet as at
31 December.

	Before revaluation £	After revaluation £
Fixed assets	600,000	750,000
Investment	40,000	40,000
Working capital	20,000	20,000
	£660,000	£810,000
	£	£
Share capital	400,000	400,000
Profit and Loss Account	260,000	260,000
Revaluation reserve		150,000
	£660,000	£810,000

Illustration 3.8   A Ltd: Balance Sheet as at
31 December (layout in accordance with Companies
Act 1985 recommendation).

Balance Sheet extract:

	£	£
Share capital		300,000
Revaluation reserve	200,000	
General reserve	100,000	
Profit and Loss Account	300,000	600,000
Shareholders' funds		900,000
Loan capital		300,000
		£1,200,000

Gearing = 300,000 : 1,200,000
= 1 to 4

Balance Sheet review

Having examined the Balance Sheet of A Ltd in detail we can now review
the complete statement set out in Illustration 3.2. Here we see the
statement headed A Ltd, Balance Sheet as at 31 December.

First we see where the investments have been made: in fixed assets
£820,000, outside investments £160,000, and net current assets £100,000
made up of current assets £495,000 less current liabilities £395,000. And
all these items add up to a total of £1,080,000. The Balance Sheet then
goes on to tell us how this total investment has been financed: by issuing
shares of £300,000, retaining profits/reserves £680,000 and by means of
borrowing £100,000, again equalling the total of £1,080,000.

The use of the Balance Sheet

It is by examining this statement that we can assess first the relative risk or
chances of each investment we have made in helping the business to make
profits, and second to examine the proportion of borrowed to owners'
funds – 'the gearing' of the business. We can find out the terms on which
such capital is provided – interest rates payable and repayment dates in the
case of loans, i.e. the extent of the pressure. After all, it is all very well
investing funds in the right place to make profits but we must remember
that funds must be obtained from the right sources. However well money
is invested, if it is obtained from the most expensive of sources much of the
profit obtained will be lost.

Present Balance Sheet format

Balance Sheet layout is a continually changing feature of financial communication. Indeed there is a different layout within nearly every advanced economy. This means that American, Japanese and United Kingdom Balance Sheets vary in their presentation. Although the same facts are being presented their order changes and their terminology may well be different.

It is not felt appropriate at this stage to set out these variations but simply to refer to them, drawing your attention to the fact that however the Balance Sheet is presented it still deals with where the money is invested and from where that same money has been funded. For your information Illustration 3.9 shows the format of a Balance Sheet recommended at the present time which varies slightly from the previous example. The figures you will see are unchanged from those shown in Illustration 3.2 except for the inclusion of the revaluation value of fixed assets to include a profit of

Illustration 3.9 A Ltd: Balance Sheet as at 31 December 19. . (layout in accordance with Companies Act 1985 recommendation).

	£	£	£
Fixed assets			
Tangibles (at revaluation value)		970,000	
Investments		160,000	1,130,000
Current assets			
Stock: Raw material	60,000		
Work in progress	140,000		
Finished goods	70,000		
Debtors	220,000		
Cash	5,000	495,000	
Less: Creditors − Amounts falling due within a year		395,000	
Net current assets			100,000
Total assets *less* Current liabilities			1,230,000
Less: Creditors − Amounts falling due in more than a year			100,000
			£1,130,000
Capital and reserves			£
Share capital			300,000
Revaluation reserve			150,000
Profit and Loss Account			680,000
			£1,130,000

Notes:
The above totals differ from those in Illustration 3.2 for the following reasons:
1. Buildings included in Fixed assets of £280,000 have been revalued at £430,000, resulting in a Revaluation reserve of £150,000.
2. The long-term loans of £100,000 are, under this recommended layout, deducted as creditors − Amounts falling due in more than a year − from the Total assets less Current liabilities.
3. All reserves and the Profit and Loss Account amounts are added up to a total of £680,000 and presented under the latter title.

£150,000 and the rewording of the other reserves to read Profit and Loss Account.

However, in the new format there are some new terms. For instance, current liabilities are referred to as 'Amounts payable within twelve months' as already mentioned, and loans and other long-term liabilities are referred to as 'Amounts payable in more than twelve months' and are deducted from the Total assets less Current liabilities of the business.

It should also be noted that outside investments are included under the general heading of fixed assets together with those items which previously went under this heading.

Intangible assets

We are also introduced to the term 'tangible' fixed assets. So what are intangible fixed assets? These are fixed assets whose value is determined at a point in time by means of market forces or cost but where their continuing value is beyond the control or prediction of the owners or managers. Examples of these are copyrights, goodwill, brand names and research and development costs. Each in turn has a value or cost at the time they are created but in no way can this be guaranteed to continue.

The copyright of the best selling author may be of great value today but if fashion changes and no one wishes to read his or her books what then is its value? A business's name and reputation may create goodwill of real value but once these are lost so is the value of its goodwill. Again the value of a brand name rises and falls with the public's opinion of the business's products – fickle at the best of times – and research and development costs would only have value if they translate themselves into a saleable product or service.

It is because of the uncertainty as to the continuing value of intangible assets that accountants recommend that they should be separately shown on the Balance Sheet and written off against profits as soon as possible. You will see an example of this being done in Illustration 3.10.

Cumulative nature of Balance Sheets

Finally – and perhaps most importantly – it must be noted that, unlike a Profit and Loss Account which is a summary of financial data for a period of time, a Balance Sheet is a statement of financial information at a single point in time. It is cumulative and therefore it is not telling us what a business has done over the last year unless it is its first year of existence.

For this reason, if we want to examine what has happened over, say, the

Illustration 3.10 A Ltd: Balance Sheets.

	Before	After
Fixed assets:	£000s	£000s
Tangible	500	800
Intangible	90	—
Investments	40	40
	930	840
Net current assets	80	80
Total assets *less* Current liabilities	1010	920
Less: Creditors – Amounts falling due in more than a year	200	200
	£810	£720
Capital and reserves:	£000s	£000s
Share capital	350	350
Profit and Loss Account	460	370 (460–90)
	£810	£720

last year we would need to extract the difference between the Balance Sheet as at the end of last year from that at the end of this. This indeed is what is set out in a Source and Application of Funds Statement referred to in the next chapter.

Balance Sheet date

It must also be remembered that because a Balance Sheet is presented as at a set date figures may be affected by the date selected. For example, stock or inventory levels, or amounts owed by debtors or receivables or to creditors or payables may vary throughout the year. However, because it is taken out at one date, a Balance Sheet may give different values for such items than if another date had been chosen.

Indeed, year ends, and therefore Balance Sheet dates, are sometimes selected so as to coincide with when such values will provide the best possible view of the business. This step is most often taken so as to present the most favourable liquidity position, but again this matter will be dealt with in more detail in future studies on interpretation.

Conclusion and consolidation

Now to test your understanding turn to Illustration 3.11. Here you will find examples of the investments and sources of capital in Companies A Ltd and B Ltd. Set out these two lists of items as Balance Sheets for each of the two businesses in the recommended format set out in Illustration 3.9.

When you have done this check your answers with Illustrations 3.12 and 3.13.

We have now completed our initial studies of the Balance Sheet, the agenda we use to consider the risk, the chances a business has of making profit. It is of course incomplete because in many areas it provides, as we have seen, merely a starting point, and there is much 'homework' still to be done. It also does not include mention of many aspects of a business which are crucial to its future profitability – the skill of its workforce and the calibre of its management, for instance. However, despite all these deficiencies it remains the only agenda we have and needs to be understood and used within its obvious limitations.

You have now completed this stage in your understanding of business finance so you are in a position to proceed to the next chapter, which is concerned with a very familiar topic for every one of us – having the ready to arrive – the Cash Flow Forecast.

Illustration 3.11 A and B Ltd: investments and sources of capital.

Business investment of A Ltd as at 31 December 19. .

	£
Outside investments	50,000
Freehold land	60,000
Merchandise stock	50,000
Fixtures and fittings	30,000
Share capital	200,000
Motor vehicles	20,000
Creditors	60,000
Bank and cash balances	45,000
Debtors	5,000
Buildings	60,000
Profit and Loss Account	60,000

Business investment of B Ltd as at 31 March 19. .

	£
Work in progress	60,000
Plant and machinery	40,000
Creditors	140,000
Share capital	200,000
Debtors	160,000
Raw material stock	10,000
Outside investments	30,000
Bank overdraft	60,000
Land and buildings	230,000
General reserve	30,000
Finished goods stock	30,000
Profit and loss account	60,000
Loans repayable in 3 years	50,000
Depreciation to date on plant and machinery	20,000

Illustration 3.12 A Ltd: Balance Sheet as at 31 December 19...

Fixed assets:		£	£
Freehold land		60,000	
Buildings		60,000	
Fixtures and fittings		30,000	
Motor vehicle		20,000	
		170,000	
Investments		50,000	220,000
Current assets:	£		
Merchandise stock	50,000		
Debtors	5,000		
Bank and cash balance	45,000	100,000	
Less: Creditors – Amounts falling due within a year		60,000	
Net current assets			40,000
			£260,000
Capital and reserves			£
Share capital			200,000
Profit and Loss Account			60,000
			£260,000

Illustration 3.13 B Ltd: Balance Sheet as at 31 March 19...

Fixed assets:		£	£
Land and buildings		230,000	
Plant and machinery		20,000	
		250,000	
Investments		30,000	280,000
Current assets:	£		
Stocks: Raw material	10,000		
Work in progress	60,000		
Finished goods	30,000		
Debtors	160,000	260,000	
Less: Creditors – Amounts falling due within a year		200,000	
Net current assets			60,000
Total assets less Current liabilities			340,000
Less: Creditors – Amounts falling due in more than a year			50,000
			£290,000
Capital and reserve:			£
Share capital			200,000
General reserve			30,000
Profit and Loss Account			60,000
			£290,000

4 | THE CASH FLOW FORECAST

Money movement – the cash flow

So far we have examined the fundamental statements produced in business to deal with the two primary financial questions raised by investors and therefore managers in every business situation, namely, what is the return on the investment, which in business we deal with in the Profit and Loss Account, and what are the chances or risk of making this return, which in business we deal with in the Balance Sheet?

However, when money is invested in a business something happens to it which is unique – it moves. After all, as we have already mentioned, when you place money on a horse the one thing you do not want to happen is for the money to move. You prefer the horse to move and the money to stand absolutely still!

In business the movement of money is crucial to its progress and to its success. In many ways having the necessary cash to meet the changing needs of a business can be likened to the fare which is required when going on a bus journey. In business we refer to the movement of money as the cash flow, which means the continual movement of money throughout the enterprise during any period of time.

The Cash Flow Forecast

An understanding of the movement of cash is essential to those running a business, because they have to realise that unless they have the money as and when it is needed the business could collapse.

The basic method of controlling cash is simply to forecast over the period ahead the cash which it is anticipated will arrive and to deduct from this the cash which it is expected will be spent. It is this forecast which enables those managing the business to examine its cash position over the period ahead. The statement setting out this situation is termed the Cash Flow

Forecast and it is divided into monthly, weekly or even daily intervals depending upon the particular needs of the business.

Construction

To illustrate this refer to Illustration 4.1. Here we see a statement headed A Ltd Cash Flow Forecast and if you look at its contents you will see that in month 1 it is planning to receive £322,000, namely £260,000 from cash sales, £60,000 from credit sales – that is cash from people or businesses who have bought goods on credit (the debtors or receivables, remember) – and £2,000 from interest on outside investments the company has made. We also see that during month 1 A Ltd is planning to spend £260,000: £90,000 to the suppliers of materials who were not paid immediately for them (the creditors or accounts payable – remember), £70,000 on wages, £60,000 on overheads and £40,000 which will be paid out to shareholders as dividends.

However, at the close of the previous month, A Ltd had cash balances to bring forward of £15,000, what is termed a positive cash flow position. The final balance carried forward at the end of month 1 is therefore arrived at by adding the receipts, subtotal A, of £322,000 to the balance brought forward, subtotal C, of £15,000, making a total of £337,000, and deducting from this subtotal B, the total expenditure for the month of £260,000. This gives the balance to be carried forward of £77,000 – again a positive cash flow position.

Illustration 4.1   A Ltd: Cash Flow Forecast.

	Month 1 £	Month 2 £	Month 3 £
Receipts			
Cash sales	260,000	200,000	
Credit sales	60,000	40,000	
Interest received	2,000	—	
Subtotal A	322,000	240,000	
Payments			
Credit purchases of materials	90,000	160,000	
Wages	70,000	70,000	
Overheads	60,000	75,000	
Dividends paid	40,000	—	
Machine purchased	—	50,000	
Subtotal B	260,000	355,000	
Balance brought forward C	15,000	77,000	(38,000)
Balance carried forward D	77,000	(38,000)	
$D = (A \pm C) - B$			
Brackets = Overdraft			

In month 2 we continue in the same manner with just a few variations. First, we do not receive any interest on investments, second we buy a new machine and the final balance carried forward becomes a minus of £38,000 – known as a negative cash flow position.

Cash, sales and debtors

In looking at this cash flow forecast it must be emphasised that our concern is confined entirely and exclusively to cash. We are not concerned with the sales we invoice, only with the cash we receive from those we sell to, and the two figures can of course be very different – remember debtors or receivables. If you remember Chapter 2 when we were dealing with the Profit and Loss Account, the sales, or turnover as it is often called, is based on what the business has invoiced irrespective of cash receipts. However, in the Cash Flow Forecast it is only the cash we receive from the customers which is of interest to us.

Cash, purchasers and creditors

This is also true of payments for materials, wages, overheads, dividends, and machines and other fixed assets purchased. These refer in each case entirely to the cash we pay out, not the costs in the Profit and Loss Account or valuations on the Balance Sheet – remember creditors or payables. We have therefore a timing and blurring difference to take into account when comparing the balances in the Cash Flow Forecast with the profit or loss in the Profit and Loss Account.

Timing difference

First, as far as time is concerned, the Profit and Loss Account is a measurement of growth or shrinkage in relationship to invoiced sales for the period, and those expenses which directly refer to the same period of time and the sales that have taken place.

However, cash is only concerned with the 'pragmatic doctrine'. Has the cash been spent or received during the period covered by the Cash Flow Forecast? If it has, it must be included; if not, it must be excluded.

Revenue/capital and cash

The second consideration is that cash does not recognise any difference between fixed assets – capital expenditure – and items of profit and loss expense – revenue expenditure. It blurs or mixes them together. There is no division, for example, in Illustration 4.1 between the purchase of a machine shown as a payment in month 2 and money spent on materials, wages and overheads during the same period from a cash point of view. Money is spent in both situations.

Profit and loss and cash

All this means that the cash flow position, whether negative or positive, will not necessarily reflect the profit or loss of the business during the same period. The business could be making a profit and yet it could be 'broke' in cash terms – that is short of money. Or it could be making a loss and yet it could be 'flush' – that is showing a healthy cash balance. This fact must be very firmly understood by all those concerned with business. It was a point we also covered in Chapter 2 when discussing the Profit and Loss Account, and if you have any difficulty in understanding this you should refer back to this previous chapter.

Depreciation and cash

Finally in comparing the measurement of cash flow with profit or loss, we must remember that we have one major expense recorded in the Profit and Loss Account which does not affect cash expenditure – depreciation.

If you again recall Chapter 2 you will remember that depreciation is an assessment of the loss – the secret shrinkage as we called it – that goes on during the life of any fixed asset which is subject to obsolescence and/or wear and tear. It is this calculated loss or shrinkage which is included as an expense in the Profit and Loss Account and by doing this the profit is correspondingly reduced or the loss increased.

But let us stop and think about this expense and compare it with all the others, like those relating to labour, materials and other expenses like advertising, rent and insurance. There is a difference, and it is of course that depreciation, unlike all the other expenses, does not reduce the cash in the business. In a business we do not take out our cheque book and write one out for depreciation as we will certainly have to do in the end for materials, wages, rent, advertising and insurance costs.

Depreciation, from a cash point of view, is therefore not an expense. It reduces the profit or increases the loss but it does not reduce the cash the business has and therefore once again we have a major difference between the assessment of profit or loss and the cash flow. It might be said that from a cash point of view depreciation is a phoney item!

Reading a Cash Flow Forecast

So let us now stand back and see what this Cash Flow Forecast tells us. First we must understand why cash is so important within a business. As we have already said it is our bus fare – and because of this it enables us to arrive! If we run out of cash we may never reach our destination at all, however attractive it may be. For instance, if we examine the cash flow forecast for A Ltd in Illustration 4.1, we see that A Ltd could be heading for a substantial profit at the close of the year, but if it has not negotiated an overdraft or a loan to become available during months 2 and 3 of at least £38,000, it may never arrive.

This is the fundamental reason for cash planning and control. It provides a view over the period ahead so that we can take appropriate action. In cash planning you need time – engineers might call it lead-time – to arrange the necessary loan facility or to curtail expenditure plans if these are felt to be more than can be afforded.

Managers must also recognise that cash directly influences all their decisions. Cash might be described as the lubrication which is needed to make every major decision. Without it, just like an engine without oil, the business seizes up! For example, if a business has no cash, its managers no longer make decisions – they are made for them! The bills cannot be paid and if this continues people and businesses owed money will take remedial action for themselves. Or managers might be tempted to buy inferior materials at a lower cost, thus affecting the quality of what is produced.

It could be said therefore that the lack of cash when it is needed reduces the options open to the decision-makers of a business. It is for this reason that perhaps the major cause of business failure is inadequate cash planning and control.

Cash planning and progressing

Having set out the Cash Flow Forecast it will then be very necessary to compare it with events as they occur – to progress the position as time goes by.

As a result of this comparison, if differences are found between actual and comparative figures, we will need to check the impact this will have on the period ahead. For example, in Illustration 4.1 in month 1, if when we compare the actual credit sales against the £60,000 we found them to be only £50,000, there is a difference of £10,000. This might well indicate slow payment of certain amounts which will be corrected in month 2, and the figure for month 2 for credit sales would then read £50,000 – that is

£40,000 plus the extra £10,000. However, it might also mean that the forecasted figures were over-optimistic and a recalculation of the future cash flow position would need to be made. Continual revision of the Cash Flow Forecast is a vital part of cash flow control as early warning of changes will provide more time to take the necessary corrective action.

We must also appreciate that effective cash flow forecasting and control requires joint action by all managers – and indeed employees – at all levels of a business. Anyone concerned with cash planning must enlist the help of every person employed within the business to ensure that the greatest possible warning – or lead-time – is given whenever any changes occur to the cash plan. For example, sales staff need to warn the business when they suspect customers will not be able to pay amounts due.

For your information the first three months of a Cash Flow Forecast setting out columns for both budgeted and actual figures is included in Illustration 4.2. In this you will see that the budgeted figures have been included and await comparison with the actual data as it becomes available. It will be necessary then, if differences occur, to calculate their impact on the future net cash flow positions over the period ahead. In other words, the business will be able to recalculate the future budgeted figures.

Illustration 4.2   Cash Flow Forecast 19...

	Period					
	1		2		3	
Receipts	Budget	Actual	Budget	Actual	Budget	Actual
	£	£	£	£	£	£
Sale of goods – debtors	50,000		60,000		40,000	
Sale of fixed assets	5,000		—		—	
Dividends/interest received	1,000		500		2,000	
Subtotal A	56,000		60,500		42,000	
Payments						
Material – creditors	30,000		40,000		41,000	
Wages/salaries	10,000		12,000		12,000	
Overheads	5,000		6,500		7,000	
Fixed assets purchases	4,000		10,000		12,000	
Subtotal B	49,000		68,500		72,000	
Balance (A – B)	7,000		(8,000)		(30,000)	
Balance b/fwd	2,000		9,000		1,000	
Balance c/fwd	9,000		1,000		(29,000)	

Cash flow – the total view

So far we have examined the cash flow on a day-by-day, month-by-month basis, but in addition to this view, we can examine it in a total way.

To illustrate this let us go back to our model set out as Illustration 1.2. Here we can see that everything is flowing into or out of cash. Cash is the centre point – it might be said that it is the fulcrum of business investment. Whatever is done within a business will eventually have an effect upon its cash position. It therefore becomes a very convenient measurement around which to examine the financial effect of business decisions, policies and plans. It is because of this fact that managers and investors have increasingly turned to the examination of the cash movement in total to trace the progress of the business investment.

In other words managers have converted their plans into an examination of their impact upon what cash will come into the business and precisely what will happen to this cash if we follow the policies agreed for the business.

Investment review and analysis

To illustrate this I want you to look at the business investment of an enterprise at two points in time by turning to Illustration 4.3. Here you will see

Illustration 4.3   A Ltd: Balance Sheets.

Last year				This year	
£				£	£
		Fixed assets			
100,000		Land and buildings		200,000	
50,000		Plant and machinery		40,000	
150,000					240,000
60,000		Investments			60,000
		Working capital			
	£	Current assets	£		
	120,000	Stock	170,000		
	200,000	Debtors	320,000		
	320,000			490,000	
		Less:			
		Current liabilities			
140,000	180,000	Creditors		120,000	370,000
£350,000					£670,000
£		Financed by:			£
250,000		Share capital			400,000
100,000		Profit and Loss Account			270,000
£350,000					£670,000

the Balance Sheets of a company setting out its position both at the beginning and end of a year. It will be remembered from Chapter 3 that in each situation we are looking at a cumulative position. The fixed assets are those A Ltd owns as at that point of time and they may well include items which have been owned for many years.

The cumulative aspect

It is this cumulative aspect of the Balance Sheet which prevents us examining precisely the changes which have occurred in the short term. However, we can overcome this problem by concentrating our view upon the changes in the short term. If we do this we can present the picture in cash terms first as regards what additional cash has come into the business, and from what sources, during the period we are looking at, and second in which areas such funds have been invested.

We can apply this approach either to a historical or to a forecasted situation. However, in what ever way it is viewed, it will have the effect of concentrating attention upon the changes which have taken or are planned to take place within the particular business. It will take us away from the cumulative view.

The Source and Application of Funds Statement

To demonstrate this let us turn to Illustration 4.4 whilst at the same time keeping an eye on Illustration 4.3.

In Illustration 4.4 we have a summary or statement of the differences between this and last year's figures set out on the Balance Sheets shown in Illustration 4.3. This is what we call a Source and Application of Funds Statement.

Sources

In this particular example it tells us that during the year £150,000 has come into A Ltd from additional share capital and £170,000 from retained profits, a total of £320,000 from these two sources.

Applications

The Statement then goes on to describe how during this same period £90,000 has been invested in fixed assets, nothing in outside investments and £230,000 in working capital. Again the total of all these applications

Illustration 4.4 A Ltd: Source and Application of Funds Statement for the year 19...

Sources of funds			£	£
Share capital			150,000	
Profits retained			170,000	£320,000

Application of funds	Increase	Decrease		
	£	£		£
Fixed assets				
Land and buildings	100,000			
Plant and machinery		10,000	=	90,000
Working capital				
	Increase	Decrease		
	£	£		
Stock	50,000			
Debtors	120,000			
	170,000			
Creditors		60,000	=	230,000
				£320,000

Note:
A reduction in credit taken (creditors) is an application of funds (or an increase to the investment made in the business).

comes to £320,000. This is why it is called a Source and Application of Funds Statement. It describes where we have invested our money and the sources from which that same money has been obtained. We can of course express this statement in much more detail depending upon our needs, and certainly if we were planning future investment, it would be necessary to obtain the fullest possible picture.

Sources and depreciation

We have also over-simplified the picture by ignoring the effect of depreciation. What I mean is that, as we have already said about depreciation, it is not a cash expense. It reduces a business's profits but it does not reduce its cash flow.

We can demonstrate this if we set out Illustration 4.3 in more detail as in Illustration 4.5. Here we are assuming that the depreciation deducted during year 2 amounted to £60,000, and this means that we would have a further source of cash for investment, a source that if we wish to have a full view of the increase to money invested must be included. The sources of money must be increased by the amount held back as depreciation for the year.

However, if this is done we must also adjust the fixed assets figure. This is because the difference of £90,000 shown in Illustration 4.4, between the fixed assets at the beginning and end of the year, is given after deducting this additional depreciation of £60,000 in arriving at the second figure for the year for the fixed assets.

For this reason the true investment in fixed assets during the year should have read £150,000. This is the £90,000 already calculated plus the £60,000 depreciation. The revised Balance Sheet for A Ltd which includes this adjustment is set out in Illustration 4.5, and a revised Source and Application of Funds Statement based on this is set out in Illustration 4.6. You will also see that Illustration 4.6, lumps everything under the heading Current assets *less* Current liabilities as one figure, which it describes as Working capital.

Working capital detailed

A more detailed example of a Source and Application of Funds Statement prepared from the Balance Sheet of B Ltd shown in Illustration 4.7 is set out as Illustration 4.8. In this case the working capital changes are set out in detail as are those that apply to the fixed assets.

You will also notice that in this illustration the company concerned,

Illustration 4.5   A Ltd: this year and last year's figures (including depreciation).

£			£	£	£
				Less	
				Depreciation	
			Cost	to date	
		Fixed assets			
100,000		Land and buildings	200,000	—	200,000
50,000*		Plant and machinery	180,000	140,000	40,000
150,000					240,000
60,000		Investments			60,000
	£	Current assets			
	120,000	Stock	170,000		
	200,000	Debtors	320,000		
	320,000			490,000	
		Less:			
		Current liabilities			
140,000	180,000	Creditors		120,000	370,000
£350,000					£670,000
		Financed by:			
250,000		Share capital			400,000
100,000		Profit and Loss Account			270,000
£350,000					£670,000
		*Made up as follows:	£		
		Cost	130,000		
		Less: Depreciation to date	80,000		
			£50,000		

Illustration 4.6 A Ltd: Source and Application of Funds Statement (after inclusion of depreciation £60,000).

Source of funds	£
Share capital	150,000
Profits retained	170,000
Depreciation	60,000
	£380,000
Application of funds	£
Fixed assets	150,000
Working capital	230,000
	£380,000

Illustration 4.7 B Ltd: Balance Sheets as at 31 December.

Last year			This year	
£	£		£	£
		Fixed assets		
	120,000	Land and buildings	170,000	
210,000	90,000	Plant and machinery	110,000	280,000
170,000		Investments		160,000
		Current assets	£	
	90,000	Stock	150,000	
	160,000	Debtors	140,000	290,000
	250,000			
		Less:		
		Current liabilities		
150,000	100,000	Creditors	90,000	200,000
£530,000				£640,000
		Financed by:		
	300,000	Share capital		500,000
	160,000	Profit and Loss Account		50,000
	70,000	Loans		90,000
£530,000				£640,000

Note: Depreciation on Plant and machinery for the year is £50,000.

B Ltd, has made a loss in the year but the presentation is in all other ways similar to that already given in Illustration 4.4.

Cash balance change

In all the examples we have so far seen, no reference has been made to the cash and bank balances and it is changes to these which are the specific purpose of the Source and Application of Funds Statement.

Its purpose is not just to dissect differences but to highlight whether the

Illustration 4.8 B Ltd: Source and Application of Funds Statement.

Sources of funds			£
Profit and Loss Account			(110,000)
Depreciation			50,000
From operations			(60,000)
Share capital			200,000
Loans			20,000
			£160,000

Application of funds	Increase	Decrease	
Fixed assets	£	£	£
Land and buildings	50,000		
Plant and machinery	70,000		
Investments		10,000	= 110,000

	Increase	Decrease	
Weekly capital	£	£	
Stocks	60,000		
Debtors		20,000	
Less: Creditors		10,000	= 50,000
			£160,000

Note: A reduction in credit taken (creditors) is an application of funds or an increase to the investment made in the business.

sources for investment are equal to or less than the investments made during the selected period of time. After all, if the investments made are less than the sources more cash will have been created than used and the cash and bank balances should reflect this fact. In the same way if the sources of funds are less than what has been invested the bank and cash balances will have been reduced. Illustrations 4.9 to 4.12 provide you with two examples of how these statements are more usually presented so as to highlight the changes in the cash/bank position. It is from the layout of the Source and Application of Funds Statement set out in these illustrations that you can see whether or not the business has, what might be termed, 'lived within its means'. Illustration 4.11 shows that sources of £105,000 exceed the C Ltd's applications of £97,000 by £8,000. On the other hand, Illustration 4.12 shows that sources of £390,000 are less than the application of funds of £405,000, in which case D Ltd has 'lived beyond its means' by £15,000.

Again as in so many financial situations there is nothing wrong or right about either situation but it is a fact that needs to be known so that the right questions can be asked. For example, in Illustration 4.11 cash/bank balances are shown to have increased by £8,000. How are these funds, not applied within the business, planned to be used or invested? Again, in Illustration 4.12 where cash/bank balances are shown to have reduced by £15,000, are the funds required to finance or source the applications being

Illustration 4.9   C Ltd: Balance Sheet as at 31 March.

Last year				This year	
£				£	£
		Fixed assets			
100,000		Land and buildings		130,000	
70,000		Plant and machinery		90,000	
170,000					220,000
20,000		Investments			25,000
	£	Current assets	£		
	10,000	Stocks	20,000		
	110,000	Debtors	120,000		
	20,000	Cash/bank	28,000		
	140,000			168,000	
		Less: Creditors: amounts falling due			
	60,000	within one year		78,000	
80,000		Net current year			90,000
270,000		Total assets *less* Current liabilities			335,000
30,000		*Less:* Loans			65,000
£240,000					£270,000
£		Capital and reserves			£
140,000		Share capital			140,000
100,000		Profit and Loss Account			130,000
£240,000					£270,000

Depreciation charge for year = £40,000.

Illustration 4.10   D Ltd: Balance Sheet as at 30 September.

Last year				This year	
£	£			£	£
		Fixed assets			
	500,000	Land and building		750,000	
	60,000	Fixtures and fittings		120,000	
580,000	20,000	Investments		40,000	910,000
		Current assets	£		
	40,000	Stocks	75,000		
	5,000	Cash/bank	—	75,000	
	45,000	*Less:*			
		Creditors: amounts falling due within one year			
	50,000	Trade creditors	90,000		
	—	Overdraft	10,000	100,000	
− 5,000		Net current liabilities			25,000
575,000		Total fixed assets *less* Current liability			885,000
120,000		*Less:* Creditors falling due in more than a year			150,000
£455,000					£735,000
£		Capital and reserves			£
250,000		Share capital			300,000
205,000		Profit and Loss Account			435,000
£455,000					£735,000

Depreciation charges for year = £80,000.

Illustration 4.11 C Ltd: Source and Application of
Funds Statement for year to 31 March

Sources	£	£
Profit and Loss Account	30,000	
Depreciation	40,000	
From operations		70,000
Loans		35,000
		105,000

Applications			
Fixed assets (details below)		95,000	
Working capital	£		
Stocks	10,000		
Debtors	10,000		
	20,000		
Less: Creditors	18,000	2,000	97,000
Changes to cash position			£ + 8,000

Analysis	£
Cash position: at beginning of year	20,000
at end of year	28,000
Cash position improved by	£8,000

Fixed assets	£
Land and buildings	30,000
Plant and machinery	20,000
Depreciation	40,000
Investments	5,000
	£95,000

found out of normal bank overdraft facilities or are bank balances
becoming dangerously low?

Summary of cash controls

We have therefore two basic controls of cash flow: first, the day-by-day,
month-by-month, assessment of cash available by means of the Cash Flow
Forecast, and second the overall assessment of cash movement by means of
the Source and Application of Funds Statement. This latter statement is
particularly useful in looking at the pattern of investment changes within
a business over past periods and in the translation of plans for a business
into cash terms for the future.

Consolidation of studies

We have now examined the last of the three fundamental financial infor-

Illustration 4.12 D Ltd: Source and Application of Funds
Statement for year to 30 September.

Sources		£
Profit and Loss Account		230,000
Depreciation		80,000
From operations		310,000
Share capital		50,000
Loan capital		30,000
		390,000

Applications	£		
Fixed assets (details below)		410,000	
Working capital	£		
Stocks	35,000		
Less: Creditors	40,000	5,000	405,000
Changes to cash position			£ – 15,000

Analysis		£
Cash position: at beginning of year		5,000
at end (overdraft)		– 10,000
Position worsened by		£15,000

Fixed assets	Increase
	£
Land and buildings	250,000
Fixtures and fittings	60,000
Add back: Depreciation	80,000
Investments	20,000
	£410,000

mation statements. In Chapter 2 we reviewed the measurement of return on business investment by means of the Profit and Loss Account, in Chapter 3 we looked at the risk or the chance of a business making a profit and we learned how to consider the chances or risk of a business making profits through the Balance Sheet. Now finally we have looked at cash, the raw material of investment, its control and its flow.

We have now gained a basic understanding of business finance but to consolidate and reinforce this knowledge turn to Illustration 4.13 which is a case study based on all your studies up to this point. First, attempt the question stage by stage without reference to the solution, and then check your work with the model answer as it is set out in Illustrations 4.14 to 4.16. Remember at each stage of the question to trace through the logic and recognise when and if errors occur in your work – the errors you make will be *illogical*.

Once you have worked through this case study pose yourself the supplementary questions below which test your knowledge of business finance up to this point.

Illustration 4.13 Financial case study.

It is planned to form A Ltd on 1 July with share capital of £40,000, of which it intends to invest £25,000 in fixed assets — plant and machinery etc. — and the remainder leave as cash £15,000. Its plans for the first six months are as below and you are asked to translate these into:

1. A monthly Cash Flow Forecast.
2. A forecasted Profit and Loss Account for the six months.
3. A forecasted Balance Sheet as at 31 December.

Sales for six months	£600,000
Materials in sales	£240,000
Labour in sales	£180,000
Other expenses including depreciation £2,000	£140,000
Materials purchases for the period	£260,000

Cash receipts and payments for six months:

	Sales receipts £	Materials payments £	Overheads and wages
July	40,000	60,000	
August	50,000	60,000	Paid
September	50,000	20,000	evenly
October	70,000	20,000	each
November	120,000	20,000	month
December	150,000	20,000	
	£480,000	£200,000	

Special note: It must be particularly noted that every figure is a *forecast*.

Illustration 4.14 A Ltd: Cash Flow Forecast.

	Jul. £	Aug. £	Sept. £	Oct. £	Nov. £	Dec. £
Receipts						
Sales	40,000	50,000	50,000	70,000	120,000	150,000
Share capital	40,000					
Subtotal A	80,000	50,000	50,000	70,000	120,000	150,000
Payments						
Materials	60,000	60,000	20,000	20,000	20,000	20,000
Wages	30,000	30,000	30,000	30,000	30,000	30,000
Overheads	23,000	23,000	23,000	23,000	23,000	23,000
Fixed assets	25,000	—	—	—	—	—
Subtotal B	138,000	113,000	73,000	73,000	73,000	73,000
Balance (A − B)	(58,000)	(63,000)	(23,000)	(3,000)	47,000	77,000
Balance b/fwd	—	(58,000)	(121,000)	(144,000)	(147,000)	(100,000)
Balance c/fwd	(58,000)	(121,000)	(144,000)	(147,000)	(100,000)	(23,000)

Illustration 4.15 A Ltd: Forecasted
Profit and Loss Account for the six
months ended 31 December.

	£	£
Sales		600,000
Less: Materials	240,000	
Labour	180,000	
Overheads	140,000	560,000
Trading profit		£40,000

Illustration 4.16 A Ltd: Forecasted Balance Sheet as at
31 December.

	£	£	£
Fixed assets	25,000		
Less: Depreciation	2,000		23,000
Current assets			
Stock	20,000		
Debtors	120,000	140,000	
Less: Current liabilities			
Creditors material	60,000		
Bank overdraft	23,000	83,000	57,000
			£80,000
Financed by:			
Share capital	40,000		
	40,000		£80,000

The Cash Flow Forecast

Once you have completed your answers and compared them with those provided in Illustrations 4.14. to 4.16, ask yourself, in the case of the Cash Flow Forecast, if you were a bank manager and this company came to you for a loan to help it over this six month period, would you say yes or no? Base your answer on what you see in the Cash Flow Forecast.

Think this through – your answer should be no, first because there is insufficient security, which seems to be confined to the fixed assets purchased in July for £25,000, and second because of commitment. The shareholders are only putting into the business £40,000 whilst you, as a banker, are being asked to lend nearly four times more than that by October.

These then are the two facts you look for before you lend money – first security and second commitment: you want sufficient security to cover the amount lent and enough commitment from the owners to indicate the risk they are taking. A textbook bankers' rule is never lend anyone more than 50 per cent of what they could lose themselves – which in our example would be no more than £20,000 (50 per cent of share capital of £40,000), a long way short of what is needed! However, textbook rules are often broken!

So if A Ltd cannot borrow the money it needs let's pose the next supplementary question. If it were your business would you welcome friends who might be willing to put in £150,000 as share capital?

Again you should say no, and again there are two reasons: first because, of course, your friends would then control the business, and if it were your ideas and energy going into the enterprise you might very well not wish this to happen!

However, there is a second and much more important reason for saying no and that lies in the nature of the sources of capital. If you remember from Chapter 1, share capital is permanent, and looking along the bottom line of the Cash Flow Forecast you certainly do not need £150,000 permanently. A Ltd only needs it in October. Before and after that it has very different needs. In fact by the time it gets to the end of December it only requires £23,000. So if you had accepted your friends' money as share capital, you would not only have lost control of your business, but by the time you reach the end of the six months you will have £127,000 sitting in your bank account which you no longer require.

Having dealt with these supplementary questions it can be seen that it is certainly not going to be easy to get a loan, and additional share capital, even if it were forthcoming, is not an alternative answer. So what should we do – give up? Well, before we do that let us see if it is going to be worth the effort. In other words the Cash Flow Forecast shows us that there is going to be a real need for cash help and that to get it is not going to be easy – impossible you might think! However, before we get too depressed let us see if it is going to be worth the effort by looking at the Profit and Loss Account. After all, if this shows that the business would make large profits, it might be worth putting a bit of effort into getting hold of the money from somewhere.

The Profit and Loss Account

So let's pose the first supplementary question about the Profit and Loss Account shown in Illustration 4.15: what do you think of the profits shown of £40,000? Do you think it is good, bad or indifferent? And I hope you will answer very good indeed. This should be because you have compared this profit, not with the sales figure of £600,000, but with the capital employed of £40,000. A return on capital employed of 100 per cent in six months.

In fact it is so good that if you were a sensible manager you would look to see if such a profit is possible. This means you would look for compar-

Illustration 4.17 A Ltd: Revised Forecasted Profit and Loss Account for the six months ended 31 December.

	£	£
Sales		600,000
Less: Direct materials	240,000	
Direct labour*	60,000	300,000
Gross profit		300,000
Less: Overheads		260,000
Trading profit		£40,000

*It is assumed that the labour cost of £180,000 shown in Illustration 4.15 is divided as follows:

	£
Direct labour	60,000
Overhead labour	120,000
	£180,000

Illustration 4.18 A Ltd: Forecasted Source and Application of Funds Statement.

Sources	£	£
Share capital	40,000	
Profit	40,000	
Depreciation	2,000	82,000
Applications		
Investment		105,000
Negative cash flow		£23,000

isons to see if other companies operating in the same type of business are making a similar profit. Then you would want to look at profit in comparison with the sales. In fact you would want to get the Profit and Loss Account analysed as we discussed in Chapter 2.

You can see this in Illustration 4.17 where the expenses have been divided between those which are variable and those which are fixed, the direct costs and overheads as they are termed in the example. In this illustration a gross profit is shown of £300,000 which represents a ratio of 50 per cent on sales. It would be this percentage that we could then compare with similar businesses to see if their gross profit percentages work out at approximately the same figure. If this is so, we could then say that although, having started A Ltd, we would certainly have a considerable cash flow problem (it would be skint in the first six months), it would at the same time be making a very large profit. In fact whatever effort is required to get the money would be well worth it!

The Source and Application of Funds Statement
These two statements together tell us something which is shown in the

Source and Application of Funds Statement set out in Illustration 4.18. This shows that the sources of funds during the six months would amount to £82,000: share capital £40,000, profits £40,000, plus depreciation £2,000. However, we have seen from the Cash Flow Forecast that we are short of cash. We have a loan requirement at the end of December of £23,000. This therefore means that we must have invested £105,000.

The Balance Sheet

In order to determine in which area this investment will take place we need to examine the forecasted Balance Sheet shown in Illustration 4.16. Now you have done this we will pose the final supplementary question. We already know that, if A Ltd is started it will have an investment problem: it will be investing more funds than it is creating. So, looking at the Balance Sheet, where precisely will this be happening, in which particular investment area or areas?

The answer is obviously in the credit it is giving its customers – its debtors – which by 31 December will amount to £120,000. This might then lead us on to considering whether this money could be brought in quicker or whether we could find bankers who might lend A Ltd money on the security of its unpaid invoices.

Summary and conclusion

We have just been explaining how from a simple business plan – in this case that referring to A Ltd – we have been able to use our knowledge gained so far, linked with our common sense, to arrive at some logical conclusions – or at least better questions! After all we are looking at a totally logical subject which stems entirely from the market-place. That is why we began our studies by understanding the way money works in every business by means of the balls model, and then followed this by studying the three primary questions we need to ask about the investment of money in any business:

1. The return as given by the Profit and Loss Account;
2. The risk as given by the Balance Sheet; and finally
3. The ready as given by the Cash Flow Forecast.

So is this all? Have we finished? Well, not quite. After all there are still more questions, questions we shall discover when we go on to study management accounting in Chapter 5 which deals with the supplementary questions which stem from these three primary financial statements.

5 | THE DEVELOPMENT OF MANAGEMENT ACCOUNTING

The evolution of financial information

In the previous three chapters we described the three primary information statements produced to measure and explain business investment – the Profit and Loss Account, the Balance Sheet and the Cash Flow Forecast. We are now going to extend this understanding by showing how further financial information is developed for managers within a modern business – information which goes under the title of management accounting. However, to help you do this turn first to Illustration 5.1 which sets out what might be termed the evolution of financial information. You will notice that reading from the left – Area 1 – the first step is described as 'Understanding money in any business' and certainly anyone who wishes to understand business finance must begin at this point.

Sources and investment of money in business

They must understand where money comes from and where it goes to, and if you turn to Illustration 5.2 there you will see the financial model again that we have become very familiar with. In this model we describe the fact that in any business money comes in from yourself and what you may borrow. This will, in the case of a limited company, be its share capital and loan capital – and this is set out as circle 1. We then go on to describe that once the money is in a business it goes into three main areas: fixed assets which are things we have no intention of selling, outside investments often these days included as one of the fixed assets, and working capital.

Working capital
Working capital is money which is invested in labour, materials and overheads, which in their turn are converted into finished goods, saleable merchandise or services. These are then sold either directly for cash, or to people or businesses who hesitate before they pay – who we refer to as debtors and Americans call accounts receivable.

Illustration 5.1   The evolution of financial information.

Area 1	Area 2	Area 3	Area 4	Area 5
The first step	Primary financial information	Derivative financial techniques	Comparative techniques	

Understanding money in any business	1. The return: given in the Profit and Loss Account	1. Analysis of profit and loss:
		  – Costing
		  – Full
		  – Marginal
			Budgetary control	Interpretation of data

	2. The Risk: given in the Balance Sheet	1. Project appraisal 2. Working capital analysis	Standard costing	
	3. The ready: given in the Cash Flow Forecast	1. Source and Application of Funds Statement		

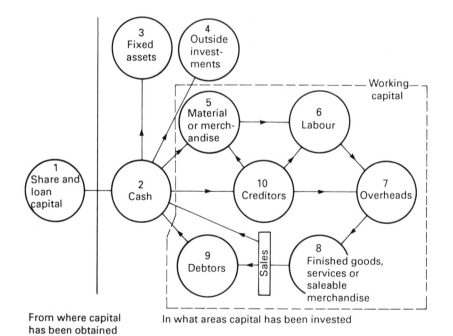

From where capital has been obtained

In what areas capital has been invested

Illustration 5.2   Financial model.

It will also be remembered that a business itself hesitates before it pays for the materials or merchandise, labour and overheads it uses – we refer to the people or businesses who are waiting for their money as the creditors, or as the Americans would say accounts payable.

Primary questions

If we then return to Illustration 5.1 you will see that the second area reading from the left is headed 'Primary financial information'. The primary financial information stems, as we have seen from our previous studies, from the three primary questions raised by anyone concerned with business investment.

The Profit and Loss Account and Balance Sheet

First there are the two questions every investor asks whenever money is invested anywhere – what is the return, and what is the risk? It is in response to these questions in business that the Profit and Loss Account – which deals with the question what is the return – and the Balance Sheet – which creates the basis from which we can assess the risk, the chances of

Illustration 5.3 A Ltd: Profit and Loss Account for the year ended 30 September (layout in accordance with Companies Act 1985, Format 1).

		£000
Turnover		170,000
Less: Cost of sales*		100,000
Gross profit		70,000
	£000	
Less: Distribution costs (these include sales expenses)	12,000	
Administration costs	18,000	30,000
Trading or operating profit		40,000
Add: Non-trading income		
Investment income	5,000	
Profit on sale of machinery	500	5,500
		45,500
Less: Non-trading expenses		
Interest on loans	7,000	
Loss on sale of equipment	1,000	8,000
Profit on ordinary activities before taxation		37,500
Less: Taxation		12,500
Profit on ordinary activities after taxation		25,000
Less: Proposed dividend		5,000
Retained profit		£20,000

*Includes the cost of: materials, manufacturing labour, manufacturing expenses, i.e. factory rent, rates, depreciation of plant and machinery, etc. If a retailer, this would include merchandise cost only.

(If shares issued numbered 100,000,000, earnings per share = 25p.)

making profit – are supplied. Examples of both these financial statements are set out as Illustrations 5.3 and 5.4.

However, in a business situation we find that answering these two primary questions is not enough because central to the understanding of business finance is the fact that when money is put into a business it moves or flows. It is continually changing position and growing or shrinking, depending on how the money flows.

This is the unique feature of business investment: the fact that money is moving and therefore the amount held is changing position all the time. This creates the need for the third primary financial statement, the one concerned with forecasting how much money as money the business will have at any particular point in time. This might be described as discovering whether the business will have 'the ready' to arrive.

The Cash Flow Forecast

We therefore have this further need – to discover what will be our cash position over the period ahead whilst we are running a business. This is not something you want to know historically. You need to discover this in advance so that you can look ahead and be prepared for any eventuality

Illustration 5.4   A Ltd: Balance Sheet as at 31 January (layout in accordance with Companies Act 1985, Format 1).

		£000	£000
Fixed assets:			
Tangibles (at revaluation value)		900,000	
Investments		60,000	960,000
	£000		
Current assets:			
Stock: Raw material	5,000		
Work in progress	8,000		
Finished goods	17,000		
Debtors	40,000		
Cash	10,000	80,000	
Less: Creditors – Amounts falling due within a year		60,000	
Net current assets			20,000
Total assets *less* Current liabilities			980,000
Less: Creditors – Amounts falling due in more than a year			250,000
			£730,000
Capital and reserves:			
Called-up share capital			270,000
Revaluation reserve			150,000
Profit and Loss Account			310,000
			£730,000

Illustration 5.5   A Ltd: Cash Flow Forecast 19. . .

	Period					
	1		2		3	
	Budget £	Actual	Budget £	Actual	Budget £	Actual
Receipts:						
Sale of goods – debtors	50,000		60,000		40,000	
Sale of fixed assets	5,000		—		—	
Dividends/interest received	1,000		500		2,000	
Subtotal A	56,000		60,500		42,000	
Payments:						
Material – creditors	30,000		40,000		41,000	
Wages/salaries	10,000		12,000		12,000	
Overheads	5,000		6,500		7,000	
Fixed assets purchases	4,000		10,000		12,000	
Subtotal B	49,000		68,500		72,000	
Balance (A – B)	7,000		(8,000)		(30,000)	
Balance b/fwd	2,000		9,000		1,000	
Balance c/fwd	9,000		1,000		(29,000)	

which may occur. Illustration 5.5 sets out the statement that deals with
this – the Cash Flow Forecast.

These then are the three primary financial statements which we dealt
with in previous chapters. You are recommended to tackle Illustration 4.13
again if you require revision.

The derivative techniques

Having understood these three primary statements it is now necessary to
take the next step, which is to say to ourselves, if we were supplied with
all this primary information, would it in itself be enough or would we ask
for more?

In response to this question I shall first explain the evolution of accounting information available within the modern business, and to deal with this
we shall begin again at the very beginning. We shall take each of the three
primary financial statements which we have just described and ask ourselves for each one the question: if we got this information is it enough in
itself or do we want to know more? The purpose of this is to illustrate the

natural – the logical – evolution of financial information to meet the needs of the interested parties – managers, investors, and indeed the world at large it might be argued. So let us begin with the Profit and Loss Account.

Techniques derived from the Profit and Loss Account

Turn to Illustration 5.3 which sets out a typical example of this statement and consider the trading or operating profit of £40,000,000.

The need for analysis – costing

Now suppose this was the Profit and Loss Account of your own business showing this trading or operating profit, and suppose at the same time that this business is concerned with selling many different products or merchandise or providing many different services. Now the question you should answer is, given this situation, would it be enough to know that you have made this profit or would you want to know more about it? No doubt what you would want to know is where the profit is being made. Where is it coming from – from which product or type of merchandise or service – and how much?

In other words a central concern of anyone looking at a Profit and Loss Account is the need to find out where the profit or loss is being made, to find out in our example where the £40,000,000 profit has been made. And to do this it will clearly be necessary to analyse the sales income and the trading or operating costs of materials or merchandise, labour and overheads so as to determine which applies to which particular product, type of merchandise or service. It is this analysis which is referred to as costing.

Costing, then, is the financial technique which has been developed to meet the very natural desire of anyone looking at a Profit and Loss Account to find out from where the trading or operating profit or loss has been made.

Full and marginal costing

We shall be looking at the details of this technique in later chapters but at the present time I would like to draw your attention to one particular feature regarding trading or operating expenses. If you extend the analysis of expenses to the units we are selling or the services we are rendering you will see that such expenses move in two ways. First there will be those which can be attributed directly to such units and services, and second there will be those which are incurred irrespective of the activity of the business.

For example, there will be the materials, merchandise and labour which can be traced directly to the particular products, merchandise or services sold, whereas many other expenses – often termed the overheads – such as the rent, insurances and salaries cannot be so directly attributed.

It is this division of expenses that has to be understood when considering the two types of analysis termed full and marginal costing. Full costing is the system of expense analysis which attempts to analyse all the trading or operating expenses of the business, whilst marginal costing confines its analysis to the direct expenses, those trading or operating expenses which move in sympathy – or as they say vary – with what is produced and sold.

Simple examples of both a full and marginal cost are set out in Illustrations 5.6 and 5.7 and we shall be dealing with each method of costing in the next two chapters.

Techniques derived from the Balance Sheet

Having considered the techniques which arise from the desire to learn more about the Profit and Loss Account we shall now consider what stems from

Illustration 5.6 Full cost analysis.

	Unit cost
	p
Direct material	5
Direct labour	4
Direct expenses	3
Prime cost	12
Indirect works expenses	3
Works cost	15
Indirect administrative expenses	4
Production cost	19
Selling and distribution expenses	5
Total cost	24
Profit	4
Sales price	28

Illustration 5.7 Marginal cost analysis.

	Unit cost
	p
Direct material	5
Direct labour	4
Other variable expenses	8
Marginal cost	17
Contribution or margin	11
Sales price	28

the Balance Sheet, the statement which is concerned with the risk or chances of a business making a profit. Once again ask yourself the question, if you received this statement would it be enough for the purpose of examining risk?

Of course, to deal with this question you have got to recognise the nature of the Balance Sheet. It is a summary of from where the business has obtained its capital and how this same capital has been invested.

It is the areas in which the business is investing its money which calls for management's greatest concern. This is because their day-to-day activities involve the continual investment and reinvestment of the funds of the business.

Investment areas

It will be remembered that when considering how money was invested in a business we say that money, very broadly, is either being put into things we have no intention of selling – the fixed assets, including outside investments – or it is being put into the money-go-round – the working capital – the area in which the money is being spent on materials, or merchandise, labour and overheads which are then converted into the finished goods, saleable merchandise or services to be sold.

Because money is going into these two diametrically different areas managers have very different questions regarding each. To emphasise and revise this division of investment in business tackle the question set out in Illustration 5.8, and when you have completed this check your answer against Illustration 5.9.

Fixed assets

We will begin our examination of the investment techniques by taking the fixed asset area first. Here, the point for managers and investors to recognise is that, by the time they read a Balance Sheet telling them what fixed assets the business owns, it is too late! After all, because fixed assets are not purchased for resale once they are acquired, the business is in a way 'stuck with them'! It is for this reason that the primary need managers have in this area is to look before they leap!

Project appraisal techniques

In other words they need enough financial data available before the investment is made to help them consider its benefits to the business once it is owned. It is to meet this obvious requirement that over the past years 'project appraisal techniques' have been developed.

These techniques consider the facts that are known about the particular investment before it is made, and from these the desirability or otherwise

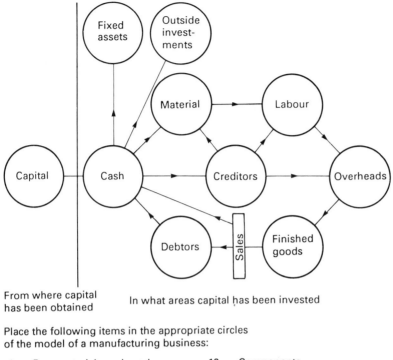

From where capital
has been obtained   In what areas capital has been invested

Place the following items in the appropriate circles
of the model of a manufacturing business:

1	Raw material purchased	12	Components
2	Marketing expenses	13	Land and building
3	Delivery vehicles	14	Share capital
4	Office salaries	15	Consultants' fees
5	Loans to business	16	Research and development costs
6	Bank overdraft	17	Salesmen's salaries
7	Amounts due to material suppliers	18	Investment in another business
8	Plant and machinery	19	Wages of employees
9	Rent	20	Auditors' fees
10	Labour employed to extend store	21	Amounts due from customers
11	Office equipment	22	Finished goods in warehouse

Illustration 5.8   Model of a manufacturing business.

of the investment is judged. We will be considering these techniques later
in Chapter 8 where we examine their application to this business
investment area.

Working capital – minimising the investment
In the second area of the Balance Sheet – the working capital – we have
the continuous requirement which we described in the very first chapter –
of minimising the investment. In this chapter we saw that every business
wishes to minimise its working capital so that it can maximise the return
on the capital employed and also so as to minimise the working capital
required to support its sales. Remember how we described the working

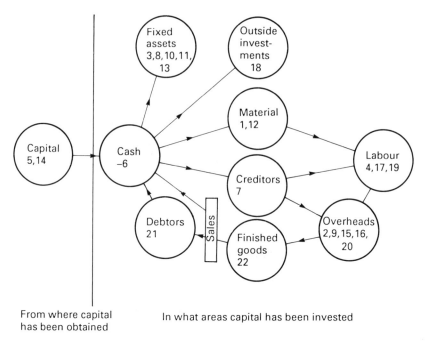

From where capital
has been obtained

In what areas capital has been invested

Notes:

1 Item 10 is an example of an expense which becomes capital because
what it is concerned with is extending the store.

2 Item 16 is an 'intangible' item and is therefore written off as a
revenue expense – see Chapter 3.

3 Item 15 is treated as an overhead but it could be a fixed asset or
capital expenditure in certain circumstances, for example architects'
fees in respect of the construction of a new factory.

Illustration 5.9 Answer to Illustration 5.8.

capital investment as the financial luggage a business carries on its journey
to a sale?

To achieve this we also saw that a business needs to control time: to
shorten the time it takes for its money to move from materials, merchandise, labour and overheads back into cash, and at the same time to maximise the time the business takes to pay for such materials, merchandise
labour and overheads. It is the analysis and control of the time money is
invested in working capital that we shall be considering in Chapter 9 which
is concerned with this subject.

Techniques derived from the Cash Flow Forecast

Having now seen the techniques that have been derived from the Balance

Sheet we shall return once again to Illustration 5.1 and consider the third primary financial statement, namely the Cash Flow Forecast. In this statement we are trying to discover exactly what money will be available throughout the running of the business.

It should be particularly noted that in this area of cash we are dealing with the one certain financial commodity – money itself. After all, we talk about profits and losses and we examine Balance Sheets but we handle money! It is perhaps because of our familiarity with money that over the years managers and investors have used money as a very central means of control.

Cash as a medium of explanation

What has happened is that managers and investors have recognised that if they translate all their plans into cash terms they will obtain a very convenient medium through which to review and control their entire business operation. It is therefore out of the Cash Flow Forecast that a technique has been developed for looking at businesses in cash terms by means of statements which examine the sources and applications of money within the business situation for given periods of time.

The Source and Application of Funds Statement

These Source and Application of Funds Statements, as they are known, summarise the business's progress, either over the past or into the future, in such a way as to highlight whether or not it is living within or beyond its means. This was illustrated in Chapter 4 on the Cash Flow Forecast and will be referred to again when we consider the interpretation of financial information in Chapter 12.

The derivative techniques – summary

We have now considered the main derivative techniques which arise from the three primary financial statements, all of which are summarised in Illustration 5.1 under the heading Area 3.

(a) First, in the case of the Profit and Loss Account, we have the need for analysis which leads to the techniques termed costing – both full and marginal.

(b) Second, in the case of the Balance Sheet, we have the need to look at and control investments as we make them. As regards fixed assets, including outside investments, the techniques of project appraisal have been developed to help us look before we leap! And in the case of working capital, we have the continual need to control and analyse time so as to minimise the amount invested in this area.

(c) Finally, in the case of the Cash Flow Forecast, we have the need to use cash in making clear the overall effect of a business's past actions and future plans on its cash position, in other words to highlight whether or not the business is 'living within or beyond its means'.

The need for comparisons

Having looked at what we have termed the derivative techniques it is now necessary to turn to the next area of concern to managers and investors alike – the continual need for comparison. In every financial situation, whether you are considering your salary, your car or your house, the natural desire is to compare!

Budgetary control

Certainly when you are presented with financial information about a business there is not only a desire but a logical compulsion to compare so as to review its progress. It is because we have this need to compare and review that in business we have produced techniques to assist us with this. The first or primary comparative technique is the one termed budgetary control which is the overall technique of financial comparison within business.

It is concerned primarily with translating the policies and plans pertaining to the business into their financial consequences. These take the form of the projected Profit and Loss Accounts, Balance Sheets and Cash Flow Forecasts which will arise from such plans and comparing these with the actual figures as they become known. However, as well as budgeted Profit and Loss Accounts, Balance Sheets and Cash Flow Forecasts, budgets can be arranged throughout the business to suit particular needs. For example, budgets can be arranged around managers and around functions as well as produced within the context of the business as a whole.

Budgetary control therefore meets the natural desire to compare and contrast actual against budgeted performance in financial terms and once such comparison has been made to take whatever corrective action is necessary or possible. It must be understood that budgetary control is fundamentally concerned with the conversion of plans and policies into financial measurements, but its use falls under two main heads: first in proving the financial credibility of the policies of the business as a whole, and second to compare the performance of management throughout the organisation against agreed targets or budgets of performance. Both these objectives will be dealt with in Chapter 10 on budgetary control.

Standard costing

Having considered the overall comparison technique of budgetary control we must recognise that the desire for comparison in one particular area of business finance – namely costing – calls for a very analytical approach. In this area managers do not just wish to compare, they wish to take effective action as soon as possible to correct things that have gone wrong or continue things that have gone right.

In order to obtain information to meet this requirement a technique of comparison has been developed termed standard costing. Standard costing is not a different form of costing as it may sound from its name, but a method of comparison which isolates and defines the reasons that have caused the differences, or variances as they are called. It entails much detailed analysis and control and will be dealt with further in Chapter 11.

Interpretation

If you now return to Illustration 5.1 you will see that we have arrived at the final area of financial understanding, the area entitled interpretation. The interpretation of financial data is the sum of all the financial understandings we have obtained up to this point. Interpretation is therefore based on the accumulated knowledge we get from all the other financial techniques and statements we have introduced up to this stage.

We shall be looking at interpretation in Chapter 12 and then we shall be considering the application of ratios and other analytical techniques. It is also then that we shall see that in the interpretation of financial information both our financial and non-financial knowledge must be harnessed. After all, it must never be forgotten that all financial information is expressing a practical business situation and therefore whatever is being reported must represent this. It is for this reason that whenever managers examine financial data they must at the same time bear in mind the practical event which is being reported. For example, if an engineer considers that the cost information regarding a product is at variance with the engineering practicalities then he or she must be willing to challenge the financial data.

It must never be forgotten that it is this interplay or practical knowledge with financial understanding which is vital in the interpretation of financial data. It must also be brought very much to mind that the accounting information that we have discussed in this and previous chapters provides managers with better questions, not answers. We hope these questions will certainly lead to better answers but this does not imply that financial information in itself provides them. Answers must always depend upon the judgement of managers.

Illustration 5.10 Functional contribution to preparation of financial data.

List the contribution beneath each heading:

1. *Buying*

2. *Work study department*

3. *Credit control*

4. *Drawing office*

5. *Sales representatives*

6. *Production foreman*

7. *Administration*

Illustration 5.11 Examples of functional contribution to preparation of financial data.

1. *Buying*
   Prices for cost and estimate purposes
   Stock valuation

2. *Work study department*
   Times for cost and estimate purpose

3. *Credit control*
   Provision for bad and doubtful debts
   Debtor and creditor times for working capital

4. *Drawing office*
   Data for estimates of new products
   Data for capital project appraisal

5. *Sales representatives*
   Sales analysis data
   Credit control intelligence

6. *Production foreman*
   Control data on material in manufacture
   Time control and analysing of labour
   Work in progress and finished goods valuation

7. *Administration*
   Control data for administrative costs

Conclusion

Finally, turn to Illustration 5.10 and list out the contribution of each function to the preparation of financial data. When you have done this compare your answers with those suggested in Illustration 5.11. Once this test has been completed we can proceed with our studies of management accounting, the first of which will deal with full costing.

6 | FULL COSTING

As we have seen, in business there are three primary financial questions leading to the three primary statements: what is the return, leading to the Profit and Loss Account; what is the risk, leading to the Balance Sheet; and do we have the 'ready', the available money to arrive, leading to the Cash Flow Forecast.

However, even when these statements are available, it becomes clear to anyone interested that they are not enough in themselves. In the last chapter we saw the evolution of financial information. For example, if we know the profit or loss a business has made this will obviously pinpoint the return on the investment, but if that business is selling many different goods, types of merchandise or rendering many different services this answer would certainly be insufficient. Those concerned would want to know where it was making its profit or loss, whether it is making more profit on one item it sells or service it renders than another. It is in response to this very obvious question of 'where am I making my profit or loss' that the techniques known as costing have been developed.

Cost and profit analysis

The purpose of costing is to pinpoint where the profit or loss is being made so that you can manage, organise and run your business more profitably. The desire for this analysis has been with us for a very long time. After all, Adam and Eve would surely have wanted to know which kilo of apples was giving them the greatest profit! Costing is not therefore a modern invention – it is one that has been part of the fabric of business life since the beginning of time.

It is from this analysis of profit that we organise our business policies, because from it, we can find out where we are making our profit or loss. It is also from this analysis that we can build up data when we are estimating new work. It is therefore for these purposes that costing has been developed. It is also because of these that costing holds within itself enormous benefits – and equally enormous dangers, discussed later when we consider the question of credibility.

Mechanics of analysis

Having described its purpose let us now look at the mechanics of costing. First we must understand that there are two systems of costing based on the desire or otherwise to analyse fully the trading expenses. All costing systems are concerned with analysing the expense and income within the trading area, and the two systems that we use are equally concerned with this but to a different degree. In the first method – the one termed full costing – an attempt is made to analyse all the expenses contained in the trading or operating section of the Profit and Loss Account. However, in the second or partial system – which is known as marginal costing – the analysis is confined to those expenses that move in sympathy or, as they say, vary with what the business produces and sells. We shall deal with marginal costing in a later chapter – for the present we will concentrate on full costing.

Benefits and dangers

The benefit of costing is, as I have already explained, in determining where the profit or loss is being made and therefore it assists us in planning a business enterprise on the most profitable lines.

The danger of costing lies in whether or not we are able to believe the information it presents. Central to any examination of costing must be the question – can we believe it? Is it credible? If the answer to this question is 'no' we could be using very dangerous information. After all, if our costing data makes us believe that one particular product, type of merchandise or service is better than another but the information on which it is based is incorrect, that is not just a shame or a nuisance, it could be ruinous. In fact some cynics have said 'that more businesses have gone bust because they have had costing than because they have not'. This is obviously far too cynical a view to accept but there is an element of truth in it!

It must also be remembered that cost analysis is not only concerned with the past, it may affect the view of the future. For instance, when a new estimate is called for, it is often found necessary to use facts already available from costs of similar products or services. This means therefore that not only will poor cost analysis provide a wrong view of present but also future profitability.

Full cost analysis

To understand full costing it is necessary to run through the build up of a full cost statement. We shall do this with reference to Illustration 6.1.

The unit of cost

In the first place in any costing system one has to choose a suitable unit of cost to which costs can be analysed, and this in turn will be determined by the business itself. For instance, in the building or construction industry we might use the building contract as the unit, in a solicitor's practice we might use the particular piece of litigation – the divorce, the writ, the claim for damages, etc., whereas for a retail operation we might use the particular department. On the other hand in a mass production engineering company we might use the cost of a unit within the production line. To do this the total cost of what is produced for the period, say the week, is first determined and then this is divided by the units produced in that period to arrive at a unit cost.

All this means that we choose the unit to suit the business. In a manufacturing business this will normally follow the production unit whereas in a service industry it will follow the service that is rendered. To test your understanding of units of cost you should tackle the question set out in Illustration 6.2 and compare your answer with the solution in Illustration 6.3.

Nature of expenses

Having chosen the unit of cost it is then necessary in a full costing system to examine the nature of the expenses themselves. Once this is done it

Illustration 6.1 Full cost statement.

	Unit cost
	p
Direct material	5
Direct labour	4
Direct expenses	3
Prime cost	12
Indirect expenses	6
Total cost	18
Profit	7
Sales price	25

Illustration 6.2   Deciding on suitable unit costs.

Consider the following businesses in relationship to the unit of cost most suitable to each.

1. Department store
2. Brick works
3. Chemical manufacturer
4. Insurance agency
5. Motor repairer
6. Hospital
7. Mass production car manufacturer

Illustration 6.3   Suggested answer to Illustration 6.2.

1. Cost per department
2. Cost per quantity of bricks
3. Cost per process of manufacture
4. Cost per type of insurance
5. Cost per job
6. Cost per hospital bed
7. Cost per car coming off production line

becomes clear that, as already mentioned, they broadly fall into two categories. First there will be those expenses which are directly attributable to the chosen unit, and second there will be others which are there whether or not we produce the particular unit to which we are attempting to analyse the expenses.

Direct expenses

We refer to the ones that directly relate to the unit as direct expenses and these we record as the unit is being produced or the service is being rendered. These are set out in Illustration 6.1 as direct material 5p, direct labour 4p and direct expenses 3p. Direct material and labour are the material and labour that can be traced directly to the unit we are costing and would be calculated from information received from those concerned with the use of material or the control of labour.

We may also find that there are other direct expenses, such as a royalty we have to pay to a designer on the manufacture of a particular unit, or the travelling expenses of a solicitor's clerk in obtaining necessary information regarding a search prior to the completion of a property conveyance. As we have said, we call these expenses direct and the total of these, as you will see from Illustration 6.1, is termed the prime cost.

Credibility

We will now return to our central consideration which you will remember is the credibility of the information. Whenever anyone looks at a cost this must be their first question and it must be a recurring theme in understanding and using cost data. On arriving at the prime cost the credibility will depend very largely on how accurately the direct costs have been analysed and recorded, and this will depend in turn very much on the grass-root recording within the business. In slang terms, more damage can be done by careless recordings by 'the bomb-happy storeman/foreman syndrome than any triple distilled cost accounting system that you could meet in a day's walk'.

Accuracy of material and labour recordings

Now what is meant by this is that the credibility down to the prime cost is very much dependent upon the accurate recording of data as and when this takes place. The direct material cost in a manufacturing process will be made up from all the information recorded within the manufacturing processes, and a wrong entry of material issued, returned or transferred will mean that the direct material cost shown will also be wrong.

Equally, with labour, the accuracy of this will depend upon the basic recording of the labour which goes into the manufacture of the goods or the rendering of the services. It is therefore essential that time recordings are accurate. If the recordings by those concerned with the manufacture of the unit or the rendering of the service are inaccurate then inevitably the cost information will also be wrong.

Accuracy of prices and rates

At the same time we must realise that costing is historical (hysterical at times even!) and so the value of the material and the labour cost going into the cost unit will also be historical. If, therefore, the price of materials or the rates of pay of labour are changing then what is set out in the cost may well be an unrepeatable bargain!

Material pricing

This problem of changing price is particularly important when considering direct material costs during a period of frequent price changes. This is set out in Illustration 6.4 where a material has been purchased at different prices throughout the month of March. The question arises: at what price

Illustration 6.4   Material prices.

	Purchases for March				Issues for March				
Date	Quantity kilos	Price per kilo p	Total £	Date	Quantity		Price per unit		
						FIFO		LIFO	
						Qty kilos	Price p	Qty kilos	Price p
3	1,000	50	500	4	500	500	50	500	50
10	1,500	52	780	12	1,600	500	50	100	50
						1,100	52	1,500	52
14	2,000	54	1,080	15	2,200	400	52	200	50
						1,800	54	2,000	54
20	1,600	55	880	21	1,400	200	54	1,400	55
						1,200	55		
	6,100	211	£3,240						

Basis of calculating:
Simple average price method = 211 divided by 4 = 52.75p
Weighted average price method = 3,240 divided by 6,100 = 53.1p

should the material be included in those costs in which it must be included. Basically there are four positions that can be taken.

FIFO and LIFO
First, the materials can be priced out in logical sequence. This is shown in Illustration 6.4 under the heading FIFO (First In First Out method). Second, the materials can be priced so as to reflect the most recent prices – again shown in Illustration 6.4 under the heading LIFO (Last In First Out method).

LIFO is much favoured during periods of rising prices as the cost will then reflect the increasing material costs. However, FIFO is more logical and therefore is often found easier to apply by clerical staff.

Average price and weighted average price
There are also the third and fourth methods shown in Illustration 6.4 which reflect the average price and the weighted average price methods.

Rising prices and rising rates of pay

We shall be dealing with the problem of rising costs in a broader context when we discuss current cost accounting in Chapter 12. However, at the present time you need to be aware that the historical prices of materials and rates of pay for labour may well need to be revised if costs are to be looked at realistically.

The use of cost data

However, what is realistic depends upon the use for which the cost is being produced. For instance, if we are using the cost data to look ahead so as to estimate what it will cost us next time we make the product or render the service, we must be careful to take this fact into consideration. We have therefore got to be particularly careful in determining whether or not the cost relates to a current, historical or future cost, and select the data with care depending on how we intend to use it. For example, if the cost data is to be used to determine the future cost of producing the product or rendering the service, care must be taken to apply those rates of pay and material prices which it is considered will apply at the future time.

Indirect expenses

We have so far looked at direct expenses but if we look at all the expenses deducted from sales before arriving at the trading or operating profit in a Profit and Loss Account we will see that there are still many other expenses apart from these. There are indeed a large number which do not relate directly to any particular unit of cost, for instance the insurance of the buildings, the salaries of the supervisors, the wages of people who clean the offices and sweep up the factory and move the materials, the rent of the retail shop, salaries and fees of directors and so on. All these expenses are necessary in order to arrive at our trading or operating profit but they are not directed at one particular unit of manufacture, merchandise or service. These expenses are often collectively referred to as the overheads in the Profit and Loss Account and as indirect expenditure in costing.

Indirect expense/overhead absorption

However, in order to arrive at a full cost it is necessary that all trading expenses are brought into the cost – and this must include not only the direct but also these indirect expenses. To do this it is necessary therefore to work out some way in which we can add into each unit of cost a proportion of these indirect expenses.

You will see in Illustration 6.1 that the indirect expenses are brought in at 6p, so the question arises how do we arrive at this figure? Well, quite simply by a series of forecasts or guesses! Let us take an example of what we mean by this. In the first place, before we do any costing whatsoever, those concerned will prepare estimates for the period ahead in order to arrive at two overall forecasts.

To illustrate this let us take a practical example. Supposing we are going to be costing in a particular year then towards the end of the previous year the cost office will seek answers to two questions, answers which are needed in order to establish the two forecasts required to calculate the basis for charging – or, as they say, absorbing – the indirect expenses.

The indirect expense for the period

The first of these will be how much do we think the indirect expenses will be during the period – in most cases the year – ahead in which we are going to be doing our future costing? Of course many of the indirect expenses will be known with total accuracy – for example, the rent, insurances and some wages and salaries for the particular year ahead – but there are bound to be certain expenses where a measure of forecasting will be needed. The salaries in certain circumstances may not be exactly known, and again indirect materials used in cleaning machines cannot be determined with total accuracy. This means therefore that forecasts will have to be made in many cases.

This then will be the first step – to arrive at a total assessment of what the indirect expenses are likely to be during the period in which the costing will take place. This is set out in Illustration 6.5 as forecast or guess number 1 – the forecast of the indirect expenses which we think will be incurred during the period ahead in which we are going to be producing the cost information. In this instance we are forecasting a figure of £5,000,000 for the year ahead.

The activity for the period

Having arrived at this figure it will then be necessary to work out our forecast or guess number 2, namely what we think the activity of the business is going to be during the same period? Now activity can be measured in many ways but in the first instance it is often found useful to measure it in terms of the sales that a business expects to make during the period

Illustration 6.5 Indirect expenditure recovery calculation.

1. Forecast of indirect expenditure over period ahead *say* £5,000,000
2. Forecast of activity of the business during the period ahead
     Prime cost forecast *say* £10,000,000

   Absorption rate £5,000,000 of £10,000,000 = 50 per cent.

ahead. However, once this estimate is made we might, in a manufacturing business, wish to translate it into production capacity, what is going to be produced during the year ahead to meet the sales forecast, and express this in value or in quantity such as production or machine or labour hours.

However, whatever measurement of activity is used it will be based on a forecast of what we believe is going to take place during the period ahead in which we are going to be doing our costing. As we have already seen in many cases this will be based in the first instance on the forecasted sales figure. Let us say in this particular instance that we have arrived at our sales budget for the year ahead and that we translate this back into the prime cost of production needed to meet these sales. In other words, we ask ourselves, if we know what sales are planned for the period ahead, what will that mean in terms of the prime cost of the production which will be needed to meet these sales? And we shall say that from this we arrive at a prime cost figure of £10,000,000 – again as set out in Illustration 6.5.

Basis for absorption

Having arrived at this figure we will see that we have now got our basis for absorbing or recovering our indirect expenses. What we have arrived at are two figures: first, the indirect costs for the period ahead which we have worked out to be £5,000,000, and second, the activity for this same period translated into its prime cost value which we have worked out to be £10,000,000.

This means that, if we take the forecasted indirect expenses of £5,000,000 as a percentage of the forecasted prime costs of £10,000,000 we arrive at a figure of 50 per cent, and we can apply this percentage – sometimes called the absorption rate – to arrive at a full cost. If you return to Illustration 6.1 we will see that having arrived at the prime cost of 12p we add on 50 per cent to this prime cost to arrive at the indirect expense of 6p which, added to the 12p, gives us a total cost of 18p.

Credibility of absorption rate

Now, having seen the mechanics of indirect cost recovery, let us get back to the central consideration again – its credibility. And here we find that whether or not we can believe the amount brought in as indirect expenses will depend upon the accuracy or inaccuracy of a couple of guesses or forecasts – and we all know how unreliable these can be!

The indirect expense items
For instance, supposing during the year ahead instead of incurring

£5,000,000 worth of indirect costs there were general wage and salary increases and the indirect expenditure went up from £5,000,000 to £6,000,000. If that was so then 50 per cent of the prime cost, on the basis of the prime cost remaining constant at £10,000,000, would be insufficient. It would fail to recover the £1,000,000 worth of extra indirect costs. And this would not be seen by looking at an individual cost, it would only be seen when the original estimate of £5,000,000 was compared with the actual indirect cost figure of £6,000,000 when this was known.

The activity achieved

However, even more important to understand is the problem of activity. For example, if due to a recession in the trade the activity of the business did not reach £10,000,000 prime cost but only £8,000,000, then we would be faced with the fact that 50 per cent of the prime cost of £8,000,000 would only recover £4,000,000. However, what we would also find, in all probability, is that whatever the activity may be, the vast majority of indirect expenses will not move directly – or, as it might be said, in sympathy – with this reduced activity. They will remain at £5,000,000. For example, it is very unlikely that management or supervision will volunteer to take a salary decrease should this recession occur. Equally, and even more certainly, the landlords will not reduce their rent during the same period. In other words indirect expenditure is not necessarily bound by the activity within the business. It is therefore vital for us to make sure that when we see indirect recovery rates added into a cost that we recognise the need for the forecasts on which they are calculated to be frequently checked against the facts as they become known, and everyone using full cost data must be aware of this need to reconcile the rates of recovery for indirect costs against the facts as and when these are known.

Full cost structure – recapitulation

We have now arrived at the total full cost of 18p in Illustration 6.1, a total cost which is made up of the total of the direct and indirect expenses of this particular unit.

We have seen that the accuracy of direct expenses is determined to a very large extent by the recording of material quantities and labour times within the business. We must continually be watchful that this recording is being made accurately so that the information we get is credible down to the prime cost. It must always be remembered that if we have bad labour or material control the likelihood is that we will have equally bad costing.

We must also be aware that the values placed on the direct costs of material and labour and direct expenses will be based upon historical values unless otherwise stated. This will therefore require very careful attention if we are using these costs as a basis for future estimates or for trying to determine the cost of a similar product when material prices and labour rates of pay are changing.

Beyond the prime cost point the amount introduced to recover indirect expenses depends upon guesses or forecasts, and in this area we need to be ever watchful that we are reconciling these with the facts as and when they are known. We must also realise that at the end, having arrived at the total cost, it will be this figure that will be compared against whatever we use for comparison. In the case of costing a product or a service we would be comparing this cost against its sales price or against an estimated cost, and whenever we make this comparison the difference will create an emotional response from management. It will make them favour or disfavour the particular product or service, and it is for this reason that central to all full costing will be the credibility of the information produced.

Multi-absorption rates

It must also be recognised that in Illustration 6.1 we have used a very simple example in which there is just one indirect rate of recovery for the entire business. In practice it is normally found that indirect expense recovery rates will be calculated for the different divisions of overheads, for example production indirect expenses, administrative indirect expenses and selling and distribution indirect expenses. Each of these indirect expense divisions will have a different rate of recovery, and an example of this is set out in Illustration 6.6.

We also need to understand that in many of these divisions we may wish to calculate more than one indirect recovery rate. This may be important when it is considered that a particular unit of cost uses a larger proportion of indirect expenses than another, for instance a product going through four production processes compared with one going through only two. In such a case it might be considered useful to arrive at a separate indirect expense absorption rate for each process. This means therefore that in place of a single indirect recovery rate as is set out in Illustration 6.1, in practice you could have many more.

Cost centres

When such a proliferation of analysis takes place the sub-divisions into

Illustration 6.6 Full cost statement with division of
indirect expenses.

	Unit cost
	p
Direct material	10
Direct labour	8
Direct expenses	6
Prime cost	24
Factory indirect expenses	6
Works cost	30
Administration indirect expenses	4
Cost of production	34
Selling and distribution indirect expenses	11
Total cost	45
Profit	8
Sales price	53

which the overheads are divided are often referred to as cost centres. A recovery rate per cost centre is then calculated and this is charged to the unit of cost in whatever way is felt appropriate. The reason for doing this is to arrive at a more equitable division of indirect expenses and so it is believed a more accurate assessment of the full cost.

However, the principles set out in Illustration 6.1 will still apply. Just because we have many more indirect recovery rates we still apply the same principles in arriving at each one. It must, though, be noted that if cost centres are established three judgements will be necessary. We have to arrive at first what we believe the indirect expenses will be and second what the activity will be when they are being incurred. But to these two we have to add a third judgement. This is on what basis should we divide the total forecasted indirect expenses between the different cost centres? This point is specifically dealt with in the consolidation illustrations which we shall introduce later.

Value of time recovery basis

It should also be understood that in using a measurement of activity it is often preferable to translate this into time rather than value. This is for the very simple reason that most indirect expenses relate more to time than to value, for example salaries for the month, insurance for the year and rent for the quarter. It is therefore found in practice that rates of recovery are often based on machine, labour or production hours. The reason for this is that if we use value, the amount we add on to recover indirect expenses will be increased if we use expensive direct costs, which may have no

Illustration 6.7 Effects on final cost of using direct costs time basis to calculate recovery rate.

	Platinum ring p	Brass ring p
Direct material	400	40
Direct labour	50	50
Direct expenses	10	10
Prime cost	460	100
Production time per ring	30 mins	20 mins
Indirect expenditure added on as 50% of prime cost	230	50
Total cost	690	150
Indirect expenditure added on a time basis at, say, 5p per production minute	150	100
Total cost	610	200

bearing on indirect expenditure. For instance, if we are producing brass rings and platinum rings, then if we are adding on our indirect expenses based on a percentage of the prime cost value, then the platinum rings would have to bear a very much higher proportion of indirect expenditure than the brass rings. However, this might not really be fair because it might not take you any longer to manufacture or sell platinum rings than if you were manufacturing and selling brass rings. An example of this is shown in Illustration 6.7.

Some final words of caution about full costing

Let us now summarise our studies of full costing. Full costing is really a combination of the actual cost going into the unit of cost down to the prime cost to which is added a rate or rates of recovery to bring in the indirect expenditure. These rates of recovery are based upon forecasts/budgets or assumptions of what the indirect expense will be and the activity which we believe will happen in the business over the period ahead. Full costing is not of course a combination of fact and fiction but extreme caution is necessary before it is believed and acted upon.

Direct/indirect division

We have stressed throughout that the value of any costing system is dependent upon its credibility. It should also be borne in mind that the division of expense in the first instance between direct and indirect is one by which its very nature can never be 100 per cent accurate. When we talk about expenses as being direct or indirect this division is in itself one which is determined by people's judgements. There will inevitably be items which may not exactly fit into either definition but for which a decision will have to be made as to which category they should be put into.

It could be argued, for instance, that every bit of labour from the Chairman down or up to the lift-boy could be made direct given enough detailed recording by those concerned. But in practice this is not done and a division is made between direct and indirect labour. However, what must be noted is that this division is not a uniform division – what one company in the same industry might term direct expenditure another might term indirect and vice versa.

Maximising direct costs

However, it must always be borne in mind that the objective of full costing should be to maximise the direct costs. This is for the simple reason that the higher the proportion there is of direct costs the more we are looking at costs which are determined when the data is being produced. It must be noted that when an indirect expense is absorbed into a cost we are dealing with expenses which inevitably will have to be reconciled against facts as and when these become known – and this will always be after the event. A manager will already have examined the cost before a reconciliation can be made of the indirect costs recovered against those actually incurred. This means therefore that any sensible manager must always view a full cost with a considerable measure of caution below the prime cost point.

Consolidation and conclusion

It is now time to test our understanding against the more complex exercise set out in Illustration 6.8. Here you will see a set of facts relating to the cost of three products A, B and C divided between:

1. The direct cost data provided from the control records for the three products as they are produced;
2. The forecasted or budgeted indirect expenses established for the year during which the direct cost data (1) is provided; and
3. The total forecasts or budgets for the same year for the direct materials, labour, expenses and sales of the three products; and finally
4. The bases which are to be used for the recovery of factory, administrative and selling and distribution indirect expenses.

From all these facts you are asked to produce the full cost analysis of these three products presented in the same way as set out as Illustration 6.6.

Illustration 6.8 Full cost exercise.

X Ltd produces three main products A, B and C. An analysis of the cost data for these products presents the following information:

		Product	
1. Direct cost data	A	B	C
(a) Direct material:			
Type D (15p per kilo)	12 kilos	6 kilos	14 kilos
Type E (12p per kilo)	11 kilos	11 kilos	11 kilos
Type F (5p per kilo)	13 kilos	12 kilos	6 kilos
(b) Direct labour:			
Dept G (60p per hour)	1 hr	$\frac{1}{2}$ hr	3 hrs
Dept H (80p per hour)	4 hrs	4 hrs	2 hrs
Dept I (70p per hour)	3 hrs	—	1 hr
(c) Direct expenses per unit	10p	5p	15p

2. Budgeted indirect expenses for year:

	Factory expenses £	Administrative expenses £	Selling and distribution expenses £
Salaries	15,000	131,000	48,000
Rent	3,700	1,800	1,400
Insurance	2,000		
Depreciation plant and machinery	16,000		
Indirect wages	22,100		
Telephone		700	
Stationery		1,100	
		£	
Commission (5% of sales price)		A 2,000	
		B 4,000	
		C 3,000	
			9,000
Advertising			411,000
	£58,800	£134,600	£469,400

3. Total budget for year:

(a) Direct material, say, £650,000: Materials required   D 1,890,000 kilos
  E 2,173,000 kilos
  F 2,048,000 kilos

(b) Direct labour, say, £850,000:   Available for product A   300,000 hours
  B   450,000 hours
  C   360,000 hours

(c) Direct expenses, say, £20,000

(d) Budgeted sales: A £900,000   B £1,000,000   C £900,000

(e) Selling price: A £16.00   B £10.00   C £14.00

4. Indirect factory expenses are to be apportioned on the following bases and recovered based on direct labour hours:

	A	B	C
Rent and rates		on basis of floor area	
Factory salaries	40%	30%	30%
Factory insurance	20%	60%	20%
Depreciation plant and machinery	25%	50%	25%
Factory indirect wages	40%	20%	40%
Floor area of factory used to manufacture product:			

A = 200,000 sq feet
B = 300,000 sq feet
C = 100,000 sq feet

Administrative indirect expenses will be recovered based on the budgeted works cost. Selling and distribution expenses will be recovered based on the budgeted cost of production.

You are asked to calculate:

(i) prime cost for each product;
(ii) works cost for each product;
(iii) cost of production for each product;
(iv) total cost for each product;
(v) profit/loss for each product.

Illustration 6.9   Suggested answer to Illustration 6.8.

	Products		
	A	B	C
	p	p	p
Direct material	377	282	372
Direct labour	590	350	410
Direct expenses	10	5	15
(i) Prime cost	977	637	797
Factory expenses (see 6.10)	54	20	31
(ii) Works cost	1,031	657	828
Administrative expenses (9%)	93	59	75
(iii) Cost of production	1,124	716	903
Selling and distribution expenses (27%)	303	193	244
Commission (5% of sales price)	8	5	7
(iv) Total cost	1,435	914	1,154
(v) Profit/loss	165	86	146
Sales price	1,600	1,000	1,400

Once you have completed your answer you should check this with the one given in Illustration 6.9 and trace through any errors that may occur. The ways in which the indirect costs, with particular reference to the factory indirect expenses, are recovered are set out for your information in Illustration 6.10. You should study this with particular reference to cost centres and how they are used in the recovery of the factory overheads.

Having completed this consolidation assignment we shall continue our studies of the analysis of profit and loss in the next chapter on marginal costing.

Illustration 6.10 Calculation of administrative expenses and selling and distribution expenses on cost rate.

Total budgeted costs for year:

	£	
Direct material	650,000	
Direct labour	850,000	
Direct expenses	20,000	
Factory expenses	58,800	
Works cost	1,578,800	
Administrative expenses	134,600	= say 9% of works cost
Cost of production	1,713,400	
Selling and distribution expenses:		
Less: Commission treated as a direct expense and charged to each product per unit of sales	460,400	= say 27% of cost of production
	£2,173,800	

				Products				
	Total	%	A	%	B	%	C	
Factory expenses:	£		£		£		£	
Salaries	15,000	40	6,000	30	4,500	30	4,500	
Rent (floor area)	3,700		1,233		1,850		617	
Insurance	2,000	20	400	60	1,200	20	400	
Depreciation plant and machinery	16,000	25	4,000	50	8,000	25	4,000	
Indirect wages	22,100	40	8,840	20	4,420	40	8,840	
	£58.800		£20,473		£19,970		£18,357	
Labour hours (direct)	1,110,000		300,000		450,000		360,000	
Rate per direct labour hour	5.3p		6.8p		4.4p		5.1p	
Direct labour hours taken per product			8 hrs		4.5 hrs		6 hrs	
Factory expenses absorbed per product on direct labour hour basis (to nearest p)			54p		20p		31p	

7 | MARGINAL COSTING

Having dealt with full costing we must now turn our attention to the alternative system of expense analysis known as marginal costing. To understand this system we must get back to our bar-stools – in other words examine expenses from a direct and personal trading point of view.

The breakeven chart

For example, if you were starting a business how would you think of the expense and income side of the business? Well I think the first thing you might do is recognise the relationship between cost and income with regard to what you are going to produce and sell. I want you to turn to Illustration 7.1 which sets out in a visual form the way everyone running a business must think about the relationship between trading expense and income. (You may indeed recall this diagram which we first introduced in Chapter 2 as Illustration 2.8.)

Variable expenses

Illustration 7.1 shows a horizontal axis AB which measures the volume of output/sales during a year and a vertical axis AC which is scaled into £s dealing with monetary value. Now if we look at our expense to income relationship over a year we will find that expenses will respond to sales and output very broadly in two ways. The first way is shown by the line AD which describes the fact that some expenses move in direct sympathy with what we produce and sell, for instance the materials and direct labour that go into the product, the commission which is payable to a salesman, the royalty paid to the designer every time the product is produced. All these are examples of what are termed variable expenses and it can be seen that in these cases if we produce and sell nothing they do not exist, whereas if we go on producing and selling they move in direct proportion to the activity achieved.

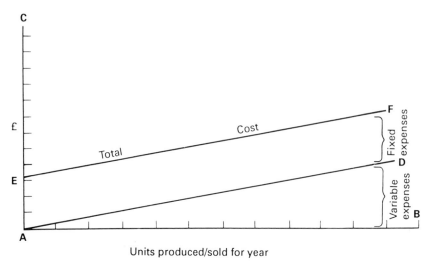

Illustration 7.1 Breakeven chart.

Fixed expenses

However, it must also be noted that we have many other expenses which are there whatever we do – the rent, the salaries of our administrators, the insurance premiums and so on. These are all examples of the other type of expense which we refer to as fixed expenses or costs. In their case if we produce nothing we are still committed to these and as we go on producing and selling they in fact remain constant for the immediate period ahead – the year in the illustration. It is these expenses which are shown on the chart as the distance AE.

Total costs

It is for this reason that fixed expenses are drawn as a band above the variable costs, the distance of which is shown on the vertical axis as AE. The total costs therefore are shown as a line running parallel to the variable expenses AD and described on the chart as the line EF, the distance between line AD and the line EF being the fixed expenses total of AE.

What we have described so far is the fact that expenses fall into two broad categories: the one which moves in direct sympathy with what we produce and sell known as variable expenses, and the other, which remains constant irrespective of what we produce and sell over a given period termed the fixed expenses. From this chart it can be seen that if nothing is sold during the year the total cost will be the fixed expenses and the total costs of whatever is sold will be read as the variable expenses relating to the particular sales achieved plus the fixed expenses for the year.

Sales income

Now let us continue by taking our view of the breakeven chart a little further and consider Illustration 7.2. Here we are including in the same chart set out as Illustration 7.1 the cumulative sales income. In other words we consider what we will get from the sales of our goods, merchandise and services over the same period. This will represent the accumulated income as and when it arrives based upon our sales for the year. To illustrate this we have put in the line AG which represents the accumulated sales value depending upon the volume of sales achieved over the year.

The breakeven point

As we can see from the chart set out in Illustration 7.2, this sales line breaks through the total cost line EF at the point H. This point H represents the point which is described in terms of the value or the volume of sales which must be achieved for the business to 'break even' depending on whether you draw the dotted line down to the horizontal or across to the vertical axes at points J and K.

Contribution

The breakeven point, as it is called, is the point at which the total income from our sales exceeds the variable expense of these by the amount of the total fixed costs for the period.

Having described the breakeven chart, as it is known, let us stand back for a minute and consider the concept which is behind this view. It is that on the sale of a unit, whether it is a unit of manufacture, merchandise or service, we do not generate profit or loss. We generate the difference between the sales price and the variable cost of the particular unit. It is this difference that may be termed the margin or the contribution.

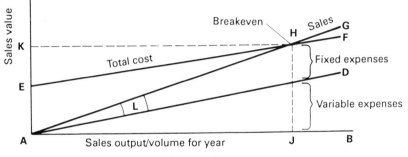

Illustration 7.2   Breakeven chart with sales income.

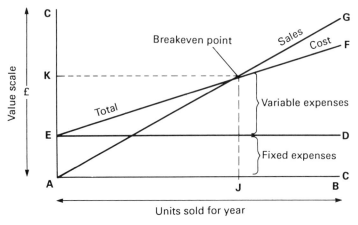

Illustration 7.3 Alternative breakeven chart.

Alternative diagram

For your information an alternative form of breakeven chart is set out in Illustration 7.3. You will see from this that the fixed and variable expense lines are drawn in reverse order and that no angle of contribution is established. It does provide a graphical translation of the breakeven point but has the disadvantage of suggesting that sales first break through the fixed expenses before recovering the variable expenses. For this reason the breakeven chart set out in Illustration 7.2 is used throughout for reference purposes.

Contribution/margin/profit

Under the concepts of marginal costing what must be recognised is that neither the margin nor the contribution is a profit. What becomes clear is that a profit is not established for any business until the breakeven point has been reached. In other words, not until all the fixed costs for the period have been fully recovered can a business consider that it has made a profit. This is because up to the point of breakeven, it is committed to its fixed expenses for the period and these will have to be met whatever volume or value of sales are achieved. In fact the critical point to examine is the angle of contribution labelled L in Illustration 7.2.

Marginal costing

Based upon the concept set out in Illustration 7.2 the system known as marginal costing has been developed. This is a system of expense analysis which over the short term – say 12 months – recognises that expenses move in the way which we have just described. Because of this it becomes evident that in examining the cost of a unit the only costs which can truly be related to it are those which are variable, because those which are fixed exist whether or not a particular product is produced or a service rendered.

Under marginal costing therefore a unit of cost does not give a business profit: it provides a contribution. Profit only happens when the total contributions gained from all that is sold equals the total of the fixed expenses for the particular period.

Now consider Illustration 7.4. Tackle the question, expressing the breakeven in units and sales value in each case. When you have done this check your answers with Illustration 7.5.

P/V ratio

From this exercise it can be seen that breakeven can be expressed in units or in sales value. It can also be seen that the contribution can be related to the sales price as a percentage and this percentage in turn can be translated into pence per £1. For example, a contribution of 30 per cent for a particular product means that for every £1 worth of sales of this product a contribution of 30p will arise.

Illustration 7.4 Expense/income relationship.

Consider the expense/income relationship for the following three businesses and calculate the breakeven point in each case:

Business	A	B	C
	p	p	p
Sale price of products	20	35	40
Variable expenses of products	15	28	22
Fixed costs	£150,000	£280,000	£360,000

Illustration 7.5 Calculations of breakeven points in Illustration 7.4.

		A	B	C
		p	p	p
Contribution of businesses		5	7	18
Breakeven = $\dfrac{\text{Fixed expenses}}{\text{Contribution}}$ =		$\dfrac{£150,000}{5p}$	$\dfrac{£280,000}{7p}$	$\dfrac{£360,000}{18p}$
	Units	= 3,000,000	4,000,000	2,000,000
	or			
	Sale value	= £600,000	£1,400,000	£800,000
Contribution/sales price	=	$\dfrac{5}{20}$	$\dfrac{7}{35}$	$\dfrac{18}{40}$
	As a % =	25%	20%	45%
	Pence per £ =	25p	20p	45p

Marginal costing is often referred to as the analysis of cost/profit/ volume. The ratio of contribution to sales price is indeed sometimes termed, rather oddly in some textbooks, as the profit/volume or P/V ratio. This ratio can be expressed as a percentage, and refers to the percentage the contribution bears to the sales value, either of one unit sold or the total sales figure of the organisation. This is demonstrated in Illustration 7.6. Some of the uses of the P/V ratio are set out in Illustrations 7.7 and 7.8.

The P/V ratio can also be used when additional expenditure is under discussion and management wishes to know what additional sales must be generated to justify the proposed outlay. For example, if the P/V ratio is 20 per cent then additional annual fixed expenses of £10,000 will increase the breakeven point measured in sales value by £50,000 (£10,000 divided by 20 per cent). This means that the business will have to increase its sales by £50,000 to recover the increased fixed costs of £10,000.

Illustration 7.6   P/V ratio.

	Unit data	Total unit data
	p	£
Contribution	30	600,000
Sales price/turnover	45	1,000,000
P/V ratio	66%	60%

Illustration 7.7   Using the P/V ratio.

The breakeven point can be determined by dividing the fixed expenses by the P/V ratio:

	£	%
Sales price	110	100
Variable costs	77	70
Contribution	33	30

P/V ratio   =   30%
If   Fixed expenses =   £750,000
Then Breakeven point = £2,500,000   (£750,000 divided by 30%)

Illustration 7.8   Using the P/V ratio.

When the breakeven point is known, profits and losses are easily determined through the P/V ratio:

	£
Budgeted sales	4,000,000
Sales value at breakeven point	2,500,000
Sales value beyond breakeven point	1,500,000

If   P/V ratio   =   30%
Then Estimated profit = £450,000 (30% × £1,500,000)

Summary

Marginal costing is therefore a system of analysis which concentrates on the variable expenses and by doing this highlights the difference between the variable cost of a unit and its sales price. This difference is called the contribution or margin.

Marginal costing, then, is concerned with an examination of the contribution. However, it must be emphasised that marginal cost does not in any way ignore fixed costs – it simply does not analyse them. To understand this point as regards marginal costing I would like you to turn to Illustration 7.9. You will see that in this illustration I am setting out a full cost analysis and alongside I am producing the equivalent marginal cost analysis. In the full cost analysis all expenses are brought into the total cost, namely direct, variable and fixed cost items, whereas in the case of the marginal cost the analysis is confined entirely to the direct or variable expenses.

Direct, variable and fixed costs or expenses

It should also be noted that the term direct cost implies that the item is indeed also a variable expense. The terms variable and direct cost, or indirect and fixed expenses, can pose a problem of definition. However, it

Illustration 7.9 Full and marginal cost layout.

	Full cost product A	Marginal cost product A
	p	p
Direct material	10	10
Direct labour	8	8
Direct expenses	2	2
Prime cost	20	20
Works expenses: Fixed	6	—
Variable	4	4
Works cost	30	—
Administration expenses: Fixed	10	—
Variable	2	2
Cost of production	42	—
Selling and distribution Expenses: Fixed	14	—
Variable	11	11
Cost of sales	67	—
Marginal cost	—	37
Net profit	8	—
Contribution	—	38
Sales price	75	75

should be recognised that, apart from materials and directly variable costs such as commissions and royalties, most other expenses are, in part, both variable and fixed. For example, labour used to render a service whilst the service is actually being rendered is variable and direct to the service, but if there is no work available and the labour is still employed such labour cost in fact becomes a fixed expense. It is indirect in respect of the particular service.

For this reason the terms direct and variable cost become interchangeable in marginal costing. Another case of duplicate jargon! Yes, and do remember the words 'cost' and 'expense' are interchangeable. 'Is there no end to this?' you might ask.

The use of marginal costing

Having taken this first view of marginal costing it is necessary to stand back and look a little closer at its meaning and significance to those using the information it provides. The first thing to understand about marginal costing is that it is used very much in the pricing and forecasting field of management. Of course it is also used in the historical view of what a unit has cost us, but inevitably, when marginal costing information is available, managers will use this in looking forward and translating their plans into profit assessments and in examining and determining their future pricing policies.

What I am emphasising here is that marginal costing is a highly dynamic technique. It is not used purely in the somewhat static role of full costing. You could say that one of the central points to understand about marginal costing is that it is not confined to the filing cabinet but will take an active part in management decisions, especially in policy-making areas such as pricing and marketing.

Limitations of marginal costing

For this reason management using marginal costing data must be aware of its limitations. If they use it without their due consideration they may form decisions and make judgements which might well lead the business to disaster. The limitations of marginal costing can be described first with regard to time and second with regard to output or sales.

Time

To illustrate the limitation of time consider the breakeven point set out in Illustration 7.2. This point is based on the facts which are available when the lines AD, AE and AG are drawn and any changes in these facts would affect the breakeven point H.

Management must make sure therefore that the facts they are using are brought up to date. Nothing is more dangerous than management discussing the breakeven point or the contributions of each unit as if they were established for all time. For example, it must be understood that the breakeven point will alter whenever there is a change in any of the costs whether they are variable or fixed, or when changes are made to the sale prices. These must be brought into account as soon as they occur.

In other words, the data on which the breakeven point and marginal costing data have been established must be continually revised and reviewed.

Output or sales

Having considered the limitation of time we must now consider the second limitation – the limitation of output or sales. This is caused because marginal costing is always based upon an assumption of a given minimum and maximum output/sales within the business situation. To illustrate this let us turn to Illustration 7.10 where we see a breakeven chart in which can be seen two vertical lines running from M to N which lies to the left of the breakeven point and O to P which lies to its right.

These two lines represent what might be described as the parameters upon which the breakeven information has been produced. The minimum limit means that the variable cost and fixed cost lines drawn in the illustration are based upon the assumption that we shall never sell less than a minimum quantity of the product. In Illustration 7.10 this is described by the line MN. It must be noted that if we do not reach this minimum output or sales point then the costs will react in a way not described in the diagram. For instance, the variable costs will not disappear to nothing as is described in the chart – they will in many cases become fixed. For example, much of the direct skilled labour will still be employed for a time, even if there is insufficient production for them to be fully employed, and their wages would therefore become a fixed cost. Equally many fixed expenses such as administrative wages and salaries might in fact be cut if the minimum output or sales is not reached.

And this is equally true at the other end of the scale. For instance, if you

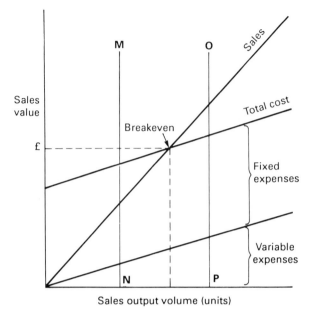

Illustration 7.10 Breakeven chart – output limitations.

get beyond a certain volume of output/sales as marked by the line OP in Illustration 7.10, then once again the variable and fixed costs will not respond in the way set out in the chart. For example, it is very likely that many of the variable costs will increase per unit produced. The business may become more wasteful with its materials or it will have to pay overtime to its labour to perform the necessary extra work. It may also be found that if it exceeds a certain normal output or sales volume the fixed cost might increase. It might have to employ more supervision or it may have to rent more space in order to obtain the extra capacity to store the goods or present the merchandise that it is now wishing to sell.

Coupled with this problem of increasing costs when a business exceeds a certain normal output/sales is the problem that if the business wishes to sell more and more of its goods or services it might well have to reduce its sale prices. It is a combination of these factors which might well mean that, although you might increase your sales and output, the result of this might be that you do not achieve the same profit level as you would normally anticipate. In fact you might even make a loss in what might be termed a trading pincer movement! This is set out in Illustration 7.11 by the continuation of the total cost and sales lines which show how changes in fixed and variable costs and sale prices affect the total profitability of the business.

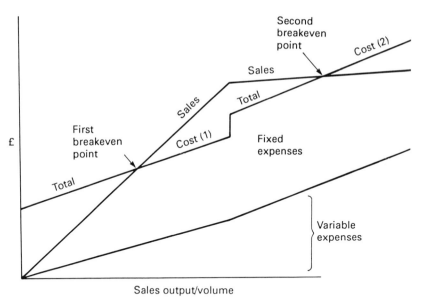

Illustration 7.11   Breakeven chart – cost changes.

Historical use of marginal costing

Now that we understand the limitations of marginal costing we can go on to examine the marginal cost structure of a unit of production, merchandise or service, and see how the marginal cost of a unit deducted from its sales value reveals the unit contribution towards the fixed cost of the business. Remember at the same time to bear in mind the limitations already discussed regarding the data.

However, as already mentioned, in addition to its use in analysing historical cost marginal costing has a very wide application in the policy areas of marketing and pricing. To illustrate these applications first let us consider the trading and pricing picture of business over the past years, because what we find is that, whenever we look at these, we find an application for marginal costing.

Marginal costing and pricing policy

Market domination

To illustrate this let us go back one hundred years or so and consider the situation that arose when many of the larger enterprises began to establish dominance in their particular marketing fields. To do this turn to Illustration 7.12 which sets out the costs of two units. We will assume that these represent the costs of units produced by two different manufacturing companies in the same industry and we will also assume that product A is produced by a large multi-product manufacturer, whereas product B is produced by a smaller manufacturer of a single product. It will be clear when you look at these two costs that whereas product A costs 10p and is sold for 12p with a profit of 2p, product B with a total cost of 8p is sold for 10p and has therefore the same profit of 2p from a full cost point of view.

What we see here is that a small company producing the single unit is selling that unit at a lower sales price than the larger manufacturer competing in the same market-place. It is also clear that, in this situation, if the larger manufacturer wished to dominate the market-place in the sale of this particular unit, it would have to eliminate the opposition. How best could this be done?

Obviously one of the more effective ways would be to reduce the sales price, but before this could be done the larger company would need to know what minimum sales price it could adopt. It is in establishing that 'minimum sales price' that marginal costing – which analyses costs into those which are variable as opposed to those that are fixed – becomes so useful. We can see from Illustration 7.12 that if the large manufacturer does this the variable cost of the unit is 6p and the fixed cost 4p. Having established this fact it is an easy step to recognise that if the larger manufacturer sells more than one type of unit it could, for a limited period, decide to recover its fixed costs from these other units. It could then decide to sell product A at something which will recover its variable costs and perhaps be satisfied with making only a very small contribution above that.

For instance, the large manufacturer in Illustration 7.12 might decide to sell A at 7p, which would then leave the small manufacturer in a very difficult position because it has no other products over which it can spread its fixed costs. In this situation the minimum sales price it could sell its product for without making a loss would be 8p.

It was based upon this view of pricing and the treatment of fixed costs that many monopolies were established at the turn of the century. For a limited period of time a large enterprise was willing to reduce its sales price so as to capture a market from its smaller 'annoying' competitor(s).

Pricing during a recession

If we go on from this point of time to a period of recession and slump, once again we see the need to establish minimum sales prices to meet the marketing problem. In such a situation if the market-place no longer wants

Illustration 7.12   Unit costs.

	Large company Product A		Small company Product B
	p		p
Direct costs	4		4
Variable cost		6	
Indirect costs	6		4
Fixed cost		4	
Total cost	10	10	8
Profit	2		2
Sales price	12		10

your goods, merchandise or services then once again it may well be necessary to try and attract business by means of bringing sales prices down. It might even be argued in this situation that any sales price which recovers some of the fixed costs is better than a sales price which does not sell anything at all! After all the fixed costs are going to go on whatever happens.

We can trace this view by again studying the breakeven chart set out in Illustration 7.2. Here you will see that if a sale is made or not the fixed costs will still continue, and therefore any sales price which recovers the variable costs and provides some contribution towards the fixed costs will reduce the eventual loss. It will certainly be better financially than not selling anything at all!

The 'other label' approach

The third application of marginal costing to processing policies can be seen in the use of 'brand label' switch techniques in marketing. What we find is that many businesses may go through short-term recessions or high competition periods, in which the production, storage or service rendering capacity might exceed the sales demand. It is to meet this situation that many businesses rendering services and manufacturing or merchandising goods attract additional sales by reducing their sales prices whilst at the same time disguising such products, merchandise or services by means of 'another label'. This action obtains two objectives: more sales achieved whilst at the same time not offending past or present customers who purchased the same goods, merchandise or services as these with reduced sales prices, at a higher price.

Here once again to establish such lower sales prices the marginal cost is used to produce a reference point for the revised sales price. For an example of this situation turn to Illustration 7.13 and examine the breakeven chart set out there. In this chart you will notice that production capacity is

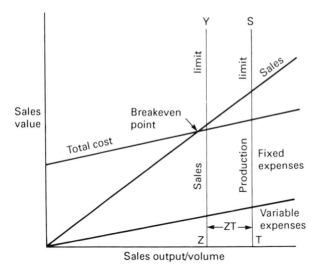

Illustration 7.13   Breakeven chart showing sales and production limits.

marked by the vertical line ST and the sales demand based on normal sales prices is marked by the vertical line YZ. We therefore have the area ZT which represents free, indeed unused production capacity. It is in order to fill this free capacity that many companies adopt the policy of marketing their excess capacity under another brand label, coupled with a price reduction, in order to attract the necessary additional sales volume.

Brand label switch problems
However, it must be understood that if a business uses such selling methods two problems exist.

(a) The first is that of establishing what is free capacity. It is easy to decide what is free capacity only to find that once you have committed yourself to filling it with work at a lower sales price you are forced, because of full capacity, to refuse higher priced work once demand flows back to the business. In other words you can over react to a short-term situation.

(b) The second problem, however, is even more important to understand and that is if you adopt the policy of selling your free capacity at lower than normal sales price you must make sure that the business maintains a strict control of the sales mix.

What is important is that you confine your lower prices to items which will fill the free capacity and you do not allow these to eat into your otherwise high profit-making capacity. Central to this problem is an understanding of the arithmetic of profit.

The arithmetic of profit

Consider Illustration 7.14. You will see that there are three products A, B and C with sales prices in column 1 of 10p, 15p and 8p respectively. You will then notice that in column 2 we have the variable cost of each product, namely 5p, 10p and 7p, which therefore gives a contribution for A of 5p, B of 5p and C of 1p. If we then relate the contribution to the sales value for each product we arrive at the following relationships given in column 4: in the case of A, 5p contribution divided by 10p sales price, gives us a relationship of 0.5; in the case of B the relationship becomes 5p divided by 15p which is 0.33; and finally in the case of C a penny divided by 8p gives us 0.125.

Each of these relationships is telling us that in the case of A whatever sales value we achieve, 50 per cent of the sales value will be contribution – in other words if we sell a pound's worth of A then 50p will be variable cost and 50p will be contribution. In the case of B for every pound we sell 33p will be contribution and 67p will be variable cost, and in the case of C $12\frac{1}{2}$p will be contribution and $87\frac{1}{2}$p will be variable cost. If you find the arithmetic confusing just remember we now have decimal currency!

The sales mix

If we then turn to the final column we will see that we have set out here first the budgeted sales mix. This is the mix of sales between the three products we are planning to sell for the period ahead. Now if we are assuming that the budgeted sales mix in the case of A, B and C is 80, 10 and 10 per cent respectively, as shown in the illustration, we could then establish the relationship of contributions to sales values within this mix by very simple multiplication and addition.

Illustration 7.14 The arithmetic of profit.

Products	Sales price (1) p	Variable cost (2) p	Contribution (3) p	Contribution to sales price (4) p	Budgeted sales Mix %	c/sp p
A	10	5	5	0.50	80	0.40
B	15	10	5	0.33	10	0.03
C	8	7	1	0.125	10	0.01
						0.44

Fixed costs = £880,000 ÷ 0.44p
Sales value to breakeven = £2 million

Sales mix and breakeven calculation

For instance, if we multiply the 0.5 that we have established for product A by 80 per cent we arrive at the figure of 0.40 of £1, and if we multiply the 0.33 we have established for product B by 10 per cent we get 0.03 of £1, and finally if we multiply the 0.12 for product C by 10 per cent we will arrive at a relationship of 0.10 of £1.

Having established the individual amounts we can then add them up to arrive at a total of 0.44 of £1. Now let us look at this overall. What we are saying is that every time we sell a pound's worth of our goods in the mix that we have just been discussing, namely 80 per cent A, 10 per cent B, 10 per cent C, we shall arrive at a contribution from each pound of our sales of 44p.

It will therefore be seen that if the fixed costs we are trying to recover for the year from our business amount to £880,000, then the amount of sales in value that we must achieve, based on a mix of 80 per cent A, 10 per cent B, 10 per cent C, to recover these fixed costs can be calculated by dividing the £880,000 by 44p. And if we do this we will arrive at the sales value of £2,000,000. The breakeven point therefore is sales of £2,000,000.

Budget/actual comparison

We can now take this a step further. We can see what will happen if we found that our actual sales do not agree with our budgeted sales, for instance if we do not achieve a mix of 80 per cent A, 10 per cent B, 10 per cent C, but in fact our mix becomes 10 per cent A, 10 per cent B, and 80 per cent C. The question we then have to solve is what does that mean as far as the sales value required to break even?

To deal with this we need to turn to Illustration 7.15. Here we see that in order to arrive at a solution we must recalculate our relationship of con-

Illustration 7.15   Revision of sales mix.

Product	Contribution to sales	Actual sales mix %	Actual contribution to sale price p
A	0.50	10	0.05
B	0.33	10	0.03
C	0.125	80	0.10
			0.18

Fixed costs   = £880,000 ÷ 0.18p
Sales value to breakeven = £4.9 million

tribution to sales price based on this new mix. In other words, we must multiply the 0.5 for A not by 80 per cent but by 10 per cent. As far as B is concerned the multiplication remains the same because the sales mix is still 10 per cent but in the case of C we must multiply 0.125 not by 10 per cent but by 80 per cent. If we do all this we come to a very different figure because this will be made up of the 0.05 for A plus the 0.03 for B and 0.10 for C giving us a total of 0.18.

What we now discover is that when we sell in this new mix, instead of arriving at a contribution of 44p per £1 we sell, we now arrive at a contribution of only 18p per £1 we sell. In other words between the budget and the actual mix every time we sell a pound's worth of our products we are losing 26p between our budget and our actual contribution figures.

We can also see that in order to break even we would have to achieve a sales value based on this actual mix of £4.9 million, which is calculated by dividing £880,000 by 0.18 – a very different figure from the budgeted sales value of £2,000,000!

All this is the arithmetic of profit which must be clearly understood by all those who seek to establish sales policies which require pricing adjustments within a sales mix. At the present time more and more businesses are entering into a much more competitive market-place and a full understanding of this 'profit arithmetic' must be established throughout such organisations.

Contribution and limiting factors

Having looked at contribution in relation to sales value it is useful to carry our thoughts on the use of marginal costing a step further. We have so far mentioned that marginal costing information provides us with minimum sales price levels below which we must not fall – namely the variable cost.

We have also seen that marginal costing gives us a way of examining the contribution of individual units in relationship to the sales value. It is in fact central to marginal costing to understand the different contributions established for each of the products or services a business produces or sells.

It is this measurement of contribution which is central to marginal costing because it defines the true difference – from a profit point of view – between products or merchandise sold or services rendered. It is because contribution is so central to product definition from a profit point of view that in many cases it is found useful to examine it, not just in relationship to sales value, but to other factors. For example, within every business there may be limitations – of time, of storage space, of value, of capital or finance – and when you arrive at one of these limitations it is useful to examine the relationship of the contribution established for each unit sold or service rendered to these limitations.

Limitation of time

To discuss this problem let us turn to Illustration 7.16 which considers the problem of time limitations in relationship to the three products that we have just been examining in Illustrations 7.14 and 7.15. We will assume that there is a demand for our products which far exceeds our production capacity. We will also assume the following facts: that it takes three minutes of manufacturing time to make A, two minutes to make B and half a minute to make C.

The problem which now arises is which of the three products is the one which we should concentrate upon during a period of limited time available for manufacture. In this situation the relationship of contribution to sales value is no longer relevant – we need to look for a measurement of contribution not to sales value but to production time. For instance, we would find if we take A, B and C that A gives us 5p divided by 3 minutes which is approximately 1.7p per minute, B 5p divided by 2 minutes or 2.5p per minute, whereas in the case of C we have 1p divided by $\frac{1}{2}$ minute or 2p.

So if we are limited by production time then from a maximisation of profit point of view, we should concentrate first of all on selling B, second on C and finally on A – in other words not quite but very nearly in reverse order of preference from that which we established when we looked at contribution to sales value in Illustration 7.14.

Price selection

However, as well as looking at established products, merchandise or services it may also be found useful to concentrate upon contribution when selecting ideal future sales prices.

To examine this situation consider Illustration 7.17. In this we see we have a product which we decide to market and we have to agree upon its

Illustration 7.16 Contribution per limiting factor of time.

Product	Contribution p	Production time (mins)	Contribution to production time (p per min)
A	5	3	1.7
B	5	2	2.5
C	1	$\frac{1}{2}$	2.0

sales price. We will assume that the marketing department advises us that depending upon the size of the market that we wish to obtain, the sales price could range from 20p to 40p. We will also assume that we select the sales prices set out in the illustration and that the variable or direct cost of this particular unit is estimated at 15p. If this is so then the contributions – depending on the sales price decided upon – would range as we see in Illustration 7.17, from 5p to 25p per unit. Suppose we then decide that this particular unit has got to give us a minimum contribution of, say, £200,000 to make it worthwhile selling at all.

The 'contribution' breakeven chart

To solve this problem we can produce what we might term a 'visual agenda' as set out in Illustration 7.18 to consider the matters involved. This shows a breakeven chart which is different from the ones we have so far examined because it is solely concerned with presenting the cumulative contributions in relationship with the volume of sales. As you will see from the chart we have two vertical lines AB and CD scaled so as to set out the value of profit above and loss below the two points X and Y. These two points X and Y are joined by a horizontal line which is scaled in units sold, the complete chart taking a form similar to a rugby goal post. In this chart the cumulative contributions attributable to the different sales prices can be traced and compared with the sales volumes predicted.

Reading and plotting the chart

For instance, the chart begins by marking off £200,000 at point E on the loss or negative portion of vertical axis AB. This indicates the minimum contribution which this unit is targeted to recover whatever sales price is decided upon. Having established this at point E the contributions from the different sales prices are then drawn to indicate the cumulative contributions they each make. These are set out in Illustration 7.19. For example, EF is the line relating to the sales price of 20p, EG to 25p, EH to 30p, and

Illustration 7.17 Contribution and price selection.

	Suggested sales price				
	p	p	p	p	p
Product	20	25	30	35	40
Variable cost	15	15	15	15	15
Contribution	5	10	15	20	25

Minimum contribution required from product – £200,000

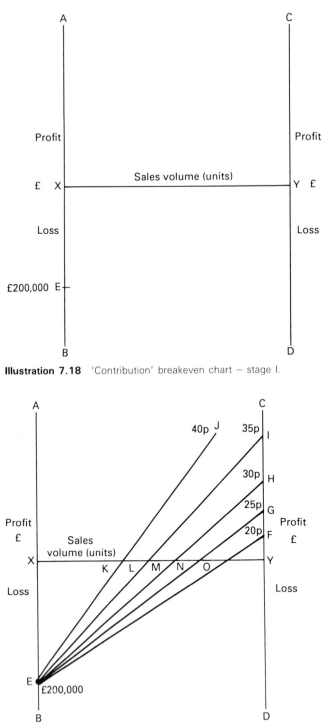

Illustration 7.18 'Contribution' breakeven chart – stage I.

Illustration 7.19 'Contribution' breakeven chart – stage II.

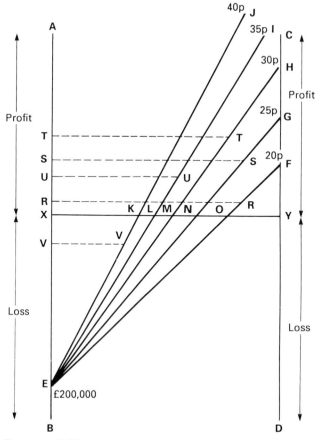

Illustration 7.20   'Contribution' breakeven chart – stage III.

so on. These lines indicate at points K, L, M, N and O the volume of sales at each sales price required to break even, that is to recover the £200,000 contribution target.

Having done this it is then possible to examine these lines in relationship to the market forecasts which are again set out in Illustration 7.20. For example, you could ask the marketing side of the business what volume of sales are anticipated at these different sales prices and mark these out as in Illustration 7.20 at points R, S, T, U and V.

From this we can then determine what we feel is the most suitable sale price by deciding which particular unit price gives us the maximum profit in relation to our production capacity. In this particular case 30p, 25p, 35p and 20p would be the order, 40p being dismissed as it does not provide a breakeven at all.

It must, however, be recognised that maximisation of immediate profit may not always be in the best long-term interest of the business. For instance, other considerations might favour a price which may not give us such a high profit as another but which might establish us in a market-place which fits into our particular range of products. Or we might wish to establish a lower price so as to attract more business, which in turn will keep the skills of the workforce more fully employed.

Summary

We have now examined marginal costing and the way in which it can be used and adapted to meet different management problems.

Definition of marginal costing

Marginal costing is a method of analysing expenses so as to highlight the fact that they move either in sympathy with what we produce and sell, or are of a fixed nature in that they are not directly influenced by sales or production volume but more by time. It must be recognised that this division is not absolute and in fact many expenses fall into neither category – in other words they are neither fixed nor variable but a bit of each. An example of this sort of expense would be depreciation on plant and machinery. This, it can be argued, varies in accordance with the use of the particular piece of plant and machinery but also contains a fixed part – the obsolescence – which is going on whether it is used or not.

We could also argue that such things as wages can often be partly variable and partly fixed. They are variable in the case of production labour so long as production continues, but once production is held up or is no longer continued, then such expenses can and often do become fixed. The skilled operator waiting for work becomes a fixed cost and it is for this reason that we must be particularly careful not to treat the division of fixed and variable expenses in too rigid a manner. The division needs to be continually reviewed in accordance with situations as they develop.

The second point to emphasise is that in the division of fixed and variable expenses the fact that marginal costing is concerned with the analysis of variable expenses does not imply that the fixed costs are being ignored. It may well be true they are not being analysed, but this certainly should not mean that they are being ignored. Throughout any system of marginal costing, contributions must be compared with fixed costs and emphasis must always be placed upon making sure that such fixed costs are being recovered by the contributions obtained from the products, merchandise or services being sold.

Having arrived at this overall view of contribution and marginal costing it is necessary to consider how this way of looking at the expense to income relationship can be used to deal with management problems. However, certain points must first be emphasised.

Limitation of data

To begin with there are the limitations which are inherent within this view of costing. What is meant by this is that, whenever we consider fixed and variable costs and the sales and breakeven points, it must be remembered that all these measurements of expense and income are based on assumptions. In other words, once we have established the breakeven point any event which alters expenses or sales prices – or indeed the sales mix – will change the breakeven point. For this reason the revision of marginal cost information must be a constant requirement by management.

Implicit assumptions

Secondly, when we look at the measurement of break even and variable and fixed costs and sales prices we must appreciate that all these are based upon an assumption of a minimum and maximum output sales level. Once a business either falls below or rises above these limitation levels the relationship between the expenses and sales may also change.

Management use of marginal costing

Having recognised very clearly the limitations and assumptions of the information we use in establishing a marginal cost it is necessary to consider the use that can be made of such data.

Sales price guidelines

The first use is in establishing sales price guidelines. For instance, to meet the different marketing situations – to take advantage of situations – we may feel that an adjustment of the sales price could be advantageous to us. If this need arises then knowing what is the variable cost of the different units we are selling could be of considerable help. It would allow us to recognise that this is the value below which a sales price would not recover the variable expense of the unit and above which we would at least make a contribution towards our fixed costs.

Establishing such a minimum sales price can be particularly useful in highly competitive market-places and could have particular application when we wish to steer our marketing policies in particular directions.

Concentration on the controllable within recognised limitations

A further point is that because marginal costing concentrates our view upon the contribution of each unit we sell, it enables us to examine our products, merchandise and services in the light of those costs which are controllable. It also enables management to study the contributions discovered in relation to particular limiting factors such as time, space or capital investment.

Illustration 7.21 Marginal costing exercise.

[B LTD]

B Ltd sells five product lines. The five products are manufactured on a bank of 60 power presses, any of which may be used on each of the five products. It is estimated that each press can produce 40 hours' work per week. The data relating to the products are as follows:

Product	Total cost £	Variable cost £	Selling price per unit £	No. of press hrs	Estimated demand per month
A	26	20	30	3	1,400
B	35	28	40	6	1,900
C	72	52	85	7	300
D	20	15	30	5	1,800
E	18	14	30	4	600

Fixed costs amount to £23,400 per month.

What combination of products would produce the maximum profit assuming the business is limited by press hours?

Illustration 7.22 Suggested answer to Illustration 7.21.

Product	Selling price per unit £	Variable cost £	Contribution £	Hours req.	Contribution per unit	Best product
A	30	20	10	3	3.3	3
B	40	28	12	6	2.0	5
C	85	52	33	7	4.7	1
D	30	15	15	5	3.0	4
E	30	14	16	4	4.0	2

To maximise the profits based on 9,600 hours per month produce:

Product	Demand	Product	Hours		Total hours	Contribution £
C	300	300	7	=	2,100	9,870
E	600	600	4	=	2,400	9,600
A	1,400	1,400	3	=	4,200	13,860
D	1,800	180	5	=	900	2,700
					9,600 hrs	36,030
					Less fixed costs	23,400
					Net profit	£12,630

Sales price selection

Finally, by the use of marginal cost analysis it is possible to review the effects of different sales prices for the same product or service by means of the revised breakeven chart set out in Illustration 7.20. This may prove a valuable way of bringing together the many considerations which have to be recognised in establishing a sales price.

Consolidation

Now to consolidate your studies of marginal costing attempt the question set out in Illustration 7.21. When you have completed it check your answer with Illustration 7.22.

Conclusion

This then completes our studies of both full and marginal costing. The question which perhaps we are still left with is why should there be two methods of analysing expense? The answer lies in the world or the market-place around us. Full costing is very much the method used when sales prices can be determined by those selling the product, the service or the merchandise. It is concerned therefore with a method of analysis by which the direct cost of each unit is established and to which a suitable absorption rate to recover overheads and profit are added so as to arrive at the sales price.

Marginal costing is, however, designed to meet a very different market-place, one which is dominated by the buyer or the competitor. Its concern, as we have seen, is in the pricing, marketing and profit measurement fields.

8 | PROJECT APPRAISAL

Introduction

In Chapter 5 we began to examine the evolution of financial information from the Profit and Loss Account, the Balance Sheet and the Cash Flow Forecast. We discussed how in order to meet the needs of the thinking manager to find out where the profit or loss is being made we have the analytical techniques of full and marginal costing.

To remind you of the pattern of this evolution look again at Illustration 5.1. We shall now return to our review of the techniques concerned by considering those which stem from the Balance Sheet. The Balance Sheet sets out from where a business has obtained its money, its capital, and where

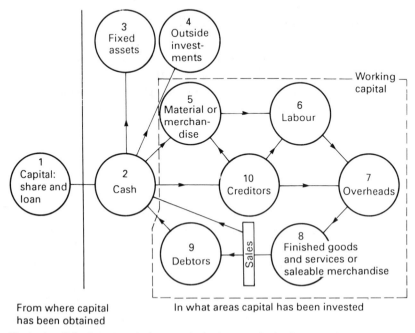

From where capital has been obtained

In what areas capital has been invested

Illustration 8.1 Investment of money in business – the business model.

this same money is invested right now. Managers are very much concerned with the areas in which the capital is invested. They may be unable to influence directly all the sources of capital but they certainly need to be aware of how it is invested. After all where it is invested is a direct result of their actions and the way managers do this will very much influence the chances or risks, of profits or losses being made. To refresh your memory of the way money is invested in business look at the form of the Business Model set out in Illustration 8.1.

Here we see the two areas of investment – fixed assets including outside investment, and working capital. So let us begin by looking at the first of these – the fixed assets, the things we buy with no intention of selling – and ask ourselves would it be sufficient to read about what we own as fixed assets on the Balance Sheet? And the answer, I think we would give, is 'No, by that time it would be too late! We would already own them.' In other words, if we had bought the 'wrong ones' it would be too late to correct the matter – we would be 'stuck' with them!

So let us look at the techniques available to help managers plan and control this investment area.

Project appraisal

In the first place we must recognise that although we can very broadly describe investment in business as either going into things we have no intention of selling – the fixed assets – or into things we do not intend to sell – the working capital – there are exceptions. There are in many businesses a certain number of investments which are neither one thing nor the other. We might term them the 'hybrid' items of investment. For example, consider an advertising campaign or an investment in long-term research and development. Both these investments are eventually going to go into what is sold but it may be some time between the investment of the money and its eventual liquidisation or return back into cash when sales or benefits relevant to such expenses are made.

We term the techniques that we use in assessing fixed assets 'project appraisal techniques'. We use this term so as to encompass not only investments in fixed assets but all investments, where the return of the money locked up back into the business is not immediate or within the normal trading cycle.

In order to study the techniques that we use in this area I would like you to put yourself in the position of an investing manager. I would like you to consider the situation that arises where managers are concerned with investing in something which they have no intention of disposing of immediately, that is putting money into a project.

Fact gathering

In examining this situation I would like you to consider what information you would require financially on which you would base your judgements. In order to approach this problem let us put a practical situation forward to consider. We shall imagine that we are considering an investment in plant and machinery which our production manager wishes to make. He approaches us and provides us first with all the technical details regarding the proposed investment.

However, when this is completed, we should also require certain financial facts about the proposition. Think through what the financial facts are that you would indeed require.

The cost

So, first of all, what is the first fact you would want to know? Of course the answer is quite simply the 'cost'. We shall quite obviously need to know exactly how much money will be required in order to purchase the particular item of plant and machinery. So the first piece of information we would seek – the cost – we will say in this case amounts to £40,000.

This may sound a nice simple round figure but it is never that easy! In fact this is often the most difficult figure of all to assess. After all it is not just the obvious cost of the machine or whatever you need to consider. There is also the supporting investment in such things as the stocks which may need to be increased to support the manufacture of the extra products which will be produced by the new machine, and the extra investment in the debtors or receivables – the customers who will buy the extra products once the new machine is operational but will not pay for them immediately – and we must not forget the training of the people who will operate the new machine!

All these and other costs will need to be taken into account in arriving at the cost of the machine. So you can see that to arrive at this first figure – the cost – will not be as easy as it might first appear.

The benefits

Now let us proceed and ask ourselves, if we know the cost, what else would we want to know? And I suggest an immediate response would be that we would want to know the effect of this purchase on our profits. In other words, what is going to be the result to us as far as the investment is concerned – what benefits will it provide the business?

Illustration 8.2   Project appraisal.

Profit and Loss Account relating to plant
and machinery investment as set out
below:

	£	£
Sales		31,000
Less: Material	15,000	
Labour	5,000	
Rent	400	
Depreciation	7,000	
Power	1,000	
Maintenance	600	29,000
Net profit		£2,000

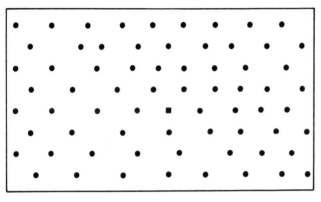

● = All other project proposals

■ = Plant and machinery (cost £40,000) proposal

Illustration 8.3   Graphic display of decision problem.

Here we have a rather odd situation because if we are to assess profit or
loss we have a particular problem when we try to trace it to a particular
project. We might begin in the way shown in Illustration 8.2. We might ask
ourselves, if we buy this machine what are the additional sales, and we
might put those down. Of course away from this amount we would have
to deduct the costs – the materials, the labour and all the other expenses
like the rent, insurance, maintenance, power, and the depreciation and so
on, which need to be deducted from these sales. We would therefore arrive
at a calculation of the profit or loss.

However, at this point I want you to stop and think this through a little
bit more and to help you to do this I want you to look at Illustration 8.3.
This is a visual illustration of the problem that confronts managers when
they are considering an investment of this nature.

What this illustrates is that managers in this situation have in front of them many projects that they have to consider, not just the particular proposition costing £40,000 marked ■ in Illustration 8.3 but all the dots (●) in the rectangle which represent other project decisions that have got to be made by the same managers. From this, what becomes clear is that the measurement which we must bring to bear upon one particular project must be one which precisely relates to it.

In other words we have got to find some measurement which will specifically pick out the project in front of us from all the others coming before us for consideration. It is when this problem is faced up to that managers find that they cannot use the measurement of profit and loss. They have to find some other measure.

Cash flow

To understand the other measurement, let us return to the financial model once again in Illustration 8.1 and ask ourselves which is the most sensitive area of all – in financial terms – when one considers anything you do in a business. In other words, which circle in the financial model will be affected whatever we do – whether we buy or sell, whether we invest in this item or not, whether we get money by bringing capital in, whether we pay bills, and so on? What we will find, if we think this through, is that the most sensitive area of all is cash itself – the pulse of the business.

Measurement of cash flow

Financially, whatever we do will eventually affect cash. It is because of this fact that when we measure the financial implications of a particular project we use cash as the medium of measurement, and this is done in a totally pragmatic way. We simply ask ourselves, when a project is being considered, exactly how will this affect the cash circulating in the business throughout the life of the particular project.

For instance, in the particular situation we are at present considering, if we invest £40,000 in the project then in Year 0 – when we purchase the item – cash will be reduced by £40,000. There will, as they say, be a negative cash flow in Year 0 of £40,000.

We then consider what is going to be the effect on cash during the project's life. To do this we must first decide in the light of the particular project its life span – in this case we shall say it is four years. So our next question is what will be the effect on the cash flow year by year over those four years if we do purchase the item?

Cash flow and profit

To illustrate the difference between cash flow and profit let us return to Illustration 8.2 and consider the difference in the figures set out when calculating the profit in Year 1 and those shown in Illustration 8.4 which sets out the gross cash flow assessment. We shall see first of all of course that, if we make sales, then this will certainly affect cash, so this amount will continue to be used in the assessment of the gross cash flow in Year 1. We can also see that the materials going into the extra units that are going to be produced from the new machine will also affect cash – so this will remain the same and so will the additional labour.

But when we come to the other expenses like rent, power and maintenance, etc., we have got to be careful. In each instance we have to ask ourselves is this additional expense, or is it an expense that would be there whether we bought this machine or not? For example, if we find that the rent is not additional it will not come into the calculation of the gross cash flow. Or again, if we find that in the case of maintenance we shall be using the same maintenance staff to look after this new machine as are used at present, with the only difference that we shall be spending a certain amount more on special repairs for this machine, then only the special repair costs should be brought into the gross cash flow calculation.

We also have to remember our studies of depreciation. Depreciation is, as we have already seen when we discussed the Profit and Loss Account and the Cash Flow Forecast in Chapters 2 and 4, an expense in the Profit and Loss Account, but it does not affect cash. Its purpose, you will remember, is to reduce the profit you could otherwise take out of the business as dividends. However, when we examine the effect upon cash in each year from this investment we would have to ignore depreciation – because depreciation is not going to affect it.

So, if we turn again to Illustration 8.4 we see the reassessment of the figures that we had shown in Illustration 8.2 as an assessment of profit into an assessment of the increase or reduction to cash.

Illustration 8.4   Cash flow assessment of project in Year 1: calculation of gross cash flow.

	£	£
Sales		31,000
Less: Materials	15,000	
Labour	5,000	
Power	1,000	21,000
Gross cash flow		£10,000

The gross cash flow

The gross cash flow is a very important measurement for us to understand and it is one which we have not used before. However, it is the only one we can use in making project decisions because of its unique ability to differentiate between one project and another by measuring its effect upon the business in cash terms. It is therefore vital that we should understand the difference between the measurement of profit and loss and that of the gross cash flow.

In order to test this understanding turn to the question in Illustration 8.5 which reinforces our studies so far. When you have completed your answer compare it with that set out in Illustration 8.6.

Profit plus depreciation and cash flow

However, to understand cash flow fully it is necessary to look just a little further at this measurement and recognise that if we are creating a growth to the gross cash flow this will indeed have an affect on the profit or loss of the business. In fact if we consider it, we will realise that the growth of

Illustration 8.5   Project appraisal exercise.

Set out the following figures in the calculation of the gross cash flows for each of the three years:

Years	1	2	3
	£	£	£
Additional sales	20,000	25,000	15,000
Material in sales	10,000	12,000	6,000
Labour in sales	5,000	7,000	2,000
Extra other expenses in sales	2,000	3,000	500
Reapportioned expenses already incurred	1,500	1,500	400
Depreciation	5,000	5,000	5,000
Additional power	300	300	100
Maintenance costs			
– reapportioned	150	150	150
– additional	50	50	50

Illustration 8.6   Suggested answer to Illustration 8.5.

Years		1			2			3
	£	£	£	£	£	£		£
Sales		20,000			25,000			15,000
Less: Materials	10,000			12,000			6,000	
Labour	5,000			7,000			2,000	
Extra expenses	2,000			3,000			500	
Power	300			300			100	
Maintenance	50	17,350		50	22,350		50	8,650
Gross cash flow		£2,650			£2,650			£6,350

cash represents the additional net profit before taxation plus depreciation that the business has charged before striking such profit.

In other words, if in Year 1 the business we are discussing does invest £40,000 in this fixed asset, then the profit of the business will be increased by £3,000 – which is £10,000 growth in the gross cash flow as shown in illustration 8.4, less the depreciation of £7,000. It also means that if this is so, then there will be taxation to pay on these additional profits – and as we all know tax affects cash!

The net cash flow

Taxation can be a very important factor in the assessment of a project because of the fact that a project such as an investment in machinery may well attract capital allowances as well as creating the need for more corporation tax payable on the additional profits. It is because taxation has to be taken into consideration before finally calculating the cash flow figure that the figure before tax is referred to as the gross cash flow (GCF) and after taxation as the net cash flow (NCF).

Detailed treatment of taxation is beyond the scope of this book so the figures used under the title net cash flow assume that taxation adjustments have already been made. These include both the corporation tax payable on the additional profits and the capital allowance benefits where applicable. They would also take account of any government grants. A simple illustration of taxation adjustments is included in Illustration 8.7 which should be studied. This presents how the gross cash flows for the four years in which the project, introduced in Illustrations 8.2 and 8.4, would be shown and sets out the relevant taxation and government grant adjustments as a note.

It is, however, emphasised that these adjustments are illustrating principles and are based on assumed taxation rates and capital allowances. In most circumstances managers would be expected to calculate the gross cash flow figures only and the financial function would supply the taxation adjustments.

As regards our project, let us now continue by considering Illustration 8.7 further. Here we see that the figures after the taxation adjustment have been placed under the head net cash flow, or NCF as it is often referred to. As we have seen, the net cash flow is the amount by which the cash is affected year by year within the business because of the particular investment. In our illustration this can be seen to show the following figures:

In Year 1 – we have a positive net cash flow of £25,000
In Year 2 –   £15,000
In Year 3 –   £10,000

Illustration 8.7 Project appraisal (*continued*).

Cost of plant and machinery	£40,000

Year	Net cash flow (NCF)
	£
1	25,000
2	15,000
3	10,000
4	5,000
Total	£55,000

Note on net cash flow calculation

Years:	1	2	3	4
	£	£	£	£
Gross cash flows	10,000	22,500	15,400	500
Less: Corporation tax @ say 50%	5,000	11,250	7,700	250
	5,000	11,250	7,700	250
Add back:				
Capital allowances at say 25% of plant and machinery cost £40,000 on reducing balance (see calculation below)	5,000	3,750	2,817	4,219
Government grant	15,000	—	—	—
Scrap value	—	—	—	600
			£10,517	£5,069
Net cash flow	£25,000	£15,000	(say £10,000)	(say £5,000)

Capital allowance calculation:

Year	Original cost	Capital allowance	Tax saving @ 50%
	£	£	£
1	40,000	10,000	5,000
1	10,000		
2	30,000	7,500	3,750
	7,500		
3	22,500	5,625	2,817
	5,625		
4	16,875	8,438	4,219

In the fourth and final year, which includes the scrap value at the end of the machines' life of £600 approximately, we have a positive net cash flow of £5,000.

We shall now look at how this information can be used in appraising a particular project and again we shall return to our questioning situation.

The payback period

First, I should like you to think about how you might look at the financial data that we have in front of us in Illustration 8.7 and ask yourself if you were in the position of making the 'yes' or 'no' decision what would it be?

And before you rush into an answer to this I want you also to consider the fact that as an investor you would find – as all investors have found – that you would need to steel yourself with a certain amount of caution before accepting or rejecting any particular investment idea. This is because it has got to be understood that from the beginning of time anyone in a position to finance an investment has always found that those putting forward propositions want them to say 'yes'!

It is for this reason that investors have always tried to arm themselves with a certain amount of depression, so as to make the judgement as dispassionately as possible. It is to create, perhaps, just such a flattening approach that investors have sought a quick measurement in looking at projects. What they have looked for is how quickly will they get their money back.

If you consider this approach you will see that the response of an investor is precisely the same as that of any person when they are heading for a situation in which once the commitment is made it will be final. It is not important what the situation is. Anyone who is going to make a decision the result of which will be final needs to 'look before they leap'. And certainly a most useful measurement would be to consider the escape route – what you would look for is how quickly can you back out if all goes wrong?

In the case of business investment therefore the first measurement that is often used in looking at the data that we have just produced in Illustration 8.7 is to see how quickly would it take to get our money back. You are paying out £40,000 on this particular project: in Year 1 you get back £25,000, in Year 2 a further £15,000, and so on.

This means that by the end of Year 2, based on the figures in front of us, we shall have got our original £40,000 investment back as cash. It is this measurement which we term the 'payback', and it is the measurement which is perhaps most often used whenever an investment is appraised. It might be described as the first financial filter we put projects through!

Return on capital invested

However, unless someone has suggested this approach, many people looking at the figures we have just gathered together might not immediately think of using the payback method. I think many would try to calculate the return on the investment made.

Average return

Illustration 8.8 shows that in calculating the return on investment people would first add up all the net cash flows which in this case come to a total

Illustration 8.8 Average return on average capital employed.

Year	NCF		£
0	£	Cost of plant and machinery	40,000
1	25,000		
2	15,000		
3	10,000		
4	5,000		
	55,000		
Less: Cost	40,000		
Difference	£15,000		

Average return = 15,000 divided by 4   = £3,750
Average capital employed = 40,000 divided by 2 = £20,000

Average return on average capital employed $= \dfrac{3,750}{20,000} \times 100 = 18.75\%$

of £55,000. From this figure they would then deduct the original cost of the project of £40,000. They would then have discovered the amount that they are going to get back on their investment in excess of the original cost – in this case £15,000.

They would then divide this £15,000 by the number of years involved, which in our example is 4 years. This gives an average return of £3,750 per year, and they would then relate this to the average capital they were investing.

Average capital invested

They are of course not investing £40,000 all the way through the four years because by the end of the four years we have had the original money invested returned back into the business. So you might say the average amount of money invested at any time over the four years would be £20,000 – half the original cost. (This is of course based on the assumption that an equal amount of money is paid back into the business each year which in this case is not strictly true!)

Average return on average capital invested

If we then relate the average annual return of £3,750 to the average capital invested of £20,000 we would be able to calculate our average return on average capital employed. This gives us a rate of approximately 18.75 per cent and we can then compare this with the rate of return we might be looking for in our business. Or if we were going to have to borrow the money for this project we could compare this 18.75 per cent with the interest charged by the lender.

The problem of time and money

However, if we consider this particular approach for any length of time we would recognise that what we have just been doing is a financial absurdity. To illustrate the absurdness of what we have just done let us consider the question of what would we rather have – £100 now or £100 in a year's time, even assuming there is no monetary inflation?

Without any hesitation, no doubt, everyone would prefer to have the money right now, for the very simple reason that if you have money now you can use it. You can re-invest it – and it will be worth £100 plus whatever the rate of interest you can earn on that money over the year, as opposed to the alternative of exactly £100 at the end of the year.

Now if this is true of the £100 it is equally true of the figures that we have just been looking at. For instance, I would much prefer £1 of the £25,000 offered to me in Year 1 than £1 of the £5,000 in Year 4 in Illustration 8.7. After all the sooner we get the money back into circulation the sooner we can re-invest it and therefore the sooner we can in fact get a further return on the money. It is because this is true that what we have just illustrated in our previous approach, in calculating the average return on average capital employed, does not in fact meet our needs. Remember all we did was add up all the years' net cash flows into a single total irrespective of when they arose.

Discount factors

It is for this reason that in the area of investment in projects people have sought out discount factors, which can be used to meet this problem of time and money.

To help understand what discount factors are turn to Illustration 8.9 and study the examples. If you look you will see that we have the factors for 0–5 years and for different rates of interest from 8–16 per cent. To illustrate their use let us take the discount factors for 10 per cent.

It will be seen that the factor in Year 1 is 0.909. This means that if you

Illustration 8.9 Discount factors.

Year	8%	10%	12%	14%	15%	16%
0	1.000	1.000	1.000	1.000	1.000	1.000
1	0.926	0.909	0.893	0.877	0.870	0.862
2	0.857	0.826	0.797	0.769	0.757	0.743
3	0.794	0.751	0.712	0.675	0.658	0.641
4	0.735	0.683	0.636	0.592	0.572	0.552
5	0.681	0.621	0.568	0.519	0.497	0.476

invest 0.909 of £1 now, in one year's time at 10 per cent interest it will grow to £1. In Year 2 you will find the factor for 10 per cent stands at 0.826, and again this means that if you invest 0.826 of £1 now in Year 0 then in two years' time at 10 per cent compound interest it will grow to £1, and so we could go on.

It is useful to become familiar with these discount factor tables. In order to reinforce your knowledge look at Illustration 8.10. This sets out a question for you to tackle to become familiar with how to read these factors. Once you have completed this you should then check your answers with Illustration 8.11 before proceeding.

Using discount factors

Having explained the meaning of discount factors we shall now see how they can be applied to the problems of investment appraisal. To illustrate this in the context of what we have been examining throughout this chapter we shall say in the first instance that we require a return of 16 per cent on our investment in this particular project. That 16 per cent is our criterion. And if this is the case then what we can do is use the appropriate discount factors for 16 per cent which we will find set out under the 16 per cent discount factor column in Illustration 8.9. These are:

Year 1   0.862
Year 2   0.743
Year 3   0.641
Year 4   0.552

Illustration 8.10   Discount factor exercise.

Set out the discount factors for the following:

1. 12 per cent in Year 4.
2. 15 per cent in Year 3.
3. 16 per cent in Year 5.
4.   8 per cent in Year 1.
5. 14 per cent in Year 2.
6. 10 per cent in Year 4.

Illustration 8.11   Solution to Illustration 8.10.

1. 0.636
2. 0.658
3. 0.476
4. 0.926
5. 0.769
6. 0.683

Illustration 8.12 Discount factors for
NCFs in project appraisal.

Year	Net cash flow	Discount factors
	£	16%
0	(40,000)	1.000
1	25,000	0.862
2	15,000	0.743
3	10,000	0.641
4	5,000	0.552

Illustration 8.13 Calculation of present values.

Year	NCF		Discount factors		Present value
	£		16%		£
0	(40,000)	×	1.000	=	(40,000)
1	25,000	×	0.862	=	21,550
2	15,000	×	0.743	=	11,145
3	10,000	×	0.641	=	6,410
4	5,000	×	0.552	=	2,760

Indeed you will see, that if you turn to Illustration 8.12 that these factors
have been placed against the net cash flow figures for each of the four years.

Having arrived at these factors we can then proceed to the next stage
which is to multiply the amounts we have calculated as the net cash flows
for each of the four years by the appropriate discount factor set out in Illustration 8.12. This multiplication is shown in Illustration 8.13, and by it we
arrive at the amount we need to invest now in Year 0 to give us the net cash
flows for each of the four years.

The present values

What we have in fact done by multiplying the net cash flows by these
factors is that we have discovered how much we need to invest now in Year
0 at 16 per cent to arrive at the appropriate net cash flow forecast for each
year. For example, in order to arrive at £25,000 at the end of Year 1,
assuming a rate of interest of 16 per cent, we would have to invest £21,550
in Year 0.

Again to arrive at £15,000 at the end of Year 2 – assuming a rate of
16 per cent compound interest – we would have to invest £11,145. And
in order to arrive at £10,000 at the end of Year 3 – assuming a rate of
16 per cent compound interest – we would have to invest £6,410 now in
Year 0. Finally, in order to arrive at £5,000 in four years' time, we would
need to invest £2,760 now, assuming a rate of 16 per cent compound
interest.

Illustration 8.14 Discounted cash flow calculation.

Year	NCF		16%	Present value	
	£		DF	£	£
0	(40,000)	×	1.000 =		(40,000)
1	25,000	×	0.862 =	21,550	
2	15,000	×	0.743 =	11,145	
3	10,000	×	0.641 =	6,410	
4	5,000	×	0.552 =	2,760	41,865
			Positive net present value		£1,865

We call the individual results of this multiplication the 'present values' as they represent the present value of investment in Year 0 required to give us the forecasted net cash flows for each year based on the interest rate chosen.

Having arrived at these individual values we can finally add them all up, and if we do this, we will see from Illustration 8.14 that we come to a total of £41,865. This is the total amount that we would have to invest now in Year 0 at 16 per cent compound interest to give us the amounts that we have calculated as the net cash flows for each of the Years 1–4 in our illustration.

Discounted cash flow appraisal technique

However, as we know, we are only being asked to invest £40,000 now so in financial terms we have a bargain! We are getting more than 16 per cent as a return on the £40,000 investment because at 16 per cent we would have to invest more – in fact £41,865. This means therefore that if 16 per cent is our criterion we would agree to the investment because we are getting a higher return than 16 per cent on £40,000.

This technique we refer to as the discounted cash flow method. What is being done by this approach is that the net cash flows for each of the years in question are being multiplied by the discount factors for the particular rate of return required. It is by doing this that we arrive at the amount that we would have to invest to give us these net cash flows.

In this particular example it amounts to £41,865, which we are then comparing with the proposed investment amount which in this case is £40,000. It is from this comparison that we are then able to see whether or not the investment is giving us the appropriate return. From this it can also be seen that by using discount factors for percentages in excess of 16 per cent we could find out precisely what return we are getting on £40,000. In other words we could find the discount factors for the appropriate percentage which would convert £25,000, £15,000, £10,000 and £5,000 into a total present value of precisely £40,000.

Internal rate of return

You will see from Illustration 8.15 that the appropriate percentage is 19: this is what is termed the internal rate of return (IRR). However, if we were simply seeking a return of 16 per cent then Illustration 8.14 sets out the fact that we are obtaining at least this. We have, what is termed, a positive net present value or NPV as it is known – the positive values equal £41,865 against the negative value of £40,000.

Consolidation

Now in order to reinforce your knowledge so far turn to Illustration 8.16 which sets out three different investment proposals together with the appropriate discount factors for 15 per cent. Make the necessary calculations to

Illustration 8.15 Calculation of internal rate of return.

Year	NCF	19%	Present value	
	£	DF	£	. £
0	(40,000) × 1.000 =			(40,000)
1	25,000 × 0.840 =		21,000	
2	15,000 × 0.706 =		10,590	
3	10,000 × 0.593 =		5,930	
4	5,000 × 0.499 =		2,495	40,015
		Positive net present value		15

The internal rate of return (IRR) is therefore approximately 19%.

Illustration 8.16 Investment proposal decision.

From the following financial facts regarding three different proposals calculate whether or not they meet the discounted cash flow criteria.

	1	2	3
	£	£	£
Investment cost	30,000	28,000	45,000
Net cash flows			
Year 1	15,000	12,000	20,000
2	10,000	8,000	30,000
3	10,000	6,000	10,000
4	5,000	6,000	5,000
5	–	4,000	–

The rate of return required = 15%

Discount factors for 15% Year	1	0.870
	2	0.757
	3	0.658
	4	0.572
	5	0.497

Illustration 8.17   Answer to Illustration 8.16.

Proposal:			1	2	3
			£	£	£
Investment cost:			30,000	28,000	45,000
Year	DF	NCF		NCF	NCF
	15%	£		£	£
1	0.870 × 15,000 =	13,050		12,000 = 10,440	20,000 = 17,400
2	0.757 × 10,000 =	7,570		8,000 = 6,056	30,000 = 22,710
3	0.658 × 10,000 =	6,580		6,000 = 3,948	10,000 = 6,580
4	0.572 × 5,000 =	2,860		6,000 = 3,432	5,000 = 2,860
5	0.497 ×	— = —		4,000 = 1,988	— —
			30,060	25,864	49,550
NPV			+ 60	− 2,136	+ 4,550

Recommendation: Accept proposals 1 and 3, reject proposal 2.

assess whether or not you would agree to the investment based on these financial facts using the discounted cash flow method. Once you have completed this task compare your answers with Illustration 8.17 before continuing.

Management considerations

Having examined the arithmetic of project appraisal techniques we shall now look at them from a decision-making point of view. The first necessity is for us to return to one of the principles discussed in Chapter 1. This was that accountants do not provide answers, they provide better questions. It is this point that must be very strongly kept in mind when using project appraisal techniques. What must be understood is that, whatever the arithmetic answer arrived at from the information presented, it is wholly dependent on the accuracy or inaccuracy of the net cash flow calculations. And we must remember that these are built up on a series of forecasts or guesses! It must always be noted that in the case of nearly every project which has to be considered, there are certain facts which cannot be financially evaluated, or if they can, it is very difficult to arrive at them with any real degree of accuracy or even certainty.

Risk analysis

To illustrate the difficulty of arriving at accuracy in assessing the net cash flows, consider the point that in assessing any project there must be an optimistic and a pessimistic view. For this reason it is very important in assessing any project based upon financial data to look at the likelihood, i.e. the chances or the risk, of the figures arrived at actually happening.

Factors may arise which are completely outside the control of managers such as monetary inflation or changes in the world economy, or the invention of newer and better methods of operation or technology, and so on. All these will change the forecasted cash flows.

Non-financially measurable considerations

Again it must always be remembered that there are certain features in any project which will be difficult – and in some cases impossible – to assess financially with any degree of accuracy but which are central to any judgement. For instance, how do you assess the ability of the person in charge of a project to overcome a future crisis? After all anyone concerned with decision-making must recognise that, however well planned a project may be, it will inevitably hit a crisis, whether that project is in the simple purchase of a piece of plant and machinery or in the more complex investment areas such as research and development or marketing.

Projects inevitably bring with them crises and when they occur it is the calibre and qualities of the person in charge of the project – or even luck! – which will become central to its success or failure. It is for this reason that management must guard against an over-glib assessment of projects that once having met the criteria set for a project under a discounted cash flow (or, as we call it, DCF) or a payback calculation then all is well! What is vital is that managers using project appraisal techniques should realise that their decisions must be assessed from many standpoints.

In other words, although the financial data may corroborate the decision, many other considerations are required outside the financial measurements set out in this chapter. This is not to say that such techniques as discounted cash flow and payback are not important, but they must not be considered omnipotent. They are corroborating not determining evidence.

Rate of return

Finally we must consider the rate of return that is used. How do we choose the 16 per cent or whatever? In the first instance we must look very closely at what we expect to get on the funds we are employing in the particular project, and it is therefore necessary for management to consider the source of the funds which are being invested. For instance, if the money being used to finance a project is being borrowed then the rate of return which must be sought must be one that covers the interest on the borrowed capital. In other words, if you are borrowing money at 14 per cent then the rate of return must be in excess of 14 per cent.

However, after allowing for a measure of safety – say in this instance 16 per cent – it must be recognised that anything in excess of 16 per cent is a rate of infinity as far as the shareholders of the company are concerned. They are getting that extra percentage on no investment on their own part at all. On the other hand if the funds are being provided by the shareholders of the company themselves, then the rate of return which will satisfy them must be the managers' decision.

It must also never be forgotten that the managers, although responsible to investors, have a very large measure of freedom in meeting this responsibility. There is no reason why management should not ask for different returns from different projects, some above and some below the overall shareholders' target. After all, so long as the total return on the capital employed satisfies investors then the manner in which this is made up among the projects, is of no concern to them.

Summary of project appraisal

The net cash flow

To summarise project appraisal we first gather together the financial facts regarding the particular project, and the measurement we use is the net cash flow.

The first thing required is the investment cost. It must be understood in this calculation that all additional investment must be brought into consideration, for example working capital in the form of stocks and debtors which may have to be increased on the installation of a new piece of plant and machinery. This will have to be brought in as part of the data being considered in calculating the cost of the new machine because it is necessary to find out the effect upon the total net cash flow year by year.

This entails very careful assessment of the cash effect of the project with regard to both its inflows and outflows. To this end we must make sure we ignore expenses already being incurred, and we must also add back depreciation as it does not affect cash. Finally, we must ensure that the effects of taxation are included in the calculation.

When we have brought these financial facts together it is then necessary to use our particular yardstick in the appraisal of the investment.

The appraisal methods

There are three such yardsticks that can be used. The first, based upon the healthy cynicism of investors, is the method we refer to as payback –

looking to see how quickly we get our money back or reinstated for further use. The second is the very simple average return on average capital employed method, which has the great disadvantage of ignoring when the money is flowing into the business. And finally we have the discounted cash flow (DCF) method which takes into account the timing of the annual net cash flows (NCF) as well as compound – as distinct from simple – interest.

Further considerations

However, whichever technique we use we must recognise the fact that project appraisal techniques do not give us answers. They provide us with better questions and therefore a better approach to the investment decision.

The basis of data

If I look at an investment and see from a project appraisal assessment that the answer is yes or no, this is not the end from a management decision point of view. It must be recognised that the data on which the financial facts are considered are based upon forecasts and these may be wrong because of over-optimism, or over-pessimism, or because certain facts are not fully known at the time of making the decision.

Management must also understand that in project decision-making certain highly relevant facts cannot be quantified financially – the ability or otherwise of project leaders to overcome crises, the sensitivity to error of the data on which the project appraisal assessments are based. Such considerations must be held very firmly in the minds of managers.

Monitoring data

It is also vital that once projects have been agreed the data contained in the appraisal is monitored as the years go by to see how near or far it turns out to be from the facts as they emerge. Such post-project audits (as they are sometimes termed) can serve as useful reminders of where errors can occur and can be used to improve future project proposals.

Buying or leasing

Before we end this chapter I want finally to turn to the problem of buying or leasing. This problem involves two separate questions: the first of assessing the benefit of the investment to the business, and the second of deciding whether, if it is worthwhile, should the investment be bought or hired. In doing this you must avoid the temptation to mix the two judgements. For instance, you must separate the assessment of whether or not

Illustration 8.18   Data for lease or buy decision.

Rate of interest required	12%
Cost of computers if bought	£60,000
Rental if hired	£15,000 per annum
Period of rental agreement	5 years
Annual maintenance cost if bought	£650
Scrap value at end of 5 years	£10,000
at end of 6 years	£5,000
Free maintenance if hired	£500 per annum
Savings per year if computers introduced	£20,000
Period computers will be used if bought	6 years
Corporation tax	take as 50% (for simplicity's sake only!)

Calculate whether to buy or hire/lease.

Illustration 8.19   Project appraisal – calculation of net cash flow.

Stage I: If bought

Year:		1	2	3	4	5	6
		£	£	£	£	£	£
Capital allowances							
Savings on corporation tax @ 50% say		7,500	6,250	4,050	3,000	2,300	1,500
Scrap value							5,000
Annual savings	£20,000						
Less: Maintenance	650						
	19,350						
Less: Tax @ 50%	9,675	9,675	9,675	9,675	9,675	9,675	9,675
		£17,175	£15,925	£13,725	£12,675	£11,975	£16,175

Stage II: If bought and not hired

Year:		1	2	3	4	5
Capital allowances (as above)		£	£	£	£	£
		7,500	6,250	4,050	3,000	2,300
Annual rental payable	£15,000					
Tax @ 50%	7,500					
	7,500					
Less: Free maintenance	500	7,000	7,000	7,000	7,000	7,000
Scrap value						10,000
		£14,500	£13,250	£10,050	£10,000	£19,300

you should obtain a new machine from whether or not you should buy or lease it. These are two very separate management decisions.

Whether to obtain the item

If you turn to Illustrations 8.18, 8.19 and 8.20 you will see how these two considerations must be kept separate. In the first instance, described as Stage I in Illustrations 8.19 and 8.20, you will see that we assume that we are going to buy and we consider the facts based on the buying situation. We take as an example an investment in computers costing £60,000 from which we then show the appropriate net cash flows year by year, in this case the saving to the business of clerical costs by its use.

Having calculated the net cash flows we come to the decision that the answer is yes, we should obtain the new computers. Go through Illustration 8.18 and Stage I of Illustrations 8.19 and 8.20 carefully as they set out all the principles we have discussed in this chapter so far.

Illustration 8.20   Project appraisal – lease or buy calculation.

Stage I: If bought

Year				£
0	Cost of computers			60,000
		Discount	Present	
	NCF	factor	value	
	£	12%	£	
1	17,175 ×	0.893	= 15,337	
2	15,925 ×	0.797	= 12,692	
3	13,728 ×	0.712	= 9,772	
4	12,675 ×	0.636	= 8,061	
5	11,975 ×	0.568	= 6,802	
6	16,175 ×	0.507	= 8,201	60,865
		Positive net present value		£865

Stage II: If bought and not leased

Year				£
0	Cost of computers			60,000
		Discount	Present	
	NCF	factor	value	
	£	12%	£	
1	14,500 ×	0.893	= 12,949	
2	13,250 ×	0.797	= 10,560	
3	11,050 ×	0.712	= 7,868	
4	10,005 ×	0.636	= 6,360	
5	19,300 ×	0.568	= 10,962	48,699
		Negative net present value		£11,301

Conclusion based on data provided is to lease computer.

Whether to buy or lease the item

It is then necessary, having decided that we are going to proceed with the investment, to go to the next stage and decide whether we should buy or lease the computer. You will see from Stage II in Illustrations 8.19 and 8.20 that we have a whole series of new facts in front of us on which to make this decision. In considering the hiring or the buying question the important

Illustration 8.21 Data for lease or buy decision.

Cost of machine if bought	£120,000
Rental if hired	£40,000 per annum
Annual maintenance cost if bought	£5,000
Maintenance provided free by rental firm worth per annum	£1,000
Scrap value at end of 6 year life	£10,000
Scrap value at end of 5 year life	£12,000
Savings per year if machine introduced	£50,000
Rate of interest required	12% per annum

Illustration 8.22 Project appraisal – calculation of net cash flow.

Stage I: If bought

Year:		1	2	3	4	5	6
		£	£	£	£	£	£
Capital allowances Savings on corporation tax @ 50% say		20,000	10,000	7,500	5,625	4,110	3,100
Scrap value		—	—	—	—	—	10,000
Savings per year	£50,000						
Less: Maintenance	5,000						
	45,000						
Less: Tax @ 50%	22,500	22,500	22,500	22,500	22,500	22,500	22,500
		£42,500	£32,500	£30,000	£28,125	£26,610	£35,600

Stage II: If bought and not leased

Year:		1	2	3	4	5
Capital allowances		£	£	£	£	£
(as above)		20,000	10,000	7,500	5,625	4,110
Savings: Annual rental	£15,000					
Tax @ 50%	20,000					
	20,000					
Less: Value on free maintenance	1,000	19,000	19,000	19,000	19,000	19,000
Scrap value						12,000
		£39,000	£29,000	£26,500	£24,625	£35,110

fact to bear in mind is that we must ignore anything which is common to both situations. We need to say to ourselves if we buy what is the difference between that or hiring/leasing?

The first difference obviously is that if we buy we will incur the cost of £60,000 which we will not incur if we hire. We then go on year by year and say to ourselves what is the difference in Year 1 between buying and leasing. You will see that we totally ignore the benefit that we are going to get from the new office computers, because this is common to both situations. In fact the only benefits that we bring in are first of all the fact that if we buy we will save the annual rental, and second we will lose the benefit of the annual maintenance which the rental firm provides us free of charge if we hire. In addition we will lose the tax benefit of being able to charge the rental against our profits for tax purposes, but we will obtain the tax benefit of the capital allowance if we buy.

You will see all these calculations set out in Stage II of Illustrations 8.19 and 8.20 so that year by year we are able to put in a net cash flow figure showing the difference between buying and leasing. You will also see the

Illustration 8.23 Project appraisal – lease or buy calculation.

Stage I: If bought

Year		£
0	Cost of machine	120,000

Year	NCF £	Discount factor 12%	Present value £	
1	42,500 ×	0.893 =	37,953	
2	32,500 ×	0.797 =	25,903	
3	30,000 ×	0.712 =	21,360	
4	28,125 ×	0.636 =	17,888	
5	26,610 ×	0.568 =	15,136	
6	35,600 ×	0.507 =	18,049	136,289
		Positive net present value		£16,289

Stage II: If bought and not leased

Year		£
0	Cost of machine	120,000

Year	NCF £	Discount factor 12%	Present value £	
1	39,000 ×	0.893 =	34,827	
2	29,000 ×	0.797 =	23,113	
3	26,500 ×	0.712 =	18,868	
4	24,625 ×	0.636 =	15,662	
5	35,110 ×	0.568 =	19,942	112,412
		Negative net present value		£7,588

Conclusion based on data provided is to lease machine.

period of comparison is linked with the rental agreement of five years, bringing into the final year our assessment of the scrap value of the computer as a benefit which arises to the buyer and not the hirer.

Examine these illustrations very carefully and then test your understanding by tackling the final question set out in Illustration 8.21. Compare your answers with Illustrations 8.22 and 8.23.

Having completed our studies of project appraisal we can now proceed to the next area of investment, that concerned with working capital.

9 | THE CONTROL OF WORKING CAPITAL

Introduction

In the previous chapter we discussed the methods which have been developed to examine the fixed assets set out in the Balance Sheet known as project appraisal techniques. Now let us turn our attention to the second and perhaps the most difficult, but no less important, area of investment to control – the working capital.

The working capital of a business, shown in Illustration 9.1, is concerned with the investment of money in materials or merchandise, labour and overheads, pending its return back to the business when the finished goods, merchandise or services are sold and paid for. It is made up of the money tied up in materials or merchandise, labour and overheads less the amount that may be owed at any time to those from whom we have purchased them.

Working capital is therefore a net area of investment. If we return to Illustration 9.1 we can see that it is made up of the total invested in circles 4, 5, 6, 7 and 8, less what is owed in circle 9.

Working capital in manufacturing industry

For a manufacturing business we can examine working capital as set out in Illustration 9.2. Here is shown the investment in labour, materials and overheads as raw material, work in progress and finished goods stocks. To this we add the debtors or receivables – the amounts due to us from our customers to whom we have sold our goods but who have not yet paid for them – less the credit taken from our creditors or payables for the materials, labour and overheads which have gone into such stocks, debtors and sales but who have not themselves yet been paid.

In the first chapter when we discussed working capital we pointed out that, from the point of view of managing or investing in a business, it should be everyone's ambition to minimise the amount of money tied up

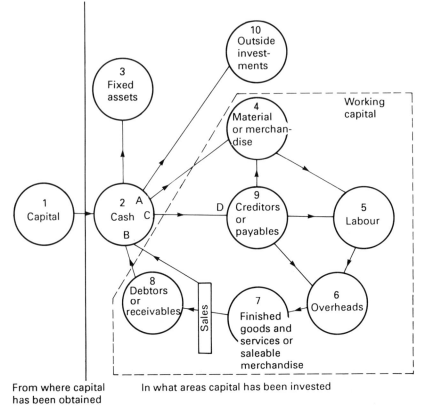

From where capital   In what areas capital has been invested
has been obtained

Illustration 9.1 Business model showing working capital area.

in this area for two major reasons. The first was that everyone's investment goal is to maximise the return on the capital employed, and if we can make the same profit with less working capital it must be better than having more!

However, there is the second reason why people wish to minimise working capital, which is far more dynamic than the basic need to max-imise the return on capital employed, although it does indeed lead to this as well. This is that if you wish to expand a business then it is vital to make sure that you are not held back because of a lack of capital.

Every business, whatever its size, is limited in the end by the total capital that it can obtain – get its hands on – but within the parameters of this capital a business is continually being limited by two barriers to progress: what it can sell – the problem of the market-place – and/or what it can produce, present as merchandise or render as services – the capacity of its fixed assets. However, if it needs working capital this in itself could limit its progress. To illustrate the point: if a business finds that for every £1's

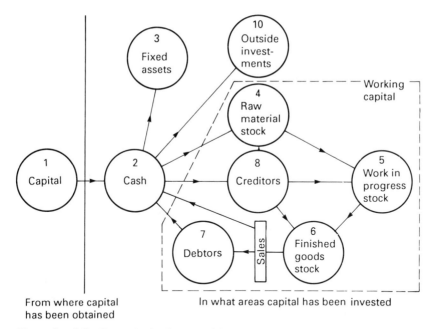

Illustration 9.2   Alternative business model setting out working capital in manufacturing industry.

worth of sales it makes it needs 10p of working capital to finance it, then that business could find itself held back, not because it could not sell and not because it could not produce, but because it had not got the necessary 10 pences.

It is not coincidental that the great business expanders always concentrate on ways of minimising the working capital. For example, Henry Ford in producing the Model T decided to paint it black and sell it to agents for cash as soon as the cars were produced. All these policies enabled him to minimise his working capital and therefore minimise the limitations to his expansion plans.

Control of working capital

Any examination of working capital points very clearly to the fact that if a business wishes to minimise this investment it must control time. If we turn to the working capital model in Illustration 9.1 it will be seen that in order to minimise working capital the objective must be to turn the materials, labour and overheads as quickly as possible back into cash and to maximise, within agreed limits, the credit it takes before meeting the amounts due to its material suppliers, providers of labour and overheads.

This then is the overall objective – to minimise working capital. We must, however, recognise that objectives such as this are not unchangeable. In fact circumstances may arise when such objectives need to be broken. For example, it might be useful in certain circumstances to hold materials over a considerable period of time where there is the fear of a commodity shortage. Or it may be useful to mass produce finished goods pending a forecasted demand explosion. But these are exceptions that in a way prove rather more than disprove the rule.

Working capital, as we explained in an earlier chapter, might be described as the financial luggage a business carries on its journey to a sale. It can also be said that the great controllers of working capital have always been sales and marketing people. They use their marketing skills to reduce the time delays that stop a business minimising its working capital. Henry Ford with his Model T was doing just that – marketing a product in such a way as to minimise the money locked up in working capital.

To control working capital we must therefore control time. But it is also necessary to recognise that the inherent difficulty in this lies in the need to coordinate the different functions responsible for each area of working capital. It has to be understood that, however dominant sales and marketing policies may be to the overall control of working capital, they are dependent upon the cooperation of the other functions.

Areas of responsibility

To understand this turn to Illustration 9.3. Here we see once again the financial model, but we have now introduced the names of the functions which will have a say in the control of time in each area. So, the control of time when materials are in store will be in the hands of purchasing, and that once material, labour and overheads are in production the time needed to convert them into finished goods will be in the hands of production (and indeed perhaps personnel). We then see that once materials, labour and overheads are translated into finished goods as saleable merchandise or services the time during which such items or services are unsold becomes the direct concern of sales and marketing. Finally we see that once finished goods, merchandise or services are sold to customers many do not pay immediately – they take time as debtors – whilst conversely the materials, labour and overheads which go into what is produced or rendered will also in most cases not be paid for immediately. The business will take time, or credit, before it pays its creditors or payables. And the control of this time given and taken becomes the concern of the finance function.

It will also be seen if we consider these areas that in each case there will be an overlap in control. That is to say that production will have a concern

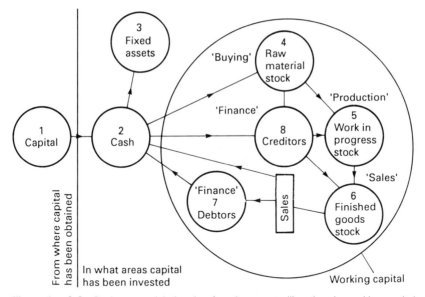

Illustration 9.3 Business model showing functions controlling time in working capital areas.

regarding the time for which material is held in store – after all it wants it when it is needed for use, and in quantities which are not too much but not too little. There will also be the concern of marketing in the credit taken by debtors as too much chasing to reduce the length of credit may make future sales difficult, even impossible. And purchasing will also be concerned with the length of credit taken before paying creditors for materials as too long a delay may jeopardise future deliveries and so the continuity of supplies.

It is this interlinking and overlapping which makes the control of working capital increasingly difficult to control once businesses grow. It is not therefore coincidental that smaller businesses can normally control their working capital much more effectively than larger concerns. This is for the simple reason that in a one-person business the same person is the buyer, the production manager, the sales manager and the accountant and can therefore keep an eye on each individual area.

However, as businesses grow and different people head the different functions we find that difficulties arise as the interlinking and overlapping grows. The orchestration of management, so vital for effective working capital control, becomes increasingly difficult as businesses expand.

It is also often found that as a business grows it is very difficult for people, who may have a very real contribution to make in controlling working capital, to see how they fit in. To illustrate this point consider the

Illustration 9.4 Control of working capital exercise.

Consider how the following functions influence the control of working capital:

1. Buying
2. Production control
3. Sales and marketing
4. Quality control
5. Accounting

Illustration 9.5 Suggested answers to Illustration 9.4.

1. *Buying*. The provision of material for the business to meet the production and sales requirements.
2. *Production control*. The conversion of material, labour and overheads as quickly as possible into saleable finished goods.
3. *Sales and marketing*. The conversion of finished goods, saleable merchandise or services into sales and cash.
4. *Quality control*. The rectification of quality problems as soon as possible so as to reduce delay to a minimum.
5. *Accounting*. The supervision of credit control so as to minimise delay from debtors and maximise the delay allowed by creditors within the agreed credit periods.

question set out in Illustration 9.4 and see if you can show the responsibility of the different functions in the control of working capital. Check your answers with the suggestions made in Illustration 9.5 before you carry on.

Working capital control in practice

Having examined working capital in an overall way it is now necessary to approach its control from a practical point of view. To do this we shall once again think through a situation for ourselves. We will consider in the first instance the problem of a manufacturing business producing goods and we will take a set of facts, from the production to the sale of the goods, to see how they fit together from the point of view of working capital control.

To do this turn first to Illustration 9.6 and follow the figures through. You will see from this illustration that we place at the top the words material, labour and overheads. What we are then going to do is to trace the time delays from the moment the materials, labour and overheads come into the business and their eventual conversion back into cash once the goods we have sold have been paid for.

The material time cycle

So let us begin at the beginning and take materials. We will say in this case

Illustration 9.6 Working capital control – time data.

Working capital areas:	Material months	Labour months	Overheads months
Raw material store	$\frac{1}{2}$	$\frac{1}{2}$	$\frac{1}{2}$
Production cycle	$\frac{1}{2}$	$\frac{1}{2}$	$\frac{1}{2}$
Finished goods store	1	1	1
Debtors/Receivables	2	2	2
Gross time	4	4	4
Less: Creditors time taken	(2)	$(\frac{1}{2})$	(1)
Net time	2	$3\frac{1}{2}$	3

that on average we hold our materials for a fortnight before they go into production. What we therefore see under the materials head is half a month against the words raw material store.

We can then proceed to the next stage where we see the words production cycle, meaning the time it takes to convert the material into finished goods. And again half a month is considered the average time of the production cycle in this particular business.

As we continue we see the third area of delay is termed finished goods stock, which is the time which finished goods on average are stored before being sent out to customers when a sale is made. And here we will say that in this case the time is one month.

Finally we come to the fourth area described as debtors or receivables, the time taken by our customers before they pay. In this case, we shall say it is on average two months.

So if we add down the materials column we come to a total of four months. However, to work out the time delay in converting materials back into cash we must deduct the time the business takes before it pays for such materials. We shall say in this case that the delay is normally two months, and we arrive at a net time of two months.

This is the time during which money will be locked up in respect of materials before it comes back when the goods into which it goes are sold and paid for.

The labour and overheads time cycle

If we now look at the columns dealing with labour and overheads time we will see that down to the gross time it is identical with materials – four months. This is because materials in a manufacturing business dominate. After all while materials are in store you will still be paying for the labour and overheads. Again while the material is in production you will also be paying for them and while your materials are being stored in finished goods, you would still have to pay for your labour and overheads. And this situation also exists while our customers are not paying you.

So we get down to the same subtotal of four months. However, when we look at the credit that we can take from our labour and our overhead suppliers we find that the time differs from that shown for materials. For instance, we normally cannot take more than a maximum of one month's credit from our employees, and in some cases this will be reduced to one week before we have to pay them. We might therefore have to accept the fact that, on average in this area, we are limited to a fortnight's credit whilst in the case of overheads we might be able to obtain, say, one month's credit before having to meet their bills!

We can see therefore that the bottom line for labour and overheads reads $3\frac{1}{2}$ months and 3 months respectively.

Functional influence on time delays

Having examined the time cycles let us now look at these so that we can begin to get to grips with a real understanding of the individual time areas. To do this turn to Illustration 9.7 where the areas for delay set out in Illustration 9.6 are repeated but in addition we have added the different functions which influence such delays.

For example, in the case of 'raw materials store', if we try to minimise the time delay between the material coming in and being used, three main functions would have to be concerned with the necessary corrective action. These would be the buying, the production and the marketing/sales func-

Illustration 9.7 Functional influences on time delays.

Working capital delay areas:	Functions which influence delay:
Raw material store	Buying Production Marketing and sales
Production cycle	Production Buying Marketing and sales
Finished goods store	Marketing and sales Production Buying
Debtors/receivables	Finance/accounting Sales/marketing
Creditors/payables	Finance/accounting Buying Labour negotiators Overhead buyers

tions. This is because if we wish to reduce time 'in store' most obviously buyers would be concerned in arranging their purchasing policies to facilitate this happening. However, we also have to be concerned with the problem of production because production would have to furnish buyers with the necessary information on which to arrange their purchasing policies. However, in addition to this it would also be vital that marketing plays its part in providing sales plans to enable production to plan and from which buyers can then create the correct buying policies to minimise the time delays making sure the material arrives 'just in time'!

Again if we then proceed to the production area. To reduce this time would also involve more than one function. Here we would be concerned with not only the production but also the other functions which would have a contribution to make. It would certainly be necessary for buyers to provide precisely the materials that are needed in order to meet day-to-day needs of production. However, sales and marketing would also be very much involved in order to ensure that the production plans can be formed based on the real needs of the marketing plans.

And again, as we come into the finished goods area we see the names of the same three functions. After all, although the control of time in the finished goods store will be very much influenced by sales and marketing there will obviously be the need for cooperation with the other functions.

Production must make sure that what is produced is precisely what the sales or marketing function requires, and to some extent buyers may also be involved in this area. This is because it may be found that the length of time goods are held in the finished goods store will be influenced by the availability of some final component or packaging device which is the responsibility of the purchasing function.

Finally we come to the credit area – both the credit we take and the credit we give. In this area the financial function will have considerable influence but even here we find that we cannot ignore the other functions. The influence of sales and marketing on the credit which is taken from us by debtors or receivables can be crucial, and indeed the contribution of buyers and those negotiating labour and overhead credit can be equally important in ensuring the maximum credit allowed is obtained.

Summary and consolidation

It is vital at this stage for us to really understand the intertwining and interweaving of functions in the control of working capital. The fact is that not only do we have different functions affecting each individual area, but we also have the overlaps between them. For example, however good the credit control may be, if production keep on producing poor quality goods

Illustration 9.8 Personal responsibility for time delays exercise.

Consider the following jobs and their responsibility in the control of working capital:

1. Storeman
2. Production controller
3. Retail salesman
4. Production inspector
5. Designer

Illustration 9.9 Suggested answers to Illustration 9.8.

1. *Storeman*. Time material in store.
2. *Production controller*. Time of converting material, labour and overheads into finished goods.
3. *Retail salesman*. Time of converting stock on shelves into cash in the till.
4. *Production inspector*. Time of correcting any production faults.
5. *Designer*. Providing designs which minimise the time of manufacture.

then customers once they have received them may express their disappointment by delaying payment. Or again, however good production control may be, if buyers never have the raw materials which are required, there can be production hold-ups creating an increase in the work in progress stock investment.

To consider this problem of time control try the exercise in Illustration 9.8. This sets out a series of jobs in a typical business and poses the question, how do the holders of each of these influence the control of working capital? In what way do they influence the time in converting materials, labour and overheads back into cash? When you have considered this question give what you consider to be the appropriate answers and then turn to the solution suggested in Illustration 9.9. Now finally consider your own influence over the working capital investment within your own business. How might you and your colleagues be able to reduce it?

Service industries and working capital

We have so far looked at working capital in the context of a manufacturing business. Let us now turn our attention to service industries. In this situation we are also concerned with converting material, labour and overheads back into cash but there may well be a different emphasis. That is, we may have little, if any, materials in a service industry being translated back into our finished services. However, the general concept underlining the control of working capital equally applies. In order that you become familiar with this and understand that the control of working capital is just

Illustration 9.10   Working capital time cycle data in a service industry.

A firm concerned with delivery of goods throughout the UK provides you with the following information regarding its working capital time cycles. Summarise these times for this business:

	Weeks
Average time between accepting delivery order and delivery	3
Average time between delivery and invoice despatch	2
Average time taken by receivables/debtors before payment	6
Credit taken — Material — Fuel etc.	4
— Labour	2
— Overheads	3

Illustration 9.11   Suggested answers to Illustration 9.10.

Working capital areas:	Material weeks	Labour weeks	Overheads weeks
Accepting order to delivery	3	3	3
Delivery to invoice despatch	2	2	2
Debtors	6	6	6
Gross time	11	11	11
Less: Creditors time taken	4	2	3
Net time	7	9	8

as vital in a service business turn to Illustration 9.10 in which the time cycles which apply to the service provided by a particular business are illustrated – in this case, the delivery of goods to customers. Then convert this into the working capital time requirements for this particular business.

When you have done this compare your answer with Illustration 9.11.

Retailers and working capital

In Illustration 9.12 you will see the timing facts regarding the working capital of a retailer. Here we see that merchandise is bought and held

Illustration 9.12   Working capital time cycle data for a retailer.

A company concerned with retailing throughout Europe provides you with the following information regarding its working capital cycle time. Summarise these times for this business:

	Weeks
Merchandise stored in warehouse	3
Average shelf-life of merchandise before sale	4
Average credit taken	2
(this is mainly caused by credit card use and other credit facilities)	
Credit taken — Merchandise	8
— Labour	2
— Overheads	4

Illustration 9.13   Suggested answer to Illustration 9.12.

Working capital areas:	Merchandise weeks	Labour weeks	Overheads weeks
Warehouse storage	3	3	3
Shelf-life	4	4	4
Debtors	2	2	2
Gross time	9	9	9
Less: Credit time taken	8	2	4
Net time	1	7	5

pending sale and that although credit is taken from the merchandise suppliers, the employees and the overhead providers where possible, no credit whatsoever is given to customers. Again work through this example and compare your answer with that shown in Illustration 9.13.

Time and money

Having examined the time cycles within working capital we will now look at the relationship of time with money. To do this turn to Illustration 9.14 in which you will see that I have set out a Budgeted Profit and Loss Account for a twelve-month period.

In this budget it is stated that the business is planning to sell goods to the value of £5,000,000 and that in relationship to these goods the materials, labour and overhead costs as percentages of such sales amount to 40 per cent, 20 per cent and 20 per cent respectively, thus leaving a profit of 20 per cent. This therefore means that the budgeted materials, labour and overhead costs would amount for the twelve months to

Illustration 9.14   Budgeted Profit and Loss Account.

	% of sales	Budgeted annual cost £	£
Annual sales budget			5,000,000
Costs:			
Material	40	2,000,000	
Labour	20	1,000,000	
Overheads	20	1,000,000	
Total cost			4,000,000
Profit	20		£1,000,000
	100		

£2,000,000 in the case of materials and £1,000,000 each in the case of labour and overheads. Having seen the basic financial facts of this particular twelve-month budget let us now apply the time cycles that we have discussed in Illustration 9.6 in relationship to this Budgeted Profit and Loss Account so as to work out the working capital requirement of this business.

Calculating the working capital requirement

Turn to Illustration 9.15 and here you will see that we are doing precisely this. We are applying the time cycles as shown in Illustration 9.6 to the values we have just seen in Illustration 9.14.

You will see that to do this we multiply the budgeted costs of materials, labour and overheads by the appropriate months calculated in Illustration 9.6 and this gives us the working capital investment that we will require to support the planned £5,000,000 annual sales. For example, if we look at materials we will see that the annual figure of £2,000,000 is multiplied by $\frac{1}{6}$ which is 12 months divided by two. We also see in the case of labour we multiply the £1,000,000, the annual figure, by $3\frac{1}{2}$ over 12 months and in the case of overheads we multiply the £1,000,000 figure by $\frac{1}{4}$ which is 3 over 12 months. These figures are then totalled to give a sum of approximately £870,000 which is the working capital this business will require to support its sales budget of £5,000,000.

In other words, what we are saying in this particular illustration is that to support £5,000,000 worth of sales we will need an investment of £870,000 as working capital. Or in simple figures, we could say that for every £1 we plan to sell we will need to generate 17p to finance the necessary working capital to support it. This is calculated by dividing the £870,000 working capital by the £5,000,000 sales.

Illustration 9.15 Budgeted Profit and Loss Statement.

Annual sales budget			£5,000,000
	%	Budgeted	Working capital
	of sales	annual costs	required (approx.)
Costs:		£	£
Material	40	2,000,000 × 1/6 =	330,000
Labour	20	1,000,000 × 3.5/12 =	290,000
Overheads	20	1,000,000 × 1/4 =	250,000
Profit	20		
	100		£870,000

Or working capital per £1 of sales: $\dfrac{£870,000}{£5,000,000} = 17p$

The limitation of overtrading

Now working capital to sales is a very vital measurement to understand because what it is telling us is that every time we sell £1's worth of our goods we would not only need to find customers to sell to and fixed assets to produce with, but we would also need to find 17p to finance the extra working capital required.

If we go back to our earlier discussions about working capital you will remember that we talked about the limitation of working capital, that if we do not minimise working capital we could be limited by this. This is precisely what this 17p means! It means that if we wish to sell an extra £1's worth of our goods, merchandise or services and we have not got whatever is needed, in this case 17p, to invest as working capital, we could be held back, not because we cannot produce the goods, display the merchandise or render the services with the fixed assets or skills we possess, and not because we cannot find customers to sell them to – but because we have not got 17p (or its equivalent in the particular situation). It is this problem that is often loosely termed 'overtrading', the situation that occurs when a business tries to sell more than it can support with its available working capital.

The consequences of saving working capital

Having examined and seen the implications of working capital, let us now take a further step and discuss the effect of saving working capital. In other words, what does it mean to us financially, when we are running a business, whether or not we can reduce this investment. To illustrate this go back to Illustration 9.6 and ask yourselves what would be the result if we could reduce the time cycle by, say, a fortnight?

Now we have already seen that the control of working capital implies the control of time, so let us now consider the financial implications of saving this fortnight. Clearly if this happened the bottom line would then be reduced for materials, labour and overheads by $\frac{1}{2}$ month in each case: material time would be reduced to $1\frac{1}{2}$ months, labour to 3 months and overheads to $2\frac{1}{2}$ months.

It would also mean, if we take the figures we have been looking at in Illustration 9.14, that the total investment in working capital would then be reduced by a fortnight of the annual cost of materials, labour and overheads. You will see that this comes to a total annual cost of £4,000,000, and a fortnight of this amount – taking a fortnight as 1/24th of a year – gives us an annual saving of approximately £170,000.

Illustration 9.16 Two approaches to the saving of working capital.

First approach:
Savings (2 weeks)	= £170,000
Return on investment expected	= 15%
Return on saving	= £25,500 (15% of £170,000)

Second approach:
Saving	= £170,000
Working capital to sales expressed as pence per £1	= 17p
Additional sales which saving can support	= £1,000,000
Profit on sales per budget	= 20% = £200,000

Now the question is, what does this mean to us financially in running a business? And to answer this let us turn to Illustration 9.16 which shows two approaches to this saving of working capital.

Investment savings

In the first instance we might look at the saving and say: 'If we can save £170,000 of working capital, we have £170,000 we can use elsewhere, and if in our business we can obtain a return of, say, 15 per cent on what we invest, then the result of this saving would be that every year we could increase our profits by £25,500 – which is 15 per cent of £170,000.'

However, even if this is true, we have still got to reduce this additional profit figure by the cost of a fortnight's saving. After all, you do not reduce the working capital time cycle by a fortnight without it costing you money. You might have to improve your material control and/or your production control and/or your credit control systems, and all this would increase expenditure in more staff, more procedures and more administration.

In fact it might well be found that if you examined the cost of the savings in comparison with the benefits that you get from the saving that there is nothing in it to justify the effort. This is certainly true in our example, set out in Illustration 9.17, where the cost of the savings is given as £30,000 per annum. Here you will see from the first part of the answer in 9.18 that the return on savings of £26,250 is less than the costs of achieving this of £30,000.

Employing savings

However, this is only one way of looking at the working capital saving and it is certainly not the way in which a dynamic business considers it. Such a business would not look at the saving of working capital in relation to the interest on money saved: it would examine the situation along very different lines. It would ask itself, as is shown in the second approach in Illustration 9.16, 'What is the effect of the saving – in this case £170,000 – on sales?' It would see that it now has £170,000 to support further sales.

We have already seen from Illustration 9.15 that the relationship of working capital to sales is 17p per £1 sold, and from this we can see that if the business can save £170,000 worth of working capital, it has this money available to support further sales. These would equal – if we take the relationship of 17p per £1 of sales – sufficient funds to support additional sales of £1,000,000. It can also be seen, taking the profits to sales set out in Illustration 9.14 of 20 per cent, that we have a possibility of additional profits of £200,000 or 20 per cent on the additional sales of £1,000,000.

Other factors

This, of course, may not in fact be the full picture. There may well be adjustments to this figure, as we have already discussed in the cost of saving the working capital. It must also be remembered if we can think back to when we were examining the Profit and Loss Account in Chapter 2, and also in Chapter 7 on marginal costing, that there are many expenses, especially those which relate to overheads, which will not move in direct proportion with sales. For this reason the profit that we obtain when our sales exceed the budget might well be in excess of the 20 per cent which we have used in this illustration. This is because although the variable costs increase in proportion with activity, the fixed expenses or overheads will be in the main more time than 'activity' related. (If this is at all unclear revise your studies of the Profit and Loss Account, and those on marginal costing, referred to above.)

The benefits from saving working capital

It can be seen from this second approach to the control of working capital that to an expanding business the benefits to be obtained from minimising working capital are very high indeed. It should also be noted that this benefit is not only the goal of the person who invests money in a business, it is also that of anyone who considers their own position within a business. After all, their salaries, wages and their entire employment conditions are very much wrapped up in the ability of the business to expand.

Turn now to Illustration 9.17 and examine the facts which are shown there together with the possible time savings, and calculate the two approaches to the benefits from saving working capital time that we have

Illustration 9.17   Calculation of saving of working capital exercise.

Question: Calculate the two approaches to working capital saving from the following facts:

Working capital required per £1 of sales	15p
Saving possible by improved time control	£210,000
Cost of saving working capital time	£30,000
Budgeted profit on sales	20%
Interest on investment expected	$12\frac{1}{2}\%$

Illustration 9.18   Suggested answer to Illustration 9.17.

First approach:

Saving	=	£210,000
Return on saving	=	£26,250 (£210,000 × $12\frac{1}{2}\%$)
Less: Cost of saving	=	£30,000
Loss from saving		£3,750

Second approach:

Saving	=	£210,000
Additional sales from savings	=	£1,400,000 (£210,000 ÷ 15p)
Profit from additional sales	=	£280,000 (£1,400,000 × 20%)
Less: Cost of saving	=	£30,000
Profit from saving		£250,000

Illustration 9.19   Calculation of working capital exercise.

The following facts refer to a manufacturing business. You are asked to prepare an estimate of the working capital required to support its sales.

	Delay time (weeks)
Raw material store	6
Production cycle	2
Finished goods store	3
Debtors	6
Creditors — Material	6
— Labour	1
— Overheads	4
Sales budget for 12 months	£12,000,000

Costs	%
Material	30
Labour	25
Overheads	20

Illustration 9.20   Suggested answer to Illustration 9.19.

	Materials weeks	Labour weeks	Overheads weeks
Raw material store	6	6	6
Production cycle	2	2	2
Finished goods store	3	3	3
Debtors	6	6	6
	17	17	17
Less: Creditors	6	1	4
Net working capital time	11	16	13
say	$1\frac{3}{4}$ months	4 months	$3\frac{1}{4}$ months

Working capital calculation

Sales budget for 12 months			£12,000,000	
Cost	%	Annual		
	of sales	£		£
Material	30	$3,600,000 \times 1.75/12$		525,000
Labour	25	$3,000,000 \times 1/3$		1,000,000
Overheads	20	$2,400,000 \times 3.25/12$		650,000
				£2,175,000

Or 18p of working capital per £1 of sales (approx).

just discussed. When you have done this and compared your answer with Illustration 9.18, turn then to Illustration 9.19. Work through the example to test your understanding of this area of financial control and when you have completed your answer check it with Illustration 9.20.

Summary and conclusion

To summarise the points introduced in this chapter we must begin at the beginning and start with the definition of working capital. It is the moving area in which our money is being converted into and out of materials, labour and overheads over a period of time. This means that its control lies in the way we manage time.

From Illustration 9.1 it is fundamental to the control of working capital to move the money as fast as we can from point A back to point B, and as slow as we can – within agreed limits – between points C and D. We must understand that those concerned with this control include virtually every person employed within a business. It is not only those in senior positions of authority but also those in seemingly unimportant jobs who may have considerable influence upon this area of investment.

Having understood working capital as an investment, it is then necessary to see the interrelationships of functions within each area. This can be done by examining Illustration 9.3 and seeing how individual functions have an influence on and relate to each other in each of the main areas of delay. Finally we must understand how the control of working capital time relates directly to the profitability of the enterprise and its ability to take advantage of marketing possibilities by reducing one of the limitations to its expansion plans – the limitation of working capital investment required to support its sales. This is shown in Illustrations 9.6, 9.14, 9.15 and 9.16, and these examples should be studied carefully before continuing to the next chapter on Budgetary Control.

10 | BUDGETARY CONTROL

Introduction

So far we have discussed the techniques which stem from the Profit and Loss Account and the Balance Sheet. These techniques have been developed to meet the demands of the thinking manager. For instance, from the Profit and Loss Account there is the need to discover where the profit or loss is being made which led to the techniques known as costing. And from the Balance Sheet there are the questions regarding investment, which led to project appraisal techniques being developed to help managers 'look before they leap' and to meet the questions regarding investment in fixed assets and other 'locked up' areas of money such as research and development and marketing before benefits arise from such expense. We also saw in the last chapter that the objective, as far as working capital is concerned, is to minimise the investment, to reduce the financial luggage – the stocks and debtors less creditors – and that that is done by the analysis and control of time, the time involved in moving the money round the working capital cycle. Finally, in Chapter 4 we saw how the detailed analysis of cash set out in the Cash Flow Forecast may be recast into a summary of immediate cash movement, a summary which is presented in what is termed the Source and Application of Funds Statement the purpose of which is to encapsulate the progress of the business in such a way as to answer perhaps the final and most pragmatic cash question of all: 'Has the business lived within or beyond its means?' We shall be referring again to this way of looking at a business's progress when we consider interpretation in Chapter 12.

However, now let us turn our attention to the recurring need of every thinking manager, when financial information is presented about what has happened: 'what can I compare it against?' It is to meet this constant need for comparison that the financial technique termed budgetary control has been developed.

Budgetary control is nothing new. It has been used from the very beginning of business life. If indeed one was to go back into the history of business it would be found that managers have always done some form of budgeting in planning and reviewing the progress of their businesses. After all 2,000 years ago Someone was quoted as saying 'What man ever built a house before first counting its cost?'

The business plan

This then is what budgetary control is concerned with: setting out the business plan in financial terms and progressing these against the facts as they become known. Imagine yourself starting a business. Inevitably you would find yourself looking at your plans and your policies so that you could see whether or not it was likely to go well. To illustrate this point refer to Illustration 10.1 which sets out a question regarding the financial situation of a company as far as its future plans are concerned. It must be stressed that in this illustration we have confined our view forward to six months, which in any real-life situation would be far too short a period. However, we shall refer to the period of a budget later in this chapter.

Illustration 10.1 Budgetary control exercise.

A Ltd is formed with share capital £140,000 of which it invests £40,000 in land and buildings, £25,000 in plant and machinery and £20,000 in motor vehicles and the remainder it leaves as cash. Its plans for the first six months are as follows:

Sales for six months		£650,000
Materials in sales		£280,000
Labour in sales		£180,000
Overheads (including depreciation):		
Plant and machinery	£5,000	
Motor vehicles	£5,000	£160,000
Materials purchased for the period		£300,000

Cash receipts and payments for six months:

	Sales receipts £	Payments material £	Overheads and wages £
July	30,000	70,000	
August	60,000	70,000	Paid
September	40,000	10,000	evenly
October	80,000	10,000	each month
November	110,000	20,000	
December	160,000	20,000	
Total	£480,000	£200,000	

Note: There is no work in progress or finished goods stocks at 31 December.

From the above facts construct the budgeted:

(a) Cash Flow Forecast for July to December;
(b) Profit and Loss Account for the six months ended 31 December;
(c) Balance Sheet as at 31 December.

You will see in the illustration that the business is planning to sell a certain volume of goods and that it estimates that these goods will cost them so much. You will also see that the business plans to raise money by issuing share capital and there are certain investments that have got to be made in items such as land and buildings, plant and machinery, and motor vehicles – in other words fixed assets. You should tackle the questions set in this illustration and see how out of this business plan we produce the three major statements – the planned or, as we say, the Budgeted Cash Flow Forecast, Profit and Loss Account and Balance Sheet.

As you tackle the questions and read through the suggested answers in Illustrations 10.2, 10.3 and 10.4 you might recall a similar illustration which we studied at the end of Chapter 4. You will recognise that what in fact is happening is that we are proving the financial credibility of the policies of this particular company. After all, it is all very well and good having great plans for the future, but they must be financially possible. Each of these three major statements are proving one aspect or other of the financial credibility of this particular business's plans.

First, if we follow this policy, what will be the return – what will the growth or shrinkage be to the money we are investing in the business? This leads us to the Profit and Loss Account. Second, if we start this business where will our money be and from where will it have been funded at any

Illustration 10.2 A Ltd: Budgeted Cash Flow Forecast: July to December.

	Jul. £	Aug. £	Sept. £	Oct. £	Nov. £	Dec. £	Total. £
Receipts:							
Share capital	140,000	—	—	—	—	—	140,000
Sales	30,000	60,000	40,000	80,000	110,000	160,000	480,000
A	170,000	60,000	40,000	80,000	110,000	160,000	620,000
Payments:							
Fixed assets	85,000	—	—	—	—	—	85,000
Materials	70,000	70,000	10,000	10,000	20,000	20,000	200,000
Wages	30,000	30,000	30,000	30,000	30,000	30,000	180,000
Overheads	25,000	25,000	25,000	25,000	25,000	25,000	150,000
B	210,000	125,000	65,000	65,000	75,000	75,000	615,000
Balance (A – B)	(40,000)	(65,000)	(25,000)	15,000	35,000	85,000	
Balance b/fwd	—	(40,000)	(105,000)	(130,000)	(115,000)	(80,000)	
Balance c/fwd	(40,000)	(105,000)	(130,000)	(115,000)	(80,000)	5,000	5,000

Illustration 10.3 A Ltd: Budgeted Profit and Loss Account for the six months ended 31 December.

		£
Sales		650,000
	£	
Less: Materials	280,000	
Labour	180,000	
Overheads	160,000	620,000
Profit		£30,000

Illustration 10.4 A Ltd: Budgeted Balance Sheet as at 31 December.

	Cost	Depreciation to date	
	£	£	£
Fixed assets:			
Land and buildings	40,000	—	40,000
Plant and machinery	25,000	5,000	20,000
Motor vehicles	20,000	5,000	15,000
	£85,000	£10,000	75,000
Working capital:			
Current assets:			
Stock raw materials	20,000		
Debtors	170,000		
Cash at bank	5,000		
		195,000	
Less: Current liabilities			
Creditors		100,000	95,000
			£170,000
Financed by:			
Share capital			140,000
Retained profits			30,000
			£170,000

point of time? In the case of the illustration we have chosen six months from the beginning of the business. We are therefore setting out the Balance Sheet, the 'snapshot', of where the money will be and from where it will have been obtained as at 31 December. Finally we need to look at whether we have the ability to arrive, the ready in cash terms? It is this that we determine by means of the Cash Flow Forecast. In fact, in constructing the budget the Cash Flow Forecast will come first. After all, in Illustration 10.1 there is a cash need of £130,000 in September and unless this need can be met there is no point proceeding to the Profit and Loss Account or the Balance Sheet. (If you find this point unclear revise your studies on cash flow forecasting in Chapter 4.)

Budgeting for policy-makers

What we have just done is to look at budgeting as it applies to the policy-makers of a business. And whether we are sitting on a bar-stool planning our own small business or whether we are sitting around a boardroom table planning the policies of a multinational corporation, we would need to subject our plans, our policies, our dreams, our ideas to these same three credibility tests of finance. What will be the return? What will be the risk? And will we have the ready – the cash – to arrive? The three Rs of finance are indeed the financial parameters of every business plan.

Budgetary control and non-policy-makers

However, we find that this form of budgeting, which we might refer to as 'Boardroom budgeting', is only part of today's budgetary control system.

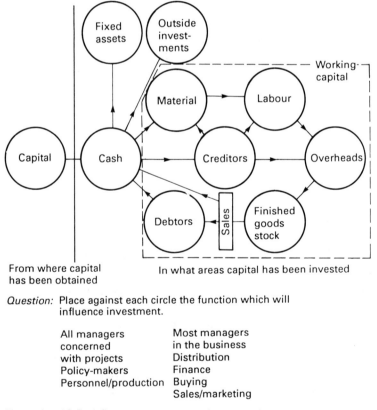

From where capital has been obtained

In what areas capital has been invested

Question: Place against each circle the function which will influence investment.

All managers	Most managers
concerned	in the business
with projects	Distribution
Policy-makers	Finance
Personnel/production	Buying
	Sales/marketing

Illustration 10.5 Influences on expenses, income or investment.

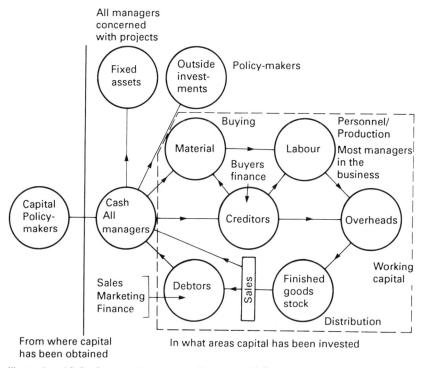

Illustration 10.6 Suggested answer to Illustration 10.5.

What we now see is that present-day business budgeting is no longer confined to the policy-makers. As businesses expand more and more people within the enterprise become concerned with the investment, receipt and expenditure of its money. It is therefore necessary, if financial control is to be effective, to extend its control to people outside the policy-makers.

It is for this reason that modern-day budgeting has taken on an additional role. We still have budgeting within the boardroom, dealing with the policy of the business, but we now see it extended to those who are not concerned necessarily with policy-making. What we find is that managers operating at different levels are more and more taking part in the budgeting process. Budgetary control is now extended to meet their needs, not as policy-makers, but as controllers of income, expense and investment within their own particular spheres of influence.

To demonstrate this point regarding the involvement of people with money in business consider the financial model set out again as Illustration 10.5. What I want you to do is place against each circle the function, e.g. buying, sales, production and finance, which will influence the expense, income or investment concerned and check your answer with Illustration 10.6.

The behavioural problem

This second role of budgeting, then, involves the setting out of forecasts of expense, income and investment which can be controlled by individual managers against which the actual expense, income and investment is regularly progressed. It is this second application of budgetary control which has brought with it a great increase in forecasting and a great deal more progressing than used to take place when budgeting was confined to the boardroom. However, perhaps most important of all, it has brought out the problem of the behavioural response to comparison. This is that when you subject anyone to personal comparison they behave in a particular way – they do not like it! And because they do not like it, they resist it.

This is the major problem which exists in this second role of budgetary control, that where managers are asked to compare their own performance against financial targets which have been prepared around their activities they react in a predictable way: because they do not wish to be personally compared they resist it. As a result of this resistance expenses may be over- and income and sales understated so that revenue budgets will easily be attained, whilst capital or fixed asset investments will be exaggerated more to increase personal prestige than for the good of the business as a whole.

We need therefore to anticipate such resistance and to try to avoid its consequences. To begin with, any business introducing budgetary control must understand that managers not only resist comparison but are well equipped to do this, because they have two well-tried 'defence barriers'. The first is irrelevance, and the second is impossibility.

Irrelevance

Irrelevance, after all, has long been used as a defence against comparisons. Take, for example, comparative religion where the excuse of those wishing to avoid it has so often been: 'his hair was longer than mine', 'he lived in the desert', 'he had no job'; not arguing its 'rightness', simply questioning its relevance. In other words this resistance barrier is nothing new and for this reason it is essential to recognise it if budgeting is to be effective. Successful budgeting presupposes that the items which managers are expected to control and progress should be relevant to them and subject to their influence.

It is therefore vital that managers take part in the preparation of their own budgets and that they are fully conversant and appreciate their influence on each expense, income and investment for which they are made responsible. It is a key point of budgeting to make sure that managers are fully involved at the planning stage. Managers should therefore agree their budgets before the period of control and progress begins so as to avoid the excuse of irrelevance. For this reason every item placed within the budget of any manager must be fully agreed and understood by those concerned.

Impossibility

Having considered the problem of irrelevance the second defence has to be tackled – impossibility. It must be noted that from a behavioural point of view budgeting has all the attributes of a game. Managers are being asked to achieve certain objectives to meet the agreed budget. Budgeting for managers has, therefore, the same characteristics as a game, and in such situations, if you are going to get people to play positively, it is essential that the game can be won!

After all if from the very start those asked to play know it is impossible to win, then the natural human response will be either to change the rules or, if that is impossible, ruin the game. You can see this if you watch children at play with adults when the adults are taking the game seriously. What you will see happening is that in order to make the game winnable children will do one of two things: they will either cheat or begin to play another game. In other words they will convert the impossible game into one which is possible to win or at least enjoyable to lose!

These are very important points to recognise in budgeting – because the identical responses will be made by managers unless great care is taken to anticipate what might be termed the 'behavioural problems of comparison'. For this reason it is important that all budgets are not only agreed with managers but that the level of efficiency, on which the budgets are set, is possible to achieve, because if this is not so managers will respond in the ways we have just mentioned. They will either cheat – in other words they will arrange the budgets in such a way that although people will think they are impossible or at least difficult to attain, they will in fact be very easy indeed – or if this is not possible they will opt out of the system. They will play another game. They will not even try, but sulk noisily!

These then are the two cardinal rules that we must apply when we are involving people in personal comparison, rules which apply to managers in a budgeting situation as much as to any human situation of comparison: the comparison must be relevant, and it must be possible to achieve.

'Below the line' items

Having set out these two behavioural rules it must be understood that in budgeting expenses, sales/income or investment it may be thought necessary to include items which, although they may not be the direct responsibility of the particular managers, they may be of interest to them. In this circumstance such items may well be referred to as 'below the line'. This means we put them in the budget report but we should not mix them with the items for which the manager is held personally responsible.

Budget presentation

A revenue budget

A typical example of a revenue budget is set out in Illustration 10.7. You will see in this illustration that the budget relates to items of expenditure within a department of a revenue nature, expenditure which will be deducted from sales before arriving at the profit or loss of the business in the Profit and Loss Account.

In the case of the revenue budget the comparison which is of major interest is normally between the cumulative figures to date because the actual monthly figures themselves can sometimes be distorted by an unusual expense in a particular month. The cumulative amounts, then, are of particular importance to those concerned with taking corrective action.

It is also useful to include space for remarks and explanations because these will bring out points which may be necessary to consider if you are going to get full value from the comparison. This is particularly important if the comparison has become distorted because of factors outside the control of the particular manager for whom the budget has been prepared.

A capital expenditure budget

If you turn to Illustration 10.8 you will see set out a budget relating to capital or fixed asset expenditure. In the case of capital expenditure, where this is of a continuing nature, it may be useful to examine the expense

Illustration 10.7 Revenue Budget for Production Department to month 6.

	This month		To date			
Expense	Actual £	Budget £	Actual £	Budget £	Variance £	Remarks
Indirect wages	9,650	10,000	65,400	70,000	4,600	Overtime less
Rent	1,000	1,000	6,000	6,000	—	
Insurance	480	500	2,800	3,000	200	
Depreciation	1,900	2,000	10,600	12,000	1,400	Plant not purchased
Electricity	1,250	1,500	9,000	8,000	(1,000)	Cost increase
Plant repair etc.	900	750	8,000	6,000	(2,000)	Major breakdown

Illustration 10.8 Capital expenditure budget.

'A' Factory

Capital project	This month		Accumulated to date		Total cost		Month 6	Remarks
	Actual	Budget	Actual	Budget	Actual cost plus estimate to complete	Total budget cost	Difference	
	£	£	£	£	£	£	£	
Extension to Parts Store	5,100	11,200	131,000	120,000	240,000	210,000	+30,000	Alteration to specification agreed per Directors Minute dated 6/12/—

to date plus an estimate of what is necessary to complete the project, compared with the total original budget. This indeed is the budget format illustrated which includes three comparisons: this month's, the cumulative figures to date, and the figures to date plus an estimate of what is still to be done to complete the project.

It should also be pointed out that capital expenditure budgets can seldom be confined to the immediate year ahead, which is the period normally selected for revenue budgets. In the case of capital expenditure many organisations budget in considerable detail over the next five to ten years, and even beyond this in outline.

Progressing budgets

After looking at the setting of budgets and the way in which budgets can be presented we shall now consider the main rules for progressing budgets. First it must be noted that budgeting is primarily a technique of communication. For this reason the progressing of budgets must fulfil the criteria of good communications or much of its advantage will be lost. For example, if you get people interested in the setting of budgets and then you proceed to bore them in the way in which the budgets are presented then you inevitably lose a great deal of the earlier advantage you may have gained. It is for this reason that care has to be put into the way in which information is progressed and in doing this we have to look at the two major rules of communication. These are the *form* in which information is communicated, and the *frequency* or *timing* of the presentation of such information.

Form of presentation

As regards the form of presentation it is necessary to consider very carefully the way which will best suit the different levels of managers who are to be involved in budgeting. Neat columns of figures may well serve the purpose for many managers, but there may also be those who do not find the 'columns of figures' approach conducive to understanding. Indeed they may well find other presentations such as the use of graphs or other visual methods more appropriate. It may also be found that it is helpful to present information in quantities as well as values. This is especially true in periods of inflation.

As an example of how graphs can be used in such situations you should turn to Illustration 10.9 which sets out two graphs, the first comparing the actual and budget value of materials used and the second comparing the actual and budget quantities used of the same materials.

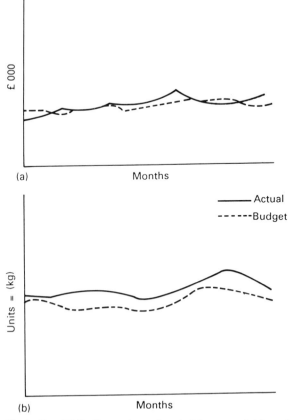

Illustration 10.9   Comparison of materials usage: (a) by value; (b) by quantity.

The Z chart

To illustrate a more comprehensive use of graphs turn first to Illustration 10.10 which sets out data relating to sales for a twelve-month period. This includes the monthly and cumulative budget sales figures accompanied by the actual sales figures as they become known. It is based on these that the graph in Illustration 10.11 is constructed.

There you will see that the figures are presented to show first the actual monthly sales as they become available compared with those that were set out in the sales budget. Second we see the same actual figures drawn up on a cumulative scale showing the cumulative actual sales month by month compared with the total budgeted sales for the twelve months. Finally we show the moving annual average sales which are based on the average monthly figures. You will see how these are calculated in the notes attached to Illustration 10.10.

Illustration 10.10 Data and calculations for graph in Illustration 10.11.

	Budget		Actual	
	Monthly £	Cumulative £	Monthly £	Cumulative £
January	5,000	5,000	5,000	5,000
February	4,900	4,900	4,800	9,800
March	5,200	15,100	5,300	15,100
April	4,800	19,900	5,400	20,500
May	5,100	25,000	4,700	25,200
June	5,010	30,010	4,800	30,000
July	4,950	34,950	4,900	34,900
August	5,100	40,050	5,200	40,100
September	5,000	45,050	5,300	45,400
October	4,800	49,850	4,700	50,100
November	5,100	54,950	5,200	55,300
December	4,900	69,850	5,600	60,900

Moving annual average calculation:
Example for June:

$$\text{Budget} = \frac{£30,010}{6} \times 12 = £60,020$$

$$\text{Actual} = \frac{£30,000}{6} \times 12 = £60,000$$

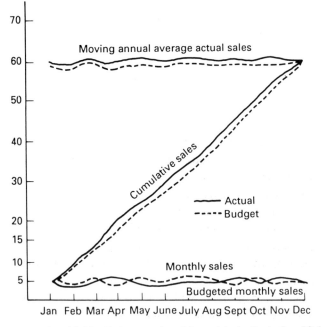

Illustration 10.11 Z chart produced from data in Illustration 10.10.

The graph in Illustration 10.11 is a way of showing the budget and actual sales figures in three ways – monthly, cumulative and the moving annual average. It is known as a Z chart.

Summarising data
There are also certain other points regarding the form of presentation which should be borne in mind. The first is that if budget information is to be summarised on one piece of paper then this can have a delaying effect upon when the information becomes available. For example, if a manager receives a summary of expenditure within his or her department at monthly intervals then if all the information is available to be presented by the end of the month with the exception of one item, which does not arrive, say, for 14 days, then everything may be delayed until that one item of expenditure is known. It therefore has to be recognised that if speedy presentation is required then summarising data can add to delay.

Personal investigation
If it is possible, managers should seek the information out for themselves and so avoid the clerical procedure of copying altogether. An initial against the source material may have its merits. For example, managers visiting the wages office at weekly intervals to initial the wages that are under their control will save the time, clerical effort and possible error of re-summarising such information on the budget statement. It may also ensure that the information is more closely studied than if it were summarised on a form convenient for parking in the pending tray!

Frequency

This brings us to the second point to consider in 'budget communication' – the frequency or timing of its presentation. In the area of communicating budgets to managers timing is often vital. For example, if a manager is told that something is going wrong regarding the expenditure or income over which he or she is responsible but is told weeks or months after the event, then the opportunity to take corrective action will be delayed if not lost altogether.

It is therefore essential to look at timing carefully to make sure that we are presenting budget/actual comparisons at a frequency which suits the managers concerned. It must be noted that what may be the right frequency for the policy-makers may not always be the right frequency for line managers or function heads. We must remember that once we take budgeting out of the boardroom then the managers most able to correct situations that have gone wrong or perpetuate those that have gone right are very

Illustration 10.12 Rules of budgetary control communication.

Types of budget:	Purpose:
Policy-makers	To provide credibility of policy
Managements	Efficiency comparison

Two cardinal rules:
Make sure comparison is — Relevant
                        — Possible

For successful communication examine:
                        — Form of communication
                        — Frequency of communication

often in reverse order to their seniority. It is the man who digs the hole too deep who will be able to get that hole the right depth as long as he is told as soon as possible the depth of the hole he just dug! We must look at the lines of communication in progressing budgets and this line must be drawn as short as possible.

The timing in which budgets are presented and progressed is central to the effectiveness of budgetary control. The rules of budgetary control communication are summarised in Illustration 10.12 which should form a checklist when considering the effectiveness of this technique within any business.

Budgeting myths

Having considered the rules of communication in budgetary control we now need to consider some of the myths which surround it as a technique.

Saves money?

The first of these is the one that claims that budgetary control saves money. This may indeed be true but it will very much depend upon the effectiveness of the system. If budgeting is not carefully introduced it can work in the reverse way, in that it may not save money, but may indeed inspire money to be spent on things which without budgetary control would never have been thought of or indeed missed! For instance, budgetary control may well become a technique which encourages managers to include more expenditure than is really necessary and less income than in fact they could achieve to avoid blame for failure to achieve targets.

One of the real problems of budgeting can be too much stress being placed on the fact that unless budgets are achieved then the manager will be subject to discipline. This means that managers may over-insure themselves in the first place in setting their budgets, and second, having over insured themselves, they will be very determined to make sure that they achieve the budget figures agreed.

It is therefore vital to avoid budgets being treated this way. Every expense and income must be looked at on its merits and rigidity should have no part to play in the system.

Flexible budgeting

We must therefore always make sure that our budgets are flexible. In Illustration 10.13 you will see an example of a budgeting situation in which in the first column the budget is based on one level of activity and it therefore shows just one set of figures against which actuals would be compared. However, if we adopt a flexible budget approach, then the budget figures would depend upon the level of activity that is actually attained.

It is this 'flexed budget' approach which is set out in the second column in Illustration 10.13. Here it can be seen that if activity alters then the variable costs – in this case direct material, direct labour and the variable overheads – should be adjusted in line with the activity obtained.

It is this flexible approach to budgeting that will make it possible to adapt the budget to meet changing circumstances and so make it usable to compare with actuals irrespective of the activity achieved. To test your understanding of flexible budgets tackle the question set out in Illustration 10.14 and then compare your answer with Illustration 10.15.

A unifying force?

The second problem of budgeting is that of making sure that it brings people together and does not split them asunder. This is the need to create within managers a sense of control and responsibility for their own sphere

Illustration 10.13 Flexible budgeting.

Fixed		*Flexible*	
Budgeted activity	24,000 units	Actual activity	18,000
Budgeted costs on above level of activity during four-week period:		Budgeted costs on actual level of activity during four-week period:	
	£		£
Direct material	30,000		22,500
Direct labour	60,000		45,000
Variable overheads	12,000		9,000
Fixed overheads	10,000		10,000
	£112,000		£86,500

Illustration 10.14 Flexible budgeting exercise.

X Ltd manufactures a product for which the activity levels in the assembly department vary widely from month to month. The following statement shows the departmental overhead budget based on an average level of activity of 20,000 units production per four-week period:

	Budget average for four-week period £
Direct material	10,000
Direct labour	20,000
Variable overheads	5,000
Fixed overheads	7,500
Depreciation	2,500
	£45,000
Production (units)	20,000

You are required to prepare a flexible four-week budget at 16,000, 22,000 and 24,000 unit levels of production.

Illustration 10.15 Answer to Illustration 10.14.

Units of production	16,000 £	22,000 £	24,000 £
Direct material	8,000	11,000	12,000
Direct labour	16,000	22,000	24,000
Variable overheads	4,000	5,500	6,000
Fixed overheads	7,500	7,500	7,500
Depreciation	2,500	2,500	2,500
	£38,000	£48,500	£52,000

of influence whilst at the same time recognising that they still fit into the business as a whole.

It must be understood by managers that a transfer of one expense from one budget to another does not eliminate or reduce the expense, it just puts it somewhere else. There must also be a sense of oneness when it comes to capital expenditure budgets. Managers must appreciate that the firm as a whole makes the profit or obtains the cash flow, and to do this requires the right investments wherever appropriate. This means that if there are scarce resources, these should be directed to those areas of investment which will bring the greatest benefit. Capital expenditure must therefore always be subject to the setting of priorities which may well cross functional barriers. A buyer's proposal to extend the warehouse may have to take second place to the production manager's requirement for new plant and machinery and so on.

Summary of budgetary control

Policy-makers' needs

Budgetary control is a system of comparison which is designed to serve two purposes: first to assess the financial credibility of the policies of the business, and as such budgeting in this area is confined to the boardroom – to the policy-makers. Budgets around policy will be developed in the context of the business as a whole and it is natural that such budgets will not be confined to the immediate period ahead. They will be made in outline over maybe three or even up to five years ahead. This is especially necessary in the case of capital expenditure where budgets over the following five to ten years are often set out in considerable detail, and even beyond this in outline. This is necessary, for example, so as to provide the required manufacturing capacity or retail outlets to meet the sales and marketing plans for the years ahead.

It must be very carefully noted that if we are to look forward, we must recognise that beyond a period of, say, twelve months, any attempt at exactness will be costly as well as in all likelihood inaccurate or inappropriate to situations as they transpire. It is therefore necessary to combine the desire to look ahead with a recognition of its clerical and managerial costs. Here as so often with financial information there is a need to strike a happy medium!

Management comparison

The second objective of budgeting, and a growing one, is to use budgeting as a method of management comparison: to use it as a way in which managers within their own area of activity can see the financial implications of what they are doing and to set these out in financial terms within a 'personal responsibility budget'. It is this area of personal comparison that creates the great behavioural problem of people not wishing to be personally compared. It is necessary therefore that when people are put into this position every effort is made to make sure that they appreciate the need for and objectives of such comparison. This also implies that the relevance and the possibility of the targets or budgets set are very carefully explained and understood by those who need to work with them.

Progressing budgets – form and frequency

Having understood this, it is equally necessary to make sure that the progressing of budgets is tailored to the needs and understanding of the different managers. This means that the form of budget presentation and its frequency should be very carefully reviewed. It must be noted that the form and frequency that might be suitable for a board of directors will not necessarily be the ideal form or frequency for a chargehand, foreman or departmental supervisor.

Budgeting myths

Finally we must be aware of the myths of budgeting. First, it will only save money if management understand and appreciate its purpose, and also only if budgets are being continually reviewed and revised – flexed – in the light of the current situation.

Second, it will only bring people together, to understand the business as a whole, if positive steps are taken, steps that will ensure people see how budgets must interlink and intermix for the benefit of the enterprise as a whole.

Present trends

The recognition of the behavioural effects of trying to avoid comparison is well illustrated in the development in recent years of approaches to budgetary control which take this into account.

One example of this is the re-forecasting of budgets at monthly intervals. Comparisons can then be made not only against annual budgets which may increasingly, through the year, become very remote from reality, but also against revised forecasts, forecasts that will reflect any current changes in income and expense levels.

Another development is that of zero-based budgeting. This technique assumes each budget starts from zero and requires that funds for each budget item of expense and investment be justified, and in some cases 'competed for' against other budgetholders.

All these developments are still very much in their initial stages but managers need to be aware of them to see whether or not they are proving effective. However, whatever may be the verdict on any particular method of budgetary control, what is clear is that it is a developing and changing field of management study and requires constant attention and concern. Certainly at the present time the suggestion that 'many firms would save thousands if they abolished budgeting' could not in all cases be challenged.

Structure of budgetary control

Finally study carefully Illustration 10.16 which sets out the structure and interrelationships of budgetary control within a business. It is not considered appropriate in this text to discuss the formulation of policy or the

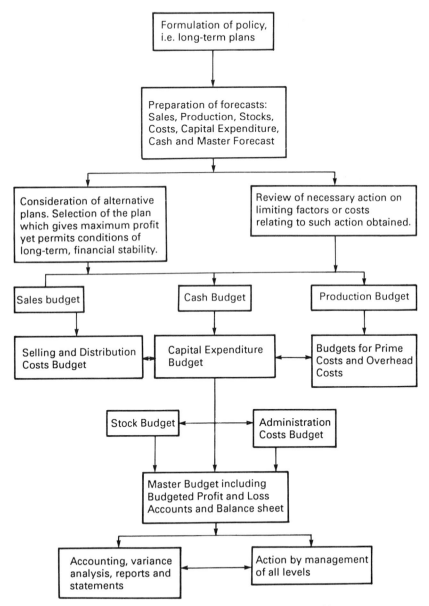

Illustration 10.16 Budgetary control: structure and interrelationships.

consideration of alternative plans and strategies. The policies or strategies of a business depend upon management as a whole, although clearly there will, in the short term, be limiting factors to the progress of the enterprise, for example the skills of the workforce, the production capacity of its fixed assets. However, within the context of such limiting factors there will be what might be termed a principal budget factor which in most cases will be sales – what the business can sell. (For those who wish to study how business policy is formed together with the strategies and limiting factors they should refer to more specialised management texts.)

However, a review of Illustration 10.16 will provide an overview of the steps required in building up budgetary control within a business. Study this illustration with particular reference to seeing how each individual budget prepared by each manager links into the final presentation of the master budget in the form of a Budgeted Profit and Loss Account, Balance Sheet and Cash Flow Forecast.

Once you have completed this review we shall continue in the next chapter to examine the second financial comparative technique – Standard Costing.

11 | STANDARD COSTING

Introduction

This chapter deals with the second financial technique concerned with comparison – standard costing. Standard costing is not, as many people think from its name, a different form of costing, but a form of comparison designed to meet the problems of managers in the cost analysis field. Such problems arise when comparison is made between an actual and a budgeted cost – the difference revealed will, in most cases, need to be analysed further before corrective action can be taken.

The analysis of difference

To illustrate this point turn to Illustration 11.1 which sets out the actual cost for a product compared with its budgeted cost. We also see that there is a third column which sets out differences under each of the four main heads of material, labour and expenses – both direct and indirect – and sales. It is this difference column that can present the problems for which standard costing is designed to tackle.

Material

For example, in the case of material, what exactly makes up this difference? How much is caused because the price of the material has changed between the actual and the budget and how much because the usage of material varies between the actual and budgeted usage?

Labour

And this is equally true in the case of labour. For instance, how much of the difference is caused because of the rate of pay changing between the actual and the budgeted rate, and how much because of the efficiency of

Illustration 11.1 Standard costing.

Product costs:	Actual	Budget	Difference
	p	p	p
Direct material	5	4	+ 1
Direct labour	4	6	− 2
Direct expenses	3	4	− 1
	12	14	− 2
Indirect expenses	6	7	− 1
Total cost	18	21	− 3
Profit	4	4	0
Sales price	22	25	+ 3

the labour? Have they done the job quicker or slower than was set within the budgeted time?

Other expenditure

This analysis will also be true of other expenditure. For example, how much of the difference between the actual and the budgeted expenditure on such things as rent, insurance, light and heat, and salaries has been caused because the expenditure itself has gone up or gone down, and how much has been caused by the activity of the business?

Activity variance

To understand this problem of activity turn to Illustration 11.2 and see how the indirect expenses – or overheads as they are often called – are arrived at in a cost. You will notice that the budgeted overhead rate of recovery set is based upon a particular expenditure – in this case £5,000,000 – and a particular level of activity forecast – in this case 10,000,000 production hours. This therefore means that failing to achieve this budgeted expense could be caused either because the expenditure incurred or the activity achieved is different from that set. For instance, if the rents have gone up, or the administrative salaries have changed, then this will obviously be one of the reasons why the actual expenditure will differ from that budgeted.

However, we also have the problem of activity. If we do not achieve – as in this illustration – ten million hours of production then we will not recover these expenses and the budgeted rate of recovery, that is 50p per hour, will be inadequate for this purpose. For example, let us assume that the actual activity was only eight million production hours. If this was so we would only recover £4 million – 8,000,000 hours × 50p per hour. However, it is to be doubted that the overheads would come down in sym-

Illustration 11.2   Indirect expense recovery calculation.

1. Budgeted indirect costs for period   £5,000,000
2. Budget activity measured in production hours   10,000,000 hours
   Budgeted indirect recovery rate $\dfrac{£5,000,000}{10,000,000 \text{ hours}}$

$$= 50\text{p per hour}$$

pathy. After all, as we explained in Chapters 6 and 7 on full and marginal costing, most overheads or indirect expenses are fixed. They continue whether or not the activity forecast is achieved.

This would mean in this case an under-recovery between the actual and the budgeted expenditure of £1 million, caused not because of any additional expenditure but because of the failure to achieve the activity budgeted.

Sales variances

The same type of problem, with different reasons for the variances, arises with sales. In fact the difference between actual sales and budgeted sales can have three causes. It could be caused because sales have not been sold at the price that was set per unit in the budget. It could also be caused because we have not reached the volume of sales that we planned to sell in the budget, or third, it could also be caused because of a failure to sell in the mix that we had planned in the budget.

Illustration 11.3   Material cost variances: usage and price.

Material budget for unit made up as follows:

Budget usage   = 10 kg
Price per kg   = £8

Budgeted material cost per unit:

= 10 kg × £8   = £80

Actual material cost per unit as follows:

Actual usage   =   9.5 kg
Price per kg   = £8.50

Actual material cost per unit:

= 9.5 kg × £8.50   = £80.75

Net variance per unit (unfavourable) 75p

Made up of:

Usage variance = (10 kg − 9.5 kg) × £8 = £4.00 Favourable
Price variance = 9.5 kg × (£8 − £8.50) = £4.75 Unfavourable
Net variance per unit unfavourable   £0.75

Price, volume and usage variances

The problems of price, volume and usage and how the differences are calculated can be seen in the case of materials for price and usage in Illustration 11.3, for labour as regards rate of pay and efficiency in Illustration 11.4, and for sales as regards price and volume in Illustration 11.5. These should be studied so that you can follow both the arithmetic and the use which could be made of this data.

Illustration 11.4   Labour cost variances: efficiency and rate.

Standard labour cost per unit made up as follows:

Standard labour hour per unit	= 9
Standard rate of pay	= £10 per hour

Therefore standard labour cost per unit = £90 (9 hrs × £10 per hr)

Actual labour cost per unit made up as follows:

Actual labour hours per unit	= 9.5
Actual rate of pay	= £9.50 per hour

Therefore actual labour cost per unit   = £90.25

Net variance = 25p (favourable)

Made up of:

Efficiency variance = (9 hrs − 9.5 hrs) × £10 per hour	= £5.00 Unfavourable
Rate of pay variance = 9.5 hrs × (£10 per hr − £9.50 per hr)	= £4.75 Favourable
Net variance per unit favourable	£0.25

Illustration 11.5   Sales variances: volume and price.

A Ltd sets its Sales Budget for Year

based on the following facts:

Standard volume of sales = 10,000 units	
Standard price per unit = £100	

Therefore Sales Budget = 10,000 × £100 per unit = £1,000,000

Actual sales achieved for year

Actual volume of sales = 10,500 units	
Actual sales price per unit = £90 per unit	

Therefore actual sales for year = 105,000 units × £90 per unit = £94,500

Total variance = (£1,000,000 − £94,500) = £55,000 (unfavourable)

Made up of:

Volume variance = (10,000 units − 10,500 units) × £100 =	£50,000 Favourable
Price variance = 10,500 units × (£100 − £90) £10 =	£105,000 Unfavourable
Net variance unfavourable	£55,000

Illustration 11.6   Sales mix example.

Products	Sales price	Variable cost	Contribution	Contribution to sales price	Budgeted Sales %	Budgeted Mix C/SP	Actual Sales %	Actual Mix C/SP
	p	p	p	p		p		p
A	10	5	5	0.50	80	0.40	10	0.05
B	15	10	5	0.33	10	0.03	10	0.03
C	8	7	1	0.125	10	0.01	80	0.10
						0.44		0.18

Fixed costs =   £880,000 ÷ 0.44   £800,000 ÷ 0.18
Sales value to breakeven: Budget £2m   Actual £4.9m (approx.)
Mix variance: 44p less 18p per £1 sales = 26p

Sales mix variance

To understand the problem of sales mix refer back to Chapter 7 where we discussed the sales mix in the context of marginal costing in Illustration 7.14. This is shown again here as Illustration 11.6 where you will see that, whereas the budgeted sales mix would have given a contribution of 44p per £1 sold, the actual sales mix produces a contribution of only 18p per £1 sold. The difference therefore of 26p between the actual and the budgeted sales mix is caused not because of the volume of sales sold and not because of the price they were sold for, but because of the sales mix. In order to refresh your knowledge of this topic, refer back to Chapter 7 on marginal costing and go through it once again very carefully.

Standard costing

We have now seen the difference between the actual and the budgeted cost of a unit could be made up of very many different reasons. It should also be understood that managers wishing to manage and control their businesses effectively need to know these reasons as soon as they occur, so they can take effective corrective action. It is to meet this requirement that the system known as standard costing has been designed.

Standard costing is a system of comparison which not only brings out the difference between actual and forecasted figures but, as we have seen, analyses such differences into their causes. It is when differences are analysed in this way that they are often referred to as variances. It is the purpose of standard costing to produce for management variances which will help them manage more effectively.

To illustrate this point turn to Illustration 11.7 which sets out an actual cost compared with a standard cost. From the information you will see

Illustration 11.7 Highlighting the variance between actual and standard costs.

	Actual cost	Standard cost	Variance
	p	p	p
Direct material	10	8	− 2 price
			+ 4 usage
Direct labour	8	9	− 2 rate of pay
			+ 1 efficiency
Variable expenses	4	3	+ 1 expense
Fixed expense	6	4	+ 3 expense
			− 1 activity

that the variances are brought out for the use and understanding of management.

Managerial requirements from standard costing

Having seen the purpose of standard costing let us look at this from a management point of view, in other words ask ourselves what is the essential requirement a manager seeks from this technique? And the answer to this question lies, once again, in the credibility that can be attached to the information disclosed. In other words, if we are to go to all the effort required to produce this detailed variance information, it is essential that the information produced is usable, and to make standard costing usable there are three essential features it must possess.

Accuracy of data

The first feature which standard costing must possess is that the actual cost data must be as accurate as possible. After all if managers looking at variances distrust the actual information upon which they have been calculated then they will take very little action, and it is the extent of the action taken which makes the system of any real value to the manager. It is therefore essential as a prerequisite of any standard costing system that the actual costs presented are believed, so that the resultant information will be used.

For this reason great care must be taken to ensure that the systems of labour, material and overhead cost controls and recordings are satisfactory before any system of standard costing is introduced.

Credibility of standards

However, having ensured that this first requirement is met there is still the second. This is to make sure that the standards which are available are recognised, understood and believed by the managers who act upon them. After all, just as the system becomes valueless if the actual data is not believed, so in exactly the same way if the standards themselves are not believed then managers will be reluctant, to say the least, to act on the information produced.

To be told that there is a variance between the actual and the standard usage of materials set and to disbelieve the standard means that once again this particular variance will be ignored. In order therefore to provide an effective system of standard costing, standards will have to be set in the best possible way. For this reason it is often found that before a standard costing system can be effectively introduced work study will have to be applied to ensure that standard times are agreed for the different labour operations.

For the same reason it may also be necessary to introduce production control to produce standard usages for materials which can be believed by those concerned with its control. And it may also be necessary for sales to set out standards which are agreed by all those concerned with sales and marketing, for example standard sales prices, volumes and mixes.

These then are the first two requirements for a successful system of standard costing – that the actual costs achieved and the standards set for them are believed so that the differences will be acted upon.

Locatability of variances

However, we still have the third and possibly the most important prerequisite for any standard costing system: that the variances are geographically located into recognisable areas so that corrective action *can* be taken. This requirement affects standard costing in three areas, namely the usage of materials, the efficiency of labour, and the volume and mix of sales.

Materials usage

To illustrate these points let us review each of these areas in turn, beginning with the usage of materials. Let us take as an example a production manager responsible for the manufacture of a product that passes through several different processes. If the manager is told that the usage of material is, say, 10 per cent greater than the standard laid down, then this is only of academic interest. Unless it can be located to a precise process or operation which can be recognised no positive action can be taken.

In other words to be told that you are wasting 10 per cent more material than you should, but to know that this is occurring over, say, two, three or even more processes, provides no help if you wish to correct the situation. You have no idea from this where you should be directing your attention to correct the situation.

Labour

Again, in the case of labour, we need to know, as far as the efficiency of labour is concerned, which particular group of labour is spending more or less time than was set out in the standard. Suppose again you are a manager told that the efficiency of your labour is better than the standard by, say, two hours. This may well be interesting, but unless you know which area of your labour is saving this time, you can take no effective action to ensure that it continues in the future.

Sales

And third, in the area of sales, once again it is essential to know where the differences are happening. To know that you have in fact improved the volume of sales or that the mix achieved gives you a lower contribution than you would have had if you had stayed within the standard mix set does not help you to control your salesforce. No corrective action can be taken until the differences are more precisely located. Is it happening in this or that product area? Is it taking place in this sales division or that? Can we trace the difference to a particular salesperson? These are the essential questions which must be answered by standard costing in the sales area.

Purpose of standard costing

Standard costing is very much a technique designed to serve the needs of the line manager. You will see in Illustration 11.8 a series of examples

Illustration 11.8 Examples of variances.

Cost:	Variance:
Material	Price
	Usage
Labour	Rate of pay
	Efficiency
Expenditure:	
Variable	Expenditure
Fixed	Activity
	Expenditure
Sales	Price
	Volume
	Mix

of variances which can be extracted to assist managers manage more effectively under each of the main cost and income heads.

It is upon this criteria that standard costing must be judged. Does it enable managers to locate the cause of the differences or variances more quickly, and if so what effective corrective action can they take? The acid test of standard costing is therefore the action it generates.

Variance calculation

Turn now to Illustrations 11.9 and 11.10 and work through the calculations of the variances under each category of expense and sales. Once you have mastered these test your understanding by tackling the similar question set out in Illustration 11.11. Your answers should be compared with Illustration 11.12.

Illustration 11.9 Standard costing variance data.

Calculate the variances which arise from the following data:

Standard product cost for 1 unit

	£
Materials: 30 kg @ 15p/kg	4.50
Labour: 4 hrs @ £1/hr	4.00
Expenses:	
Variable	0.50
Fixed (recovered at 25p/labour hour)	1.00
Standard product cost	10.00
Standard profit	2.00
Standard sales price	£12.00

Budgeted Sales for the month are 10,000 units giving rise to a Budgeted Profit of £20,000.

The actual results for the month were:

		£
Sales: 9,500 units		118,750
Less:		
Materials: 300,000 kg @ 14p/kg	42,000	
Labour: 40,000 hrs @ £1.10	44,000	
Expenses		
Variable	4,800	
Fixed	11,200	102,000
Actual profit		£16,750

Note: There are no stocks.

Illustration 11.10 Standard costing variance analysis.

			£
	Budgeted profit		20,000
Variances	Favourable	Adverse	
(a) Sales – Price	4,750		
– Volume		1,000	
(b) Materials – Price	3,000		
– Usage		2,250	
(c) Labour – Rate		4,000	
– Efficiency		2,000	
Expenses:			
(d) Variable – Expenditure		50	
(e) Fixed – Volume		500	
– Expenditure		1,200	
	7,750	11,000	3,250
Actual profit			£16,750

Workings:

(a) Sales   – Price 9,500 units × £12 – £118,750
           – Volume (10,000 – 9,500) × £2 Profit

(b) Materials – Price (15p – 14p) × 300,000 kg
              – Usage (9,500 × 30 kg) – 300,000 kg × 15p

(c) Labour   – Rates   [(£1.00 – £1.10) × 40,000 hrs
          – Efficiency [(9,500 × 4 hrs) – 40,000 hrs × £1]

(d) Variable   – Expenditure (9,500 × 50p) – £4,800

(e) Fixed   – Volume (40,000 hrs × 25p) – (9,500 × 4 hrs × 25p)
           – Expenditure (10,000 units × £1) – £11,200

Illustration 11.11 Standard costing variance analysis exercise.

Calculate the variances which arise from the following data:

Standard product cost per unit:

		£
Materials	40 kg @ 20p/kg	8.00
Labour	3 hrs @ £5/hr	15.00
Expenses:		
Variable		0.75
Fixed (recovered at £2 per hr)		6.00
Standard product cost		29.75
Standard profit		16.00
Standard sales price		45.75

Budgeted sales for the month are 30,000 units.

Actual results for the month are:		£
Sales: 32,000 units		1,408,000.00
Materials 1,400,000 kg @ 18p/kg	252,000	
Labour 8,800 hrs @ £5.10/hr	448,800	
Expenses:		
Variable	25,600	
Fixed	192,000	918,400.00
Actual profit		£489,600.00

Illustration 11.12   Answers to Illustration 11.11.

			£
Budgeted profit (30,000 units × £16 per unit)			480,000

Variances	Favourable £	Unfavourable £	
(a) Sales – Price		56,000	
– Volume	32,000		
(b) Material – Price	28,000		
– Usage		24,000	
(c) Labour – Rate		8,800	
– Efficiency	40,000		
Expenses:			
(d) Variable – Expenditure		1,600	
(e) Fixed – Volume	12,000		
– Expenditure		12,000	
	112,000	102,400	9,600
Actual profit			£489,600

Workings:

(a) Sales:

Price	£1,408,000 – (32,000 units × £45.75 per unit)	= £56,000 (unfavourable)
Volume	2,000 units × £16.00 per unit	= £32,000 (favourable)

(b) Material:

Price	(20p – 18p) × 1,400,000 kg	= £28,000 (favourable)
Usage	32,000 × 40 kg = 1,280,000 – 1,400,000 × 20p	= £24,000 (unfavourable)

(c) Labour:

Rate	(£5.10p – £5) × 88,000 hrs	= £8,800 (unfavourable)
Efficiency	(32,000 × 3 – 88,000) × £5	= £40,000 (favourable)

(d) Variable expenses:

Expenditure variance (32,000 × 0.75p) – £25,600	= £1,600 (unfavourable)

(e) Fixed expenditure variance:

Volume	(90,000 hrs (= 30,000 units × 3 hrs) × £2) – 32,000 units × £6 per unit	= £12,000 (favourable)
Expenditure (30,000 units × £6) – £192,000		= £12,000 (unfavourable)

Standard stock valuation

It should also be noted that standard costing can be used to establish standard costs not only for the products and services as a whole within a business but also in calculating the standard cost values of stocks in different

Illustration 11.13 Standard cost values for stocks exercise.

Assuming the following standard costs calculate the value of stock held at the end of each stage of production and for finished goods, assuming Stage II completes the production cycle.

Production Stage I:
Standard cost of production

Type of material	Standard quantity	Standard price per kg
X	20 kg	20p
Y	10 kg	10p
Z	5 kg	30p

Labour: 4 standard minutes at 2.5p per standard minute
Overheads: charged at 25p standard labour minute

Production Stage II:
Standard cost of production

Type of material	Standard quantity	Standard price per kg
A	5 kg	10p
B	10 kg	10p

Labour: 8 standard minutes at 25p per standard minute
Overheads: charged at 10p per standard labour minute

Final production stage:
Standard costing of packing:

Materials: standard packing cost 20p
Labour: 2 standard minutes at 50p per standard minute
Overheads: charged at 50p per standard labour minute

Illustration 11.14 Answers to Illustration 11.13.

Production Stage I	£	£	
Materials: X 20 kg @ 20p	4.00		
Y 10 kg @ 10p	1.00		
Z 5 kg @ 30p	1.50	6.50	
Labour: 4 minutes @ 25p		1.00	
Overheads: 25p per labour minute		1.00	
		8.50	Standard Value Stage I

Production Stage II			
Materials: A 5 kg @ 10p	0.50		
B 10 kg @ 10p	1.00	1.50	
Labour: 8 minutes @ 25p		2.00	
Overheads: 10p per labour minute		0.80	
		12.80	Standard Value Stage II

Final Production Stage			
Materials: 1 standard packing cost @ 20p		0.20	
Labour: 2 hours @ 50p		1.00	
Overheads: 50p per labour hour		1.00	
		£15.00	Standard Value Final Stage

Illustration 11.15 Standard cost values for work in progress and finished goods.

Assume the following standard cost data and from this calculate the value of work in progress at the end of Production Stage I and finished goods stock at the end of the finished process.

Production Stage I
Standard cost of production:

Type of material	Standard quantity (tonnes)	Standard price per tonne £
C	10	10
D	8	12
E	4	15

Labour mix	Standard times of labour	Standard rate per hour
D	2	5
E	1	6
F	3	4

Overheads: charged at 40p per total standard labour hours

Final finishing stage:

	Standard quantity	Standard price
Packing material:	1 packing case	£4.00
	1 plastic bag	£1.50

Labour: 0.5 standard hours at £4 per standard hour
Overheads: charged at £2 per standard labour hour

Illustration 11.16 Answers to Illustration 11.15.

Production Stage I:

	Type	Tonne		£	£
Materials:	C	10 @ £10		100.00	
	D	8 @ £12		96.00	
	E	4 @ £15		60.00	256.00
Labour:	D	2 hrs @ £5		10.00	
	E	1 hr @ £6		6.00	
	F	3 hrs @ £12		12.00	28.00
Overheads:		40p × 6 hrs			2.40

Standard value of work in progress per unit at end of Stage I   286.40

Final Finishing Stage:

		£	
Packing materials:	Packing case	4.00	
	Plastic bag	1.50	5.50
Labour: 0.5 hrs @ £4 per hour			2.00
Overheads: charged £2 × 0.50 hour			1.00
Standard value of finished goods per unit			£294.90

stages of production. This application of standard costing is set out in Illustrations 11.13 and 11.14 and should be studied carefully. Then test your knowledge by tackling the question set out in Illustration 11.15, comparing your answer with Illustration 11.16.

Standard Cost Profit and Loss Account

Finally, turn to Illustration 11.17 which sets out how, once standards and budgets have been established for a business, they can be used to prepare a Standard Cost Profit and Loss Account. The illustration shows that this Standard Cost Profit and Loss Account can then be compared with the actual Profit and Loss Account results once they are known so that the variances can be reviewed in detail and in total.

Illustration 11.17 Standard Costing Profit and Loss Account.

		£000
Budgeted sales		400
Less: Volume variance		10
Standard sales value of actual sales in standard mix		390
Less: Standard cost of such standard sales		240
Standard net profit of such standard sales		150

		Adverse	Favourable	
		−	+	
Variances		£000	£000	
Sales:	Price	5		
	Mix	2		
Materials:	Price	3		
	Usage		2	
Labour:	Rate	1		
	Efficiency		1	
Variables expenses:				
	Expenditure		1	
Fixed expenses:				
	Expenditure		1	
	Activity	2	−	
		13	5	8
Actual net profit				£142

Summary

Standard costing is the second of the two comparative techniques used in business finance. The first is concerned with the overall comparison between the budget set for the business as a whole, together with its individual functions and departments, with the actual results as and when they are known and is referred to as budgetary control.

The second is concerned with the analyses of the variances, tracing them to their causes so that effective corrective action can be taken speedily and effectively. This technique is known as standard costing.

Conclusion

We have now completed our study of the evolution of financial information, starting as we did from the three primary financial measurements of profit in the Profit and Loss Account, investment in the Balance Sheet, and cash in the Cash Flow Forecast. We have seen that from these have been developed the techniques of *costing* which helps us to analyse where the profit or loss is being made, *project appraisal* which helps us to examine before committing ourselves to investments in fixed assets and other areas where money will be tied up whether or not the investment is worthwhile and will lead to business profit, and *working capital control* which helps us to analyse time and therefore minimise the amount invested in this area.

We also saw when we examined the Cash Flow Forecast how out of this statement information can be summarised so as to express the central problem regarding cash as a whole within any business. Are the sources equal to or less than the applications of such cash? In other words, is the business living within or beyond its means?

And finally, we have just completed our studies of the comparative techniques of budgetary control and standard costing.

We are now ready to complete our understanding of business finance by studying the approach to and the techniques available for interpreting the information presented.

12 | THE INTERPRETATION OF FINANCIAL INFORMATION

Introduction

We now come to the final step we must take in understanding business finance, the one step possibly everyone would like to take at the very beginning – the interpretation of financial information. However, as was said in the very first chapter, financial information does not provide answers, only better questions, and these in turn presuppose knowledge. It is for this reason that interpretation must wait until the end. We have to know and understand what is available and from this draw logical conclusions – and, in many instances, pose further questions – and this is what is meant by the interpretation of financial information.

In other words there is no simple procedure to enable anyone to interpret. It is the result of all the knowledge that has been gained along the way in understanding the information presented and the techniques which are involved. There are in fact three steps set out in Illustration 12.1 which must be taken by anyone wishing to interpret financial information, each of which we shall discuss in turn.

Step 1: Data must be understood

The first step of all is to understand what we are looking at – what is available. What can never be over-stressed is that there is absolutely no possibility of interpreting information unless we fully understand it. It is indeed this failure to understand financial data which so often creates an inability to interpret its content – and this means a *complete* understanding. It is impossible to interpret financial data if it is only partially understood. For instance, if we understand only part of the Balance Sheet it means that we will never be able to interpret it. Or if we only understand part of the costing data presented we will never be able to interpret and

Illustration 12.1   Steps in interpreting financial data.

Step 1: The data must be **understood**.

Step 2: The data must be **organised** using: – Source and Application Summaries
                                                 – Full and marginal cost analysis
                                                 – Breakeven analysis etc.

Step 3: The data must be **measured** using: – Applied common sense
                                                – Ratio analysis.

   Only then can data be **interpreted**.

therefore use its contents – or if we do the consequences could be very dangerous indeed.

You can see therefore that unless you approach financial information with total honesty as to the extent of your knowledge, you will be unable to use it effectively. And what is meant by honesty in this context is whether or not there is an understanding of everything that is presented. For instance, if you have any feelings whatsoever that there are any terms or facts presented within the data which are beyond your understanding, questions must be raised and answers sought.

It must always be remembered that there is a basic problem with financial understanding which is that people do not wish to admit ignorance. They are very often inclined to hide this from other people and it is this deception which in many cases can be highly dangerous – and certainly counter-productive as far as interpretation is concerned. In finance it is essential that you understand everything presented to you, and to appreciate that even the simplest terms may require fresh definitions so as to overcome any confusion.

Throughout our previous discussions on finance we have mentioned the fact that there are many areas of confusion caused by inconsistencies and duplications regarding the meaning and use of terms. You might call it duplicate and in some cases even triplicate jargon! For example, consider the confusion regarding the words fixed assets and capital expenditure, which as you now know mean the same thing. Or sales which are often described as turnover or in some industries revenues, meaning the sales made during a period of time whether paid for or not.

We must also appreciate that within any particular business there may well be 'domestic' jargon, terms used which are not used in their usually accepted way. We must also realise that there are very few legal definitions of financial terms and for this reason a clear definition must be sought whenever there is doubt. Indeed it was to create the necessary confidence to ask questions when in doubt which formed a main purpose of many of the earlier chapters.

Step 2: Organise data

Now having understood what you are looking at, the next step is to make sure it is properly organised. Before anyone can interpret information it is vital that the information itself is first sorted out.

For instance, if you turn to Illustration 12.2 you will see a Profit and Loss Account set out for a manufacturing business for a particular year compared with last. If you look at this illustration you will see that before the reorganisation of the data very strange conclusions could be drawn. For instance, it would look very much as if the expenses as a percentage of sales were going down from 17.5 to 15.0 per cent. However, if we rearrange the information as set out in Illustration 12.3 and divide the expenses between those which are variable and those which are fixed, we find that variable expenses as a percentage of sales are in fact going up to 5 per cent, whereas if they had remained truly variable they should have been constant at 3.5 per cent.

We can also see that the fixed expenses have certainly not remained fixed as they have gone up from £448,000 to £500,000. This may be explainable, but the fact that the percentage comparison from 14 to 10 looks as if fixed expenses are being well controlled is a false conclusion. If this point escapes you refer back to your studies on the Profit and Loss Account in Chapter 2 and those on marginal costing in Chapter 7.

Illustration 12.2 'A' Manufacturing Co.: Profit and Loss Account. Profit and Loss Accounts for year 1 and year 2.

		Year 2			Year 1	
	£000	£000	%	£000	£000	%
Sales		5,000	100		3,200	100
Less:						
Materials	2,500		50	1,600		50
Labour	1,250		25	800		25
Expenses	750	4,500	15	560	2,960	17.5
Profit		£500	10		£240	7.5

Illustration 12.3 'A' Manufacturing Co.: rearranged Profit and Loss Account. Profit and Loss Accounts for year 1 and year 2.

		Year 2			Year 1	
	£000	£000	%	£000	£000	%
Sales		5,000	100		3,200	100
Less:						
Materials	2,500		50	1,600		50.0
Labour	1,250		25	800		25.0
Variable expenses	250	4,000	5	112	2,512	3.5
Contribution		1,000	20		688	21.5
Fixed expenses		500	10		448	14.0
Profit		£500	10		£240	7.5

All this illustrates the fact that before we organise information we might well draw wrong conclusions.

The Source and Application of Funds Statement

We have many techniques that we use for organising information. For instance, the presentation of changes in investment and their funding by means of the Source and Application of Funds Statement is very much for the purpose of organising the data so that we can obtain greater meaning.

To illustrate this point look at Illustration 12.4 which shows the Balance Sheet of a company B Ltd. This sets out this year's figures together with those of last. If you then turn to Illustration 12.5 you will see that the differences between these figures are set out as a Source and Application of Funds Statement.

This reorganising of the Balance Sheet allows us to see that during the present year the business has raised cash for investment amounting to £170,000 from the following sources: from internal sources retained profits plus depreciation £90,000, and from external sources a new issue of share capital plus new borrowings of £70,000 and £10,000 from the sale of investments. We can also see how this money was invested in fixed assets £120,000 and working capital of £70,000, a total of £190,000. This

Illustration 12.4 B Ltd: Balance Sheet as at 31 December.

Last year				This year	
£	£		£	£	£
		Fixed assets			
	120,000	Land and buildings		170,000	
210,000	90,000	Plant and machinery		110,000	280,000
170,000		Investments			160,000
		Working capital			
		Current assets:	£		
	90,000	Stock	150,000		
	120,000	Debtors	160,000		
	40,000	Cash/bank	20,000	330,000	
	250,000				
		Less:			
		Current liabilities:			
150,000	100,000	Creditors		130,000	200,000
£530,000					£640,000
		Financed by:			
	300,000	Share capital			350,000
	160,000	Profit and Loss Account			200,000
	70,000	Loans			90,000
£530,000					£640,000

Note: Depreciation on plant and machinery for the year is £50,000.

Illustration 12.5 B Ltd: Source and Application of Funds Statement.

		£
Source of funds		
Retained profit		40,000
Add back: Depreciation		50,000
		90,000
Share capital		50,000
Loan capital		20,000
Sale of investments		10,000
	Sub-total A	£170,000

	£
Application of funds	
Purchase of fixed assets	
Land and buildings	50,000
Plant and machinery	70,000
	120,000

Movement in working capital:

	Source £	Application £		
Stock		60,000		
Debtors		40,000		
Creditors	30,000			
	£30,000	£100,000	70,000	
		Sub-total B	£190,000	
		Negative cash flow	£20,000	(A − B)

means that part of this increase in investment has been paid for by reducing the company's bank and cash balances by £20,000, referred to as a negative cash flow.

We can also see from this that the amount of money invested in such areas as plant and machinery, office equipment, motor vehicles, etc., does not bear any relationship to the amount held back as depreciation. This in itself may not be a very important point but if we could see this analysis over the years, let us say over the last five years, it might well raise questions as to whether or not the business is keeping up with the investment required in such items. After all, as depreciation is based on the historical values of the fixed assets, you would expect the amount invested in such things to be more, that the amount invested would in fact exceed depreciation over the long term to take into account new technology, expansion and inflationary price adjustments.

We can also see from the Source and Application of Funds Statement set out in Illustration 12.5 the increase in the amount being invested in working capital. Here again, because of the reorganisation of this information, it becomes clear to us that there are increasing amounts being put into stocks and debtors and also that the business is being financed to some extent by increasing its creditors, the time it takes to pay its bills.

Again, this in itself is not conclusive evidence of things going right or wrong but it does lead us to further questions. For instance, were these increases in investments planned? Did we intend to invest all this money in these areas, or is it accidental? Again, is it to do with inflation, or is it to do with increased sales volumes? After all, if sales increase a business may well have to hold more stocks and finance more debtors or receivables. Inflation may also create a need for more investment as we shall see later in this chapter. All these are questions that can be raised once we reorganise the information in this way.

However, as well as examining where the money has come from and how these funds have been invested, the Source and Application of Funds Statements tell us more. It tells us the overall fact as to whether the business has lived beyond or within its means. In Illustration 12.5 the business has created funds of £90,000 from its own operations of profit plus depreciation, and from share issues, loans and the sale of investment funds of £80,000, a total of £170,000. However, it has invested, £120,000 in fixed assets and £70,000 in working capital, a total of £190,000. So it has 'lived beyond its means' to the tune of £20,000 and this is reflected in its cash and bank balances being reduced by £20,000.

There may of course be nothing wrong in this but it certainly calls for questions as to the effect of this reduction in liquid funds within the business. Again, if the reverse situation arose and the business invested less than the funds created the question would be – what is it doing with the surplus funds this would create?

Organising information does not of course give us answers but it does raise more searching questions. We must therefore realise that it is vital to organise information before interpretation can successfully take place.

The added value link

At this stage we could also look at the reorganisation of information in the form of the link between the creation of wealth and its distribution set out in the Profit and Loss Account, and its investment set out in the Balance Sheet.

This can be done by re-summarising the Profit and Loss Account in the form of an Added Value Statement. If you turn to Illustration 12.6 you will see an example of an Added Value Statement in which the added value is calculated at £60m – the difference between the sales for the year of £100m, and the input or 'outsiders'' costs of materials and bought-in services such as rent, heat and light, insurance, etc., which have gone into the cost of the goods we have sold, amounting to £40m.

Illustration 12.6   G Ltd: Added Value Statement for year ended 31 December.

	£000
Sales	100
Less:	
Materials and bought-in services	40
Added value	60

Distribution of added value:

Employee costs	20	⎫
Dividends	10	⎬ Needs of today
Interest	5	⎪
Taxation	10	⎭
Depreciation	5	⎫ Needs of tomorrow
Retained profits	10	⎭
	60	

Amount available for reinvestment:

Retained profits	10	
Depreciation	5	⎛ For reinvestment
	15	⎨ in fixed assets
		⎝ and working capital

Analysis of added value

We then see that of this £60m added value, £20m has gone into the wages and salaries due to the people employed within the business, that £15m has been set aside as interest and dividends on the money invested by shareholders and lenders, and that £10m is being deducted for taxation on the profits.

We can therefore see from this summary that the amount of money generated within the business during the year for reinvestment in fixed assets, working capital and outside investments or left to increase the cash and bank balances is £15m. This is created by £5m depreciation plus £10m retained profits.

This add-back of depreciation is caused by the fact that although depreciation reduces the profit or increases the loss shown in the Profit and Loss Account it does not affect the cash held or owed by the business. Indeed the purpose of depreciation, as you will remember from Chapter 2, is to reduce the amount that otherwise could be distributed as dividends, this latter amount being limited to the profit shown less taxation. It is because depreciation does not reduce the cash held that the funds created for investment, when profits are made, are the total of profits retained plus the depreciation deducted before calculating such profits.

From the Added Value Statement we can examine the amount of funds the business has generated for reinvestment and see how it compares with previous years. We can also examine the proportion which has been paid out as 'rewards' as dividends to shareholders, as wages and salaries to employees, or as taxes to the government.

All this can be seen in relationship to the total added value created and can be compared from year to year. For instance, in Illustration 12.6 wages and salaries are one third of the added value and this could be compared with previous years. The added value can indeed be said to be what the business creates for itself as it represents the difference between what it sells its products, merchandise or services for and what the input costs of these were.

Added value is sometimes used as a measurement of efficiency by comparing the added value per £1 of wages and salaries or numbers of employees employed. In Illustration 12.6 this reads £3 of added value per £1 of employees' costs, which if set against a budget of, say, £2.75 would show an improvement. However, if the added value were divided by the numbers employed, and assuming the budget was set based on £1,500 per employee, then if the actual employees for the year were 55,000, the added value per employee would be approximately £1,100 – a deterioration from budget. This latter comparison has advantages over the former when technology allows the numbers employed to be reduced whilst wages per employee increase. Both these measurements can be usefully compared from one period to another so that the trend can be examined.

At the same time we can see from the Added Value Statement the relationship between the amount invested in fixed assets and the amount being held back, both as depreciation and retained profits. This will show the proportion of such investment financed from these sources and again comparison with previous periods will show the trend.

Once again in the case of the Added Value Statement we are looking at information which does not give us answers but helps us to organise the information in such a way as to pose further and better questions.

Added value also focuses attention on the fact that much of a business's investment has to be financed not from outside but inside sources. Indeed once a business is in existence by far the majority of its future investment will have just one source – its own self-generated funds, funds created by the retention of profit and what is held back as depreciation. This means that the health of a business depends not only upon its creation of profit but its division, between what is taken out to reward its employees, investors and the whole community through taxation and what is left in for reinvestment.

Current cost accounting

It is in the judgement of what is needed for reinvestment that led accountants some years ago to consider the problem of inflation and how this should be accounted for in the division of profits. What became clear was that when inflation begins to rise above, say, 10 per cent, the amount required to replace a business's fixed assets and to maintain the same level of investment in its working capital begins to increase, not because the business is buying more fixed assets or increasing its real investment in working capital but simply because prices are rising. In other words during periods of inflation a business needs more money invested in it not to get bigger but just to stand still!

However, a problem arises when you look to see from where such extra money 'needed to stand still' is going to come. For instance, very few people will want to put money into a business for this purpose whether they are potential new shareholders or bankers lending money. It is because of this fact that accountants suggested a way of accounting termed current cost accounting which would highlight this problem and suggest a solution. This was that whatever profits are generated at such times which would otherwise have been classed as distributable – available to take out as dividends – should be reduced by three adjustments. These are set out in Illustration 12.7 and the calculations for them are detailed in Illustration 12.8. The three adjustments are concerned with:

(a) *Additional depreciation* to account for the increased cost of replacing fixed assets.
(b) *The cost of sales* to account for the increased investment required to maintain the same quantity of stocks at increased prices.
(c) *The monetary working capital adjustment* to account for a similar increase in the investment in the credit given less credit taken to maintain the same level of sales and purchases.

Illustration 12.9 sets out these three adjustments needs within the context of the business model. The amounts calculated in Illustration 12.7 total £10.05m and represent the additional investment needed to keep this business at the same level of activity. As can be seen from this illustration when such adjustments have been made the amount calculated is referred

Illustration 12.7 A Ltd: extract from Profit and Loss Account for year ended 31 December.

		£000
Profit calculated in normal way		40,000
Current cost accounting adjustments:		
	£000	
Additional depreciation	5,000	
Cost of sales	2,167	
Monetary working capital	2,883	10,050
Current cost profit		£29,950

to as the current cost profit or loss. Its purpose is to highlight how much of the profit which would otherwise be shown in Illustration 12.7 as a profit of £40m represents true growth, in this case £29.95m – in other words how much should be retained to maintain the present level of investment, which in this case is £10.05m.

Current cost accounting was tried experimentally for some three years in the United Kingdom, but since 1982 it has no longer had any widespread use. However, the need to maintain and preserve investment remains, together with the questions as to whether or not the right balance is being held between retention and distribution of profits. It is for this reason that the reorganisation of the Profit and Loss Account by means of Added Value Statements, and an appreciation of the principles which underlie current cost accounting are necessary requirements for those engaged in the interpretation of financial data.

Illustration 12.8 Calculations for Illustration 12.7.

	Historical cost £000	Replacement cost £000
Fixed assets subject to depreciation	50,000	75,000
Annual depreciation based on writing off over 5 years	10,000	15,000
Additional depreciation		£5,000

Cost of sales adjustment

	Historical value £000	Price index	Mid-year value £000
Opening stock	10,000	100	$= 10,000,000 \times \dfrac{110}{100} = 11,000$
Mid-year index	—	110	—
Closing stock	14,000	120	$= 14,000,000 \times \dfrac{110}{120} = 12,833$
	£4,000		£1,833
Cost of sales adjustment		£4,000 – £1,833	= £2,167

Monetary working capital adjustment

	Historical value £000	Price index	Mid-year value £000
Opening debtors *less* Creditors	130,000	100	$= 13,000,000 \times \dfrac{110}{100} = 14,300$
Mid-year index	—	110	—
Closing debtors *less* Creditors	19,000	120	$= 19,000,000 \times \dfrac{110}{120} = 17,417$
Difference	£6,000		£3,117
Monetary working capital adjustment		£6,000 – £3,117	= £2,883

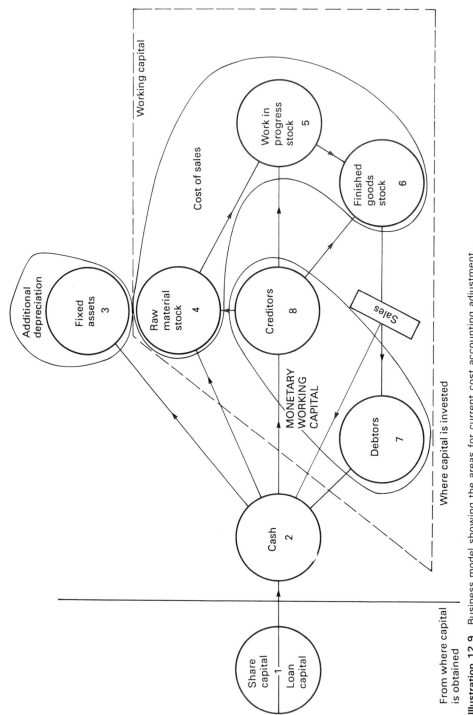

Illustration 12.9 Business model showing the areas for current cost accounting adjustment.

Revision

We have therefore seen that in the approach to interpretation the first two steps are first that we must understand the information that we are looking at, and second in many situations we may need the information itself to be reorganised. Illustrations 12.10, 12.11 and 12.12 set out a series of statements which require reorganisation to provide the fullest possible value to

Illustration 12.10   Reorganisation exercise 1.

Reorganise the following Profit and Loss Statement in a way which you feel may aid interpretation.

	£000	£000	£000
Sales			8,000
Cost of sales:			
Factory:			
Material	3,000		
Labour	1,000		
Variable expenses	640		
Fixed expenses	560	5,200	
Sales:			
Commission	800		
Variable expenses	400		
Fixed expenses	100	1,300	
Administration:			
Variable expenses	160		
Fixed expenses	140	300	6,800
		Profit	£1,200

Illustration 12.11   Reorganisation exercise 2.

Reorganise the following Balance Sheets in a way which will show the movements of funds.

		Year 2 £m		Year 1 £m
Fixed assets		200		170
Outside investments		100		60
Working capital				
Stock	60		30	
Debtors	40		25	
Cash	10		10	
	110		65	
Less: Current liabilities				
Creditors	60	50	30	35
		£350		£265
Share capital		150		125
Reserves		100		60
Loan capital		100		80
		£350		£265

someone concerned with interpretation. Try to reorganise these in your own way and compare your answers with those set out as suggestions in Illustrations 12.13, 12.14 and 12.15.

Illustration 12.12 Reorganisation exercise 3.

Reorganise the following Profit and Loss Statement to show how wealth was created and distributed in the year.

	£000	£000
Sales		7,500
Less: Materials	2,500	
Labour	1,500	
Expenses	1,000	
Salaries	500	
Depreciation	200	
Interest paid	300	6,000
Profit before tax		1,500
Taxation		750
Profit after tax		750
Dividends		250

Illustration 12.13 Suggested answer to Illustration 12.10.

Reorganised Profit and Loss Statement:

	£000	£000	£000	%
Sales			8,000	100
Less: Direct costs				
Factory:				
Material	3,000			
Labour	1,000			
Variable expenses	640		4,640	
Prime contribution			3,360	42
Sales:				
Commission	800			
Variable expenses	400	1,200		
Administration:				
Variable expenses		160	1,360	
Net contribution			2,000	25
Less:				
Fixed expenses				
Factory		560		
Sales		100		
Administration		140	800	
Profit			£1,200	15

Illustration 12.14   Suggested answer to
Illustration 12.11.

Reorganised Balance Sheets:

Source and Application of Funds Statement

Source of funds		£m
Retained profit		40
Add back: Depreciation		10
		50
Share capital		25
Loan capital		20
		95

Application of funds		
Purchase of fixed assets		40
Increase in outside investments		40

Movements in working capital

	Source	Application	
Stock	—	30	
Debtors	—	15	
Cash	—	—	
Creditors	30	—	
	30	45	15
			95

Illustration 12.15   Suggested answer to Illustration
12.12.

Reorganised Profit and Loss Statement:

Added Value Summary

		£000	%
Sales		7,500	100
Less: Input materials	2,500		
And services	1,000	3,500	47
Added value		£4,000	53

Analysis of added value:	£000	%
Wages and salaries	2,000	50
Depreciation	200	5
Interest paid	300	8
Taxation	750	19
Dividends	250	6
Retained profit	500	12
	£4,000	100

Amount available for reinvestment:	£000
Depreciation	200
Retained profit	500
	£700

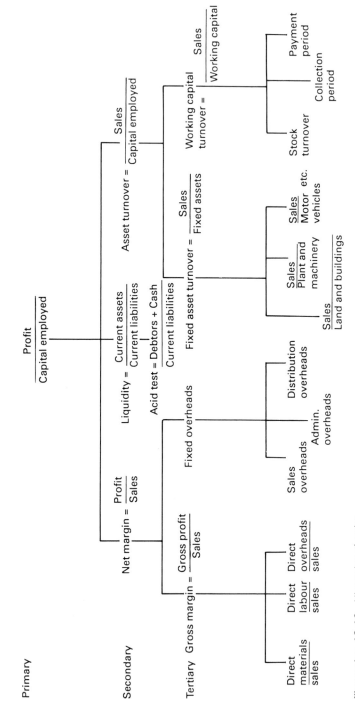

Illustration 12.16   Hierarchy of ratios.

Step 3: The measurement

Having discussed the first two steps that must be taken in the approach to interpretation, we now come to the third – the measurement of the information itself. Once we have understood and reorganised the financial data we need then to measure it and to do that we have two major devices: applied common sense and ratio analysis. Of the two, the most important is applied common sense. However, before we find out how we can use this, we will first consider the use of financial ratios.

Financial ratios

Financial ratios, as they are known, are the indices used in expressing financial data in such a way that it can be compared. Ratios may be expressed as percentages or as indices or even as ratios! However, in each case their purpose is to create data which can be used for comparison purposes, comparison which can be examined and from which questions may be raised. Illustration 12.16 sets out the main ratios in what might be termed their hierarchical order whilst Illustration 12.17 provides a summary explanation of each ratio.

Illustration 12.17   Ratio analysis.

Primary ratio
  – *Return on net assets*: Earnings before interest and taxation/Net assets (i.e. Fixed assets *plus* Current assets *less* Current liabilities)

Secondary ratios
  – *Profit margin*: Earnings before interest and tax/Sales
  – *Asset turnover*: Sales/Net assets

Tertiary ratios
  – *Profit/Expenses control*:
    – Gross profit/Sales
    – Variable expense/Sales
    – Fixed expense/Sales
    – Fixed expense/Budget
  – *Use of assets*:
    – Fixed assets/Sales
    – Working capital/Sales

Financial status ratios
  – *Liquidity/Current ratio*: Current assets/Current liabilities
  – *Acid test*: Cash + Debtors/Current liabilities

Working capital/Collection ratio
  – *Stock Turnover*: Sales/Stock
  – *Collection period*: Debtors/Sales × 365 = days
  – *Payment period*: Creditors/Purchases or Cost of Sales × 365 = days

Solvency ratios
  – *Gearing ratio*: Long-term debts/Capital employed
  – *Interest cover*: Profits before interest and tax/Interest

The primary ratio

From the illustrations it can be seen that the primary or number one ratio is profit (or return as it is often called) normally for the year related to capital employed (or net assets as it might alternatively be described) used during the same period. This is the primary measurement for all investment anywhere and in business we start from this self-same point.

The secondary ratios

We then see that to investigate this more fully we have two secondary ratios: the one concerned with profitability – profit in relation to sales – and the other with activity – sales in relation to capital employed or net assets.

The tertiary ratios

Again having struck these secondary ratios, we may wish to take our studies further. You can see how from the secondary ratios we can expand these into the tertiary ratios.

Profitability

Here you can see how profitability might be studied from the point of view of gross profit to sales as a percentage and the individual fixed overhead categories as amounts. You should recall this approach to examining profit and expenses by revising your studies in Chapter 2. Again, if we feel it useful, we could look at the contribution to sales prices of each of the individual products and merchandise sold or services rendered, and again if this point is unclear revise your studies on marginal costing in Chapter 7.

Activity

At the same time we could extend our examination of activity by comparing sales separately with fixed assets and working capital. This will reveal how many times we are turning over our investment in these two areas in relation to the sales for the period – in most cases the year. We can also in this situation break this activity ratio down to its constituent parts as suggested in Illustration 12.16.

Financial status ratios

It can also be seen that in addition to ratios concerned with profitability and activity there are those that help us study a business's financial status: the business's ability to pay its liabilities – its bills – and whether this ability is changing because of design or necessity.

Liquidity ratio

In this area we start with the overall ratio discussed when we looked at the relationship of current assets to current liabilities in Chapter 3. We also see how this can then be looked at more pragmatically or immediately by means of what is termed the acid test or quick ratio. In this we only bring into account the more liquid current assets such as the debtors or receivables and cash and bank balances before dividing them by the current liabilities. We therefore leave out stocks from this more immediate measurement.

Stock turnover, collection and payment ratios

We can also see in Illustration 12.17 that because liquidity is closely connected with working capital and its control we have three ratios concerned with stock turnover and the collection and payment periods relating to debtors and creditors. It is these three ratios that need to be read in conjunction with the liquidity ratios to see whether stocks are being controlled and credit policies altered.

Solvency ratios

Again the financial status of a business including its ability to meet its liabilities may well be affected by its gearing, the 'pressure' under which it is operating you will remember from Chapter 1. In Illustration 12.17 we set out the calculation of the gearing ratio and associated with this is the interest cover. This looks at the ability of the business to meet the interest due from the profits available for this purpose.

A worked example

Having studied the hierarchy of ratios in Illustration 12.16 with their explanations in Illustration 12.17 turn to Illustrations 12.18 and 12.19 which set out the Profit and Loss Account and the Balance Sheets for four years for a particular business. From these statements the appropriate ratios are calculated and set out in Illustration 12.20. These should be studied carefully so that you become familiar with their calculation.

Illustration 12.18   Summarised Profit and Loss Accounts for the year ending 31 December.

	Year 1 £000		Year 2 £000		Year 3 £000		Year 4 £000	
Sales		1,440		1,600		2,000		2,400
Less:								
Cost of goods sold		800		1,000		1,200		1,520
Gross profit		640		600		800		880
Selling expenses	160		190		240			
Admin. expenses (inc. 10% loan interest)	220		240		200			
Depreciation	120		130		140			
Miscellaneous expenses	20	520	20	580	20	600		700
Net profit before tax		120		20		200		180
Corporation tax (50%)		60		10		100		90
Net profit after tax		60		10		100		90
Retained profit b/f		240		280		260		300
		300		290		360		390
Dividends paid	1.4p per share	20	1.9p per share	30	3.8p per share	60	1.5p per share	70
Retained profit c/f		£280		£260		£300		£320
Market value of share at Balance Sheet date		60p		50p		65p		49p

Illustration 12.19 Summarised Balance Sheets as at 31 December.

	Year 1 £000		Year 2 £000		Year 3 £000		Year 4 £000	
Fixed assets								
Land and buildings		1,100		1,260		1,120		1,320
Plant and machinery		240		240		220		340
Motor vehicles		40		20		80		120
		1,380		1,520		1,420		1,780
Current assets								
Stock	600		640		840		840	
Debtors	480		500		640		800	
Cash at bank	180		140		100		180	
	1,260		1,280		1,580		1,820	
Less: Current liabilities								
Creditors	240		260		300		440	
Accruals	60		70		100		130	
Taxation	60		10		100		90	
	360		340		500		660	
Net current assets		900		940		1,080		1,160
Total assets *less* Current liabilities		2,280		2,460		2,500		2,940
Less: Amount due in more than 12 months								
Loans		600		600		600		600
		£1,680		£1,860		£1,900		£2,340
Capital and reserves								
Share capital								
Authorised and issued £1 Ordinary shares fully paid		1,400		1,600		1,600		1,600
Retained profits		280		260		300		320
Shareholders' funds		£1,680		£1,860		£1,900		£2,340

Illustration 12.20 Ratio analysis from data in Illustrations 12.18 and 12.19.

	Year 1	Year 2	Year 3	Year 4
Performance:				
Primary	180:2,280	80:2,460	260:2,500	240:2,940
Secondary:	7.9%	3.3%	10.4%	8.2%
PM	180:1,440	80:1,600	260:2,000	240:2,400
	12.5%	5%	13%	10%
AT	1,440:2,280	1,600:2,460	2,000:2,500	2,400:2,940
	0.63	0.65	0.8	0.82
Liquidity:				
Current	1,260:360	1,280:340	1,580:500	1,820:660
	3.5 times	3.76	3.16	2.76
Acid	660:360	640:340	740:500	980:660
	1.8 times	1.9	1.5	1.5
Tax	All 50%			
Solvency:				
Gearing	600:2,280	600:2,460	600:2,500	600:2,940
	26%	24%	24%	20%
Interest cover	180:60	80:60	260:60	240:60
	3 times	1.3	4.3	4
Control of working capital:				
Stock turnover	1,440:600	1,600:640	2,000:840	2,400:840
	2.4 times	2.5	2.4	2.9
Collection period	1,440:480	1,600:500	2,000:640	2,400:800
	122 days	114	117	122
Payment period	800:240	1,000:260	1,200:300	1,520:440
	110 days	95	91	106
Investment:				
Return on equity	60:1,680	10:1,860	100:1,900	90:2,340
	4%	1%	5%	4%
Earnings per share	60:1,400	10:1,600	100:1,600	90:2,020
	4.3p	0.6p	6.3p	4.5p
Price/Earnings ratio	60p:4.3p	50p:0.6p	65p:6.3p	49p:4.5p
	13.9	83	10.3	10.9
Dividend yield	1.4p:60p	1.9p:50p	3.8:65p	3.5p:49p
	2.3%	3.8%	5.8%	7.4%
Dividend cover	4.3p:1.4p	0.6p:1.9p	6.3p:3.8p	4.5p:3 5p
	3.1	0.3	1.7	1.3
Use of assets:				
Fixed assets/Sales	1,380:1,440	1,520:1,600	1,420:2,000	1,780:2,400
	96	95	71	74
WC/Sales	900:1,440	940:1,800	1,080:2,000	1,160:2,400
	62	59	54	48
Expense control:				
GP/Sales	640:1,440	600:1,600	800:2,000	880:2,400
	44%	38%	40%	37%
Fixed expenses/Sales	520:1,440	580:1,600	600:2,000	700:2,400
	36%	36%	30%	29%

Investment ratios

Return on equity
Finally we need to be aware that, as well as management requirements, we have those of investors. These are, of course, identical but there are certain key areas which are of particular importance to investors. These are set out in Illustration 12.21 and begin with return on equity which confines its view to the profits belonging to the shareholders. The profit after tax and interest is then related to the shareholders' funds – the share capital plus all retained profits and reserves. Using the ratio formula set out in Illustration 12.21 together with the figures presented in Illustrations 12.18 and 12.19 you can see this ratio calculated in Illustration 12.20.

Earnings per share
Next in Illustration 12.21 we come to what is often considered the central measurement of profitability from an investor's point of view, the earnings per share. It is this ratio which companies try to better year by year and calls for the effort of the whole enterprise to improve what is termed 'the bottom line'. The bottom line is the profit after tax and interest or in other words that profit which belongs to the shareholders. The calculation for this ratio is set out in Illustration 12.20 and is again based on data introduced in Illustrations 12.18 and 12.19.

Price/earnings
In Illustration 12.21 the earnings per share calculation is followed by the ratio which expresses the multiple, the number of times the price of the share exceeds the earnings per share. It is this ratio which is set out for companies with stock exchange quotations in what is termed the P/E column in the financial press. The calculation is made by dividing the company's earnings per share, which stays constant for its financial year, into the share price which is based on the daily transactions in its shares. Again the calculation of this ratio is set out in Illustration 12.20.

The net earnings value
If therefore the ratio or multiple rises or falls for a particular company this

Illustration 12.21   Investment ratios.

Return on equity:	Profit after tax and interest/Shareholders' funds (Share capital *plus* Retained profits and Reserves)
Earnings per share:	Profit after tax and interest/Number of issued shares
Price/earnings ratio:	Market price per share/Earnings per share
Dividend yield:	Dividend per share/Market price per share
Dividend cover:	Earnings per share/Dividends per share

Illustration 12.22 Net earnings valuation.

Profits for year   = £70,000
P/E ratio   = £10
Net earnings value of business = £70,000 × 10
                               = £700,000

indicates the popularity or otherwise of its shares in relationship to its last declared profits figures. It also indicates that if a company was purchased, based on its earnings, a value could be calculated from this price/earnings ratio (P/E). This is arrived at by multiplying its profits after tax and interest by the P/E multiple. This calculation can be seen in Illustration 12.22.

Dividend yield
However, as well as profitability investors are concerned with comparing their rewards – the dividends paid to them – with the market price of their shares. This comparison is what is termed the dividend yield and in a sense brings the dividend paid into perspective. What it represents is a return on the real value of the investment made, and an example of this is also included in Illustration 12.20.

Dividend cover
Finally there is the concern by investors regarding generosity, in other words finding out what proportion of the profits available for distribution have in fact been distributed. This is calculated by means of the dividend cover ratio. The higher the cover the greater the retention; the lower the greater the distribution. An example of this ratio is included with the other investors' ratios in Illustration 12.20.

You need to be fully familiar with the logic of ratios, stemming as they do from the primary through to the tertiary measurements, and with how liquidity must also be studied as central to the health of an enterprise. We must remember that a business can be heading for a profit and achieving the right investment activity but it may still have a cash or liquidity problem. At the same time, because managers are wholly responsible for the investment of money to investors, it is equally important for them to become conversant with those ratios that particularly concern investors. Having therefore explained what ratios are and how they are calculated let us consider their use.

Use of financial ratios

Ratios are particularly important when building up those questions which are vital if financial information is to be correctly interpreted. Such interpretation must never be based upon snap judgements. Ratios should be used so as to build up and summarise the evidence available and from this create a picture from which, not conclusions, but better questions can be drawn.

Ratios have a very particular part to play in summarising financial data so as to produce the right questions. It must always be remembered that they in themselves do not in any way provide answers, but they do give much better questions. We use ratios rather as detectives use questions in sorting out alibis – we have therefore got to use the same care when reviewing ratios as good detectives use with the evidence on which they assess the alibis in a particular case.

For example, if a detective asks the husband of a murdered wife where he was at the time of the murder, the husband might give as a reply that he was taking their dog for a walk. This is in a way like the first ratio that we might strike when looking at financial data. However, like good detectives this would not be enough on its own. Detectives would seek corroboration. For instance, they might well seek the evidence of people who may have been along the route of the walk, the newsagent, for example, on the corner. They might ask her 'Did you see the husband taking his dog for a walk?' Now the newsagent may say 'yes' and of course the detective must therefore look at that piece of information with care because, on the face of it, it certainly does corroborate the husband's statement. However, it may also have been given in order to help the husband's case because the newsagent and the husband may be in league. Perhaps the wife has not paid her paper bill and this has made the newsagent rather annoyed with her! On the other hand, the newsagent may say 'no', but again this does not disprove the husband's evidence because it may be that the newsagent herself was engaged in the evil act!

In just the same way the evidence of ratios must be very carefully used. It is important to decide when using ratios what should be taken as the minimum number of periods for that information. For instance, if one is looking at the annual results of a company, one would look for a minimum of three years, and preferably five, before drawing any real conclusions based on ratios.

This is equally true if one is looking at short period statements like cost summaries. Again you would want to take a minimum number before you could use ratios as evidence in creating a satisfactory judgement based on trends.

It cannot be over-emphasised that ratios simply 'spark off' intelligent questions. A great number of errors have been made by people who leapt to conclusions with insufficient evidence. Indeed ill-informed people using ratios sometimes suggest that they in themselves provide answers whereas in fact, as has been stressed, they simply pose better questions.

It must always be remembered that if making money was simply a question of following a formula or creating the right ratios we would not be wasting our time at the moment learning about business finance, we would simply be studying the formula. The creation of wealth is not accomplished by means of a formula – it is accomplished by the mixing of people with money so as to create wealth, and in that mixture there is much complication, judgement and luck!

However, it must also be pointed out that it is possible in certain situations to create minimum ratios for safety. This can be very valuable when financial judgement is required in such fields as the lending of money. In such cases minimum ratios have often been applied by, for instance bankers, who have allowed staff, who in many cases possess a very flimsy knowledge of finance, to make lending decisions.

In such situations it is quite possible to lay down certain minimum ratios that we might look for so as to indicate maximum safety, for instance that the current assets should cover the current liabilities more than twice. This could be considered to be a very safe situation, as it means the business has twice the amount of money coming into its till as it is going to have to pay out to meet its current needs. However, although it is safe it may not be good from the business's point of view. (If that is unclear to you revise your studies of working capital in Chapter 9 and the objective of minimising such investment.) You could also lay down certain minimum ratios regarding the gross profit to sales, the day's credit allowed to debtors and the turnover of stocks, etc.

These then are just examples of the ratios that can be devised to help in situations where you do not wish for too much freedom of expression in the interpretation of financial data. However, it must never be thought that such 'safe' ratios are in themselves sacrosanct – they are simply convenient to use in certain situations.

It must also be remembered that the creation of wealth involves a mixture of people with money. This means that whatever the money situation may be, the people who will be handling the money are all important, and that in the interpretation of the results of a business we must never forget the people investing, spending, and earning the money. Their study should always be central to any judgement of a business's financial progress. For instance, a good banker has always understood that behind the figures on which he or she is lending money people will be spending it. For this reason the people concerned with this must be of equal if not of more importance than the soundness or otherwise of the Balance Sheets, the Profit and Loss Accounts and the Cash Flow Forecasts that are used in evidence for the loan.

Revision

To consolidate your studies of ratios go through Illustrations 12.18 and 12.19 again, considering not so much the arithmetic of the ratios set out in Illustration 12.20 but their meaning. Jot down your ideas, indeed in some cases your questions, based on the trends the ratios show and compare your findings with the notes made in Illustration 12.23.

Illustration 12.23 Suggested comments on Illustrations 12.18, 12.19 and 12.20.

Performance
1. Profitability is inconsistent with no apparent trend during the four years.
2. Apart from year 2 the overall profit margin has remained in double figures although the expense control ratios indicate that the company has had problems maintaining its gross profit margin. This could be due to inability to increase sales prices in line with cost increases in material and/or labour.
3. The fixed expenses seem to be in reasonable control as they have decreased as a percentage of sales throughout the years. It would be helpful to see how they compare with budgeted levels of expenditure.
4. Asset turnover whilst low is on the increase. This is a healthy sign as the company has been investing in additional assets especially in year 4.

Liquidity
1. Working capital has increased each year in line with increases in sales although the requirement per £ of sales has decreased each year. This is shown by the working capital/sales ratio.
2. Both the current and acid test ratios have decreased over the four years indicating a slight weakening in the liquidity position of the company. This should not give rise to any alarm as both ratios are still in excess of the normal requirement. (2:1 for current and 1:1 for acid test.)
3. Stock turnover has improved in the last year although with a present stock turn of over 4 months there is still room for improvement.
4. The credit terms offered by the business need to be known to interpret the collection period ratio as there seems to have been slackening in collection during the last three years. Were the terms to be 30 days then customers seem to be taking on average at least three times that figure. This could lead to bad debts if the credit control policies are not regularly reviewed.
5. The company seems to have fairly patient creditors although again it would be useful to know the purchasing terms of trade. The increase in creditors this year is not too worrying.
6. The overall financing of fixed assets expenditure is good in that the extra cash has come in the main from shareholders plus the depreciation charge:

Asset investment:	Year 2	Year 3	Year 4
Opening book value	1,380	1,520	1,420
Less: Depreciation	130	120	140
	1,250	1,400	1,280
Closing book value	1,520	1,420	1,780
Net purchase during year	£270	£20	£500
Financed by:			
Extra share capital	200	—	420
Profit after tax and dividends	(20)	40	20
	180	40	440
Depreciation for the year	130	120	140
	£310	£160	£580

Investment
1. There is not a lot to encourage existing shareholders, particularly as the return on equity does not exceed 5 per cent whilst the dividend has yet to reach 8 per cent.
2. However, the company has paid a dividend each year, not covering its dividend in year 2.
3. The dividend cover is not very high and was not covered in year 2. This may make shareholders happy in the short term but could result in lower profits and dividends in the future.

The measurement of common sense

We have now seen the first of the two measurements used in interpreting financial information – ratio analysis. However, we still have to consider the second and most important measurement of all – that of common sense. It must always be remembered that whatever financial figures are presented about a business, they express a practical situation and it is the investigation and understanding of this practical situation which requires the unique gift of common sense.

For instance, behind a cost statement there is the manufacture of goods that are being sold or the services which are being rendered. This means that the first question to ask when looking at any cost statement is 'Does the information make sense in the context of the practical situation?' For instance, could that amount of material be used in the manufacture of these goods? Could that value of labour be spent in the rendering of that service? If the merchandise stocks of a retailer amount to so much could the remainder of what has been purchased during this period have been sold? We must always recognise that the financial information which has either been produced fraudulently or in error will be illogical.

It could be said that all 'con men' rely on people not applying the yard-stick of common sense or logic to the information they present. For this reason everyone concerned with financial analysis must always recognise the paramount need to apply their own common sense in assessing financial data. This means that it is not always the accountant, or the so-called financial expert who possesses the invaluable yardstick. There is always a great need to enrol the assistance of practical managers if interpretation is to be fully applied.

This can be illustrated by the situation that happened some years ago in what is still referred to as 'the salad oil fraud'. This was a case in which a company had consistently over-valued its stocks and it had done this by fraudulently manipulating its records. However, the auditors following their custom had not seen this. They had looked at all the appropriate records and evidence and found them correct. They had examined the bin cards and the store ledgers, they had even looked into the vats which contained the salad oil and seen what they presumed to be salad oil floating about and they had found nothing wrong. However, they had never considered the situation from a practical point of view.

In fact it was not an accountant who discovered the situation at all, it was someone who applied his own practical knowledge in the simplest and most direct way possible. He was a chemist and he looked at the Balance Sheet and saw the stock, or inventories as Americans call it, expressed in dollars and he did what now seems so obvious. He converted the stock that was set out in dollars into cubic feet, and this proved that no receptacles on earth would hold the quantity of salad oil revealed by the calculation.

He needed therefore to look no further! He had no knowledge of course as to whether the stock figure was fraudulent but what he did know was that that amount of stock did not exist. He did not know it from any accountancy records or any study of ratios – he knew it based on his own practical knowledge.

It can never be over-stressed that everyone within a business looking at financial information must apply their own practical experience in assessing whether or not the information is in accordance with this yardstick. Common sense will always remain the most important measurement technique used in the interpretation of financial information. Whenever information is incorrectly expressed, whether it is fraudulent or otherwise, the clue to its error will always be found to rest in the fact that the information does not express a logical picture – in other words it defies common sense.

It might even be said that the real danger to business of managers not possessing financial or commercial awareness is that they will not use their own common sense or practical skills. They will treat financial information as if it is the province of financial experts only, whereas in fact it is the essence of the business. It expresses its activities and its progress and its use requires the marketing knowledge of the sales person, the production knowledge of the engineer, the people knowledge of the personnel executive – and most of all the knowledge of the whole enterprise.

Conclusion

Now having got so far, turn to the final exercise of all set out in Illustration 12.24, a case study concerned with the interpretation of financial information. It is important to follow the rules that have been laid down in the approach work to interpretation. We must first understand clearly what we are interpreting and therefore we should read very carefully through the notes to the case study.

Next it will be necessary to reorganise the data – to get it into perspective – so that we can ask better questions. Suggestions as to this are also included.

Finally having reorganised the information it is then necessary to apply the measurements of common and practical sense, and in some cases the ratios we have described in this chapter, which will bring out a greater understanding of the way in which the business has been progressing. Both the steps of reorganising the data and calculating the necessary ratios are set out as Illustrations 12.25 and 12.26.

Work through the case study at your own speed, and once this is complete compare your 'findings' with those set out in Illustration 12.27.

Illustration 12.24 Interpretation Ltd: a case study.

The Board of Directors of Interpretation Ltd, having examined their financial statements for the last three years are worried that the present level of sales cannot continue without an increase in borrowing. They have asked you to analyse their financial performance during this time with particular reference to the industrial averages they have supplied, and the movement of funds.

Industry averages at present (constant for the last three years)

Net profit to net assets	20%
Net profit to sales	6%
Sales to net assets	3.3 times
Gross profit to sales	20%
Current ratio	2.5 times
Acid test	1.1 times
*Stock turnover	6 times
*Debtor collection period	32 days
*Creditor payment period	25 days
Gearing	10%
Debt to total assets	50%

* Based on year end Balance Sheet figures.

Operating Statements for the year ending 31 December

		Year 1 £000		Year 2 £000		Year 3 £000
Sales		6,630		6,886		7,140
Less: Cost of sales		5,304		5,508		5,712
Gross profit		1,326		1,378		1,428
Less: Expenses						
Selling	240		260		280	
Administration	270		302		332	
Distribution	102		214		306	
Depreciation	204	816	256	1,032	306	1,224
Net profit before tax		510		346		204
Taxation		256		174		102
Net profit after tax		£254		£172		£102

Balance Sheets as at 31 December

	Year 1 £000	Year 2 £000	Year 3 £000
Assets employed:			
Fixed assets			
Land and buildings	122	326	306
Plant and machinery	378	296	256
Other fixed assets	72	20	16
	572	642	578
Current assets:			
Stock and work-in-progress	766	1,276	2,066
Debtors	612	694	970
Bank balances and cash	154	72	52
	1,532	2,042	3,088
Less: Current liabilities			
Creditors and accruals	366	530	960
Bank overdraft	—	256	714
	366	786	1,674
Net current assets	1,166	1,256	1,414
	£1,738	£1,898	£1,992
Represented by:			
Share capital	918	918	918
Reserves	706	878	980
Shareholders' funds	1,624	1,796	1,898
Loan capital	114	102	94
	£1,738	£1,898	£1,992

Illustration 12.25 Interpretation Ltd: Source and Application of Funds Statement.

		Years	
	Note	1/2 £000	2/3 £000
Sources			
Net profit after tax		172	102
Add back: Depreciation		256	306
Generated from operations		£428	£408
Applications			
Net expenditure on fixed assets	A	326	242
Increase in working capital (net)	B	428	636
Loans repaid		12	8
		£766	£886
Decrease in net liquid funds	C	(£338)	(£478)
Notes:			
A Net book value previous year		572	642
Less: Depreciation this year		(256)	(306)
		316	336
Net book value this year		642	578
Net expenditure on fixed assets		£326	£242
B Increase/(decrease) in working capital			
Stock and work in progress		510	790
Debtors		82	276
Creditors and accruals		(164)	(430)
		£428	£636

	Years	
	1/2 £000	2/3 £000
C Increase (decrease) in net liquid funds		
Bank balances and cash	(82)	(20)
Bank overdraft	(256)	(458)
	(£338)	(£478)

Source and Application of Funds:
1. A significant decrease has taken place in liquidity during the last three years requiring a large overdraft from the bank.
2. The principal reason for the decrease has been the increased requirement for working capital, over £1m in two years.
3. The generation of internal cash has come mainly from depreciation rather than profit which has decreased each year.
4. The expenditure on fixed assets appears to have been financed from internal cash. The depreciation charge in both years is more than the investment in similar fixed assets.
5. The company has not sought either additional Share Capital or Long Term loans despite a net investment of £568,000 in Fixed Assets during the last two years. This has put pressure on the cash resources required for Working Capital and hence the present overdraft of £714,000.

Illustration 12.26   Interpretation Ltd: ratio analysis.

	Note	Year 1	Year 2	Year 3	Industry average
Profitability ratios:					
Net profit to net assets	A	29.3	18.2	10.2	20%
Net profit to sales	B	7.7	5.0	2.9	6%
Sales to net assets	C	3.8	3.6	3.6	3.3 times
Gross profit to sales	D	20.0	20.0	20.0	20%
Liquidity ratios:					
Current	E	4.2	2.6	1.8	2.5 times
Acid test	F	2.1	1.0	0.6	1.1 times
Activity ratios:					
Stock turnover	G	8.7	5.4	3.5	6 times
Debtor collection period	H	34	37	50	32 days
Creditor payment period	I	25	35	61	25 days
Capital ratios:					
Gearing	J	6.6	5.4	4.7	10%
Debts to total assets	K	22.8	33.1	48.2	50%

Ratio workings	Note	Year 1	Year 2	Year 3
Net profit to net assets	A	510:1,738	346:1,898	204:1,992
Net profit to sales	B	510:6,630	346:6,886	204:7,140
Sales to net assets	C	6,630:1,738	6,886:1,898	7,140:1,992
Gross profit to sales	D	1,326:6,630	1,378:6,886	1,428:7,140
Current	E	1,532:366	2,042:786	3,088:1,674
Acid test	F	766:366	766:786	1,022:1,674
Stock turnover	G	6,630:766	6,886:1,276	7,140:2,066
Debtor collection period	H	6,630:612	6,886:694	7,140:970
Creditor payment period	I	5,304:366	5,508:530	5,712:960
Gearing	J	114:1,738	102:1,898	94:1,992
Debt to total assets	K	480:2,104	888:2,684	1,768:3,666

Illustration 12.27 Interpretation Ltd: findings.

Ratio analysis

1. The only area where the company seems to be better than the industry is with its debt position, although this is now very close to the average.
2. The remaining ratios highlight a number of problem areas. These are:
   (a) *Liquidity*. Both the current ratio and acid test show a declining position and are now well below the industrial average. Unless action is taken to arrest this downward trend it is possible that the creditors and bank may put pressure on the company for payment which will affect solvency.
   (b) *Stock turnover*. This has decreased at an alarming rate and is only just above half that for the industry. It suggests:
      (i) too much stock on hand perhaps due to bad sales forecasting, production planning or buying;
      (ii) the possibility of obsolete or deteriorated stock;
      (iii) the true liquidity position could be worse than the current ratio indicates;
      (iv) the valuation may be incorrect. More information perhaps is needed on work in progress.
   (c) *Debtor collection period*. The company seems to have slipped badly in debtor collection. It suggests:
      (i) a poor credit control department in chasing debtors;
      (ii) slack credit control in accepting orders;
      (iii) an increasing possibility of bad debts.
   (d) *Creditor payment period*. The company is now more than twice the industry average time period for paying their bills, due of course to stock and debtor problems. Pressure from the creditors for payment will affect the solvency of the company.
   (e) *Profitability*. All the profitability ratios indicate that the company is less profitable than the average firm in its industry. The maintenance of the gross profit margin indicates that the company has been recovering cost increases in materials and labour in increased sales prices. The low net profit margin indicates that the sales price increase has not been enough to recover cost increases in overheads. The overhead costs look high especially distribution.

   Sales to net assets is higher than the industry average due to Interpretation's primary problem in managing its current assets. The decrease in net profit to net assets reflects the low profit margin on sales.

Summary

1. The company shows severe signs of overtrading and needs an injection of capital to support any increase on the present sales level.
2. The company can of course generate funds from its own resources namely:
   (i) net profit plus depreciation
   (ii) reduction of debtors
   (iii) reduction of stock.
3. The sales price will have to rise or overheads be cut back for funds to be generated from profits.
4. There is room for significant reductions in stock and debtors although these cannot be accomplished immediately. However, assuming the stock to be saleable and the debtors collectable, it should be possible for the firm to generate a substantial amount of funds from these sources. If the firm could reduce stock, debtors and creditors to the industry averages this would release £750,000. This would be more than enough to pay off the overdraft and increase sales without requiring additional working capital.

   This will, of course, require some effort on behalf of the management of Interpretation.

5. It would be useful to produce a Cash Flow Forecast for, say, the next six months to show the effect of the action proposed above, and particularly to show the bank manager that by continuing to trade the company can reduce the overdraft which is now probably reaching its limit.

We have now completed our understanding of business finance. There is of course much more that you can learn about finance that has not been included. However, it must be remembered that real understanding will only be gained by experience and practice, and that the best case study of all is back at work – because that is where it all happens.

INDEX